AIR STAFF HISTORICAL STUDY

THE UNITED STATES AIR FORCE:

BASIC DOCUMENTS ON ROLES AND MISSIONS

Richard I. Wolf

OFFICE OF AIR FORCE HISTORY
UNITED STATES AIR FORCE
WASHINGTON D.C., 1987

Library of Congress Cataloging-in-Publication Data

The United States Air Force basic documents on roles
    and missions.

    (Air staff historical study)
    Bibliography: P.
    Includes index.
    1. United States.   Air Force--History--Sources.
I. Wolf, Richard Irving. II. Series.
UG633.U625 1988   358.4'00973   88-19530
ISBN 0-912799-54-4 (pbk.)

United States Air Force
Historical Advisory Committee
(as of 31 December 1987)

Mrs. Anne Foreman
<u>The General Counsel,</u> USAF

Dr. Norman A. Graebner
The University of Virginia

Dr. Dominick Graham
Royal Military College

Dr. Ira D. Gruber
Rice University

Lt. Gen. Charles R. Hamm, USAF
<u>Superintendent,</u> U.S. Air Force Academy

Dr. Haskell M. Monroe, Jr. (Chairman)
The University of Missouri

Dr. John H. Morrow, Jr.
The University of Tennessee at Knoxville

Gen. Thomas M. Ryan, Jr.,
USAF, retired

Lt. Gen. C. Truman Spangrud, USAF
<u>Commander,</u> Air University

Dr. Gerhard L. Weinberg
The University of North Carolina

The Author

RICHARD I. WOLF is an historian with the Air Staff Branch, Office of Air Force History. Dr. Wolf holds the B.S degree in education (1974), and M.A. (1976) and Ph.D. (1981) degrees in history from Boston University. From 1982 to 1983 he worked in private industry, and then joined Air Force historians at Headquarters Strategic Air Command, Offutt AFB, Nebraska. In 1985, Dr. Wolf transferred to the History Office of Headquarters Tactical Air Command, Langley AFB, Virginia. In October 1985, Dr. Wolf entered his current assignment, writing the annual history of Headquarters United States Air Force.

Foreword

One of the major lessons of World War II was the need for the military services, both in the United States and elsewhere, to work together in mutually supporting ways to defeat an enemy. Changing technology and the worldwide character of the war altered the traditional boundaries between land and sea warfare, and the new elements of air power and atomic weapons even further called into question the traditional roles and missions of the armed services.

In 1947, the U.S. Air Force became independent of the Army and a National Military Establishment (which became the Department of Defense in 1949) was formed to coordinate and, after 1949, to control the services. Yet, disagreements over roles and missions continued, often exacerbated by the fiscal limitations of the post-war era. But not all roles and missions disagreements were caused by financial struggles. Genuine differences of opinion over doctrinal issues and the best means to accomplish missions often divided the services, and on many occasions the Secretary of Defense had to assign missions and adjudicate roles amid a blizzard of conflicting claims.

Dr. Richard Wolf of the Office of Air Force History has collected in this volume the most significant documents which have determined the roles and missions of the Air Force, from its birth in 1947 to the present. The documents themselves only tell part of the story, of course. Dr. Wolf provides an introductory essay to each document so that readers can comprehend the context in which the decisions over roles and missions took place. The result is a convenient and useful reference tool for anyone working with, or studying, the organizational and doctrinal basis of the United States Air Force.

RICHARD H. KOHN
Chief, Office of Air Force History

v

Preface

This volume is designed to provide a useful reference work that contains primary source documents not easily obtainable elsewhere. Thirty-seven of the most influential documents in Air Force roles and missions follow. Not all of the documents center precisely on roles and missions. Some of them involve largely organizational issues, since these issues often affected roles and missions. However, the focus of this work is not organization. The volume is arranged in the following manner: the first section presents a general overview of Air Force history as it relates to the subject at hand; followed by the bulk of the work, the documents. Each document is preceded by an introductory essay to provide the historical context for the document. Following the essay, any sources used in its compilation are cited. The document immediately follows the essay. The essays and documents have been printed in differing fonts to set them apart. The documents are identified by title at the top of the essay, and by number in the header above the document text. The pages cited in the table of contents are for the introductory essays. Editorial additions are bracketed in bold face type. Any errors or omissions are the responsibility of the author, who welcomes any suggestions for additional documents or further explanatory material. All such correspondence should be addressed to the author at HQ USAF/CHO, Pentagon, Room 5D-1018, Washington, D.C. 20330.

This project grew out of the work of others. I would like to thank my predecessors, Melden Smith and Max Rosenberg, who began the effort. My Branch Chief, Jack Neufeld guided the project from its start in October 1985, while the Office of Air Force History Publications Panel, Richard H. Kohn, Col. John F. Shiner, Herman S. Wolk, Marcelle S. Knaack, and Alfred M. Beck, provided useful suggestions on several points. Vanessa Allen ably edited the manuscript. I thank Warren A. Trest, Senior Historian, Air Force Historical Research Center, currently preparing a monograph on Air Force roles and missions, for his ideas and comments. Most of the documents were converted to computer disk using the optical character reader owned by the 7th Communications Group at the Pentagon. I would like to thank Jean Ditoto of the 1100th Resource Management Group for her assistance in typing the remainder.

TABLE OF CONTENTS

xi

Introduction

This volume is a compilation of the major documents which codified the Air Force's roles and missions since the Second World War. Documentary volumes such as this are useful in bringing together a series of original references to illustrate the evolutionary pattern of development in the contemporary writings of the participants. While an effort has been made to provide a context for each document by including introductions, interpretation of the meaning and effect of each document rests with the reader. Included are four basic categories of documents: legislation; executive orders; Department of Defense (DOD) memoranda and directives; and military department executive directives and agreements. An introductory essay precedes each document describing the document's contents and significance. Each essay contains a footnote providing reference sources for further study, except in cases where the essay is drawn solely from the document's contents. The documents were selected largely by the degree to which they shaped Air Force roles and missions and changes in them. Those documents which explained only changes in organization were excluded, except where these changes proved fundamental to mission assignments.

This project began in the early 1970s, when Max Rosenberg, the Deputy Chief Historian of the Air Force, conceived of the idea and began collecting documents. An Air Force Reserve officer, Maj. Melden Smith, took over and continued the collection effort in the mid-1970s. The project was overtaken by higher priorities after a couple of years and has essentially lain dormant since then. The current author completed the document collection, wrote the document introductions, and composed the overall introduction.

The interpretations of Air Force roles and missions have evolved over time since the service's establishment as an independent service in 1947. Today the Air Force operates under roles and missions directives which have varied very little since the last Eisenhower Administration reorganization in 1958. The youngest of the armed services, the Air Force has carved its operating arena out of responsibilities formerly possessed by the older services. As a result, conflict over roles and missions have been endemic throughout its existence. While no one could challenge the Air Force's legitimacy to operate in the aerospace environment, each of the other services has preserved a portion of that space for itself. While aerospace's overlap into other operational mediums made some conflict inevitable, the roles and missions conflicts concerned relatively narrow issues and reflected the struggle for priority within funding limitations imposed on all the services from without.

Roles and missions is a term which encompasses the broad range of service activities and specific tasks within several categories. Within the overall role of air operations, the Army Air Forces (AAF) after World War II possessed four main missions: strategic bombardment, support of ground operations, air defense, and air transport. These missions proved essential to the war effort and were necessarily carried over into the peace-time organization. While the first three missions were predominant in the pre-war era, the air transport mission grew in importance during the war to a status almost equal to the other three. During the years covered by this volume, technological advances in military hardware pushed the boundary of the Air Force operational medium into the aerospace, though not fundamentally altering the character of its assigned tasks.

GENERAL MISSION

After the end of World War II, the Army Air Forces maintained a largely autonomous existence within the War Department. This fact stemmed from the reorganization of the War Department on 2 March 1942, promulgated in War Department Circular 59. This new status, operative for the duration of the war plus six months under the terms of the First War Powers Act of 1941, conferred on the AAF equality with the Army Ground Forces and the Army Service Forces, though not the full independence desired by the airmen. The AAF mission was "to procure and maintain" AAF-unique equipment, and "provide air force units properly organized, trained and equipped for combat operations." Operational control of the forces was assigned to the theater commanders. Following the war, the AAF reorganized on 21 March 1946 **(Doc. 1)**, followed closely thereafter by the War Department on 11 June 1946. The mission assigned under this latter reorganization, promulgated in War Department Circular 138 of 14 May 1946 **(Doc. 2)** gave the AAF direction over operations and training of air commands within the United States, including direction of the Strategic Air Command (SAC). This was a slight change from the wartime mission in which the AAF provided units to theater commanders, although the AAF always controlled air operations within the United States. Later in 1946, President Harry S. Truman approved an Outline Command Plan **(Doc. 3)**(the first of what later became known as the Unified Command Plan), which removed that directive authority from the Commanding General AAF and vested it in the Joint Chiefs of Staff (JCS), who were authorized to exercise strategic direction over all elements of the armed forces. In essence, the Outline Command Plan altered the role of the AAF, later the Air Force, to training rather than operations. Operations would be undertaken by the unified commands set up by the plan, and by SAC, all of whom were under the authority and control of the JCS, who exercised their authority through one of their members acting as executive agent for the JCS. When the Air Force was created under the terms of the National Security Act of 1947 **(Doc. 4)**, its mission (assigned by Executive Order 9877 of 1947) **(Doc. 5)** was fundamentally unchanged; to "organize, train and equip air forces" for operations, not to conduct operations as a service.

STRATEGIC BOMBARDMENT

Largely as a result of its demonstrated effectiveness in World War II, strategic bombardment continued as the Air Force's major focus from its inception through the early 1960s. Its primacy was reinforced by the functional reorganization of 21 March 1946 **(Doc. 1)** which formed SAC as one of three air commands of the Army Air Forces. SAC was charged with being prepared to conduct worldwide strategic operations and reconnaissance and providing units for sustained combat.

Under the provisions of War Department Circular 138 of May 1946 **(Doc. 2)**, SAC was directed to maintain a global air striking force and train very heavy bombardment crews. The National Security Act of 1947 **(Doc. 4)** did not address the organizational level of the air commands, nor did Executive Order 9877 of July

1947 **(Doc. 5)**, although the latter assigned the Air
Force the function of organizing the strategic air
force of the United States.

The strategic bombardment mission sparked
disagreement between the Air Force and the Navy in the
late 1940s as to whether the Navy had a role in it, and
who ought to control the mission. These contentious
issues prompted Secretary of Defense James V.
Forrestal to convene a conference, out of which grew
the Key West Agreement of April 1948 **(Doc. 7)**. It
settled the dispute in favor of the Air Force, while
preserving a small measure of the bombardment mission
(tactical applications) for the Navy by allowing it to
retain an air component. The Key West Agreement, which
spelled out the functions of the armed forces, remained
in force until codified in a DOD directive in 1954
(Doc. 19). However, its effectiveness remained limited
to forestalling a Navy role in strategic air
operations. The next battlefield between the services
was control of nuclear weapons, heretofore dominated by
the Air Force. The outgrowth of a second conference,
at Newport, Rhode Island, the Newport Agreement of
August 1948 **(Doc. 10)** resolved the issue with a
compromise, giving the Navy access to nuclear weapons
and a portion of strategic operations planning, while
the Air Force gained primary oversight of the nuclear
weapons development programs.

Although the Air Force had received primary
responsibility for strategic operations, controversy
arose once again with the advent of guided missiles.
Intercontinental ballistic missiles (ICBM) promised a
new long-range strategic weapon, one without historical
precedent to guide mission assignment. As a result of
Secretary of Defense Louis A. Johnson's Guided Missile
Memorandum in 1950 **(Doc. 13)**, the Air Force was
assigned development of air-to-air missiles and
missiles for the strategic bombardment mission. In
1956, Secretary of Defense Charles E. Wilson assigned
the Air Force operational employment of land-based
intermediate-range ballistic missiles (IRBM) **(Doc. 21)**,
while assigning ship-based IRBMs to the Navy. With
these notable exceptions, the strategic bombardment
mission remained largely as it evolved in the late
1940s, with the Air Force firmly in control of two of
the three legs of what later was called the nuclear
deterrent triad -- bombers, ICBMs, and submarine-
launched ballistic missiles.

SUPPORT OF GROUND OPERATIONS

The activities subsumed under the tactical mission generally fell into three separate areas: air superiority, close air support, and air interdiction. These missions grew out of World War II experience and were organizationally confirmed in the same 21 March 1946 reorganization as the strategic mission **(Doc. 1)**. Throughout the period since its formation, the Air Force has been challenged in two areas of the tactical mission but reigned largely unopposed in the air superiority mission (though naval air forces retained a portion of the sea-based mission). The Air Force received the close air support mission per Executive Order 9877 **(Doc. 5)**, as well as further explication in the Key West Agreement **(Doc. 7)**. In 1951, the Army and Air Force secretaries were drawn towards signing an agreement **(Doc. 16)** which clearly kept the Army from duplicating Air Force capabilities in close air support, using either rotary-wing or fixed-wing aircraft. Nonetheless, the two secretaries were led to sign another agreement within thirteen months, which retained the language relating to close air support but reinstituted a weight limit for Army aircraft **(Doc. 17)**.

In 1956, Secretary Wilson found it necessary to define the use of aircraft by the Army. Once again the Army was restricted from providing aircraft for close air support **(Doc. 21)**. Additionally, the Army fixed-wing aviation program was limited to observation and liaison within the combat zone, although the combat zone was now extended to 100 miles in either direction from the contact line with enemy troops. Despite these agreements, the Army's aircraft inventory continued to grow as the Air Force allowed its air-to-ground capability to diminish in favor of multi-role fighters and air atomic operations. By the mid-1970s, the Army's helicopter force provided a large degree of the close air support required by the Army. However, in the face of directives prohibiting it, the Army promulgated doctrine which differentiated between its own organic air support and the centralized close air support provided by the Air Force. By this time the Air Force had begun to provide greater close air support than previously, as amply demonstrated by its acquisition of A-7 and A-10 aircraft. The issue of duplicative efforts prompted Congress to question the Army and the Air Force, to which the services replied in a joint letter of September 1975 **(Doc. 35)** explaining the shades of difference.

The air interdiction portion of the tactical support mission remained largely an Air Force preserve. This function was first assigned inferentially in 1947, in Executive Order 9877 **(Doc. 5)**, through the clause which charged the Air Force with responsibility for "air operations including joint operations." In the Army-Air Force Implementation Agreements of September 1947 **(Doc. 6)**, the Army continued to have tactical missile responsibility for those targets which had "a direct effect on current Army tactical operations." This could include some targets which were nominally an Air Force responsibility under close air support or interdiction responsibilities. In the Key West Agreement **(Doc. 7)**, the Air Force was assigned a primary function of furnishing support to the Army, including "interdiction of enemy land power and communications." In the 1950 Guided Missile Memorandum **(Doc. 13)**, the Army was assigned surface-to-surface missiles which extended or replaced artillery, while the Air Force received surface-to-surface missiles which replaced support aircraft for fulfillment of assigned functions, such as interdiction. The first Pace-Finletter Agreement of October 1951 **(Doc. 16)** specifically prohibited the Army from providing aircraft for the interdiction function, as did the second agreement in November 1952 **(Doc. 17)**. The codification of the interdiction role, in DOD Directive 5100.1 of March 1954 **(Doc. 19)** and subsequent updates in December 1958 and afterwards **(Doc. 25)**, carried the same language as the Key West Agreement. Despite the seemingly definitive nature of these directives, twice during the 1950s, the Secretary of Defense found it necessary to include in his roles and missions memoranda specific injunctions against Army aircraft providing interdiction in 1956 and 1957 **(Docs. 21 and 23)**. Finally, the issue appeared to be settled, with no further mention of the function save in updates of DOD Directive 5100.1.

AIR DEFENSE

Another primary mission assigned to the Air Force, and earlier to the AAF, was air defense --

6

particularly air defense of the United States. Despite its primacy, however, the Air Force has generally received assistance in this mission from both the Army and the Navy. The mission's importance was emphasized by the formation of an Air Defense Command (ADC) in the 21 March 1946 reorganization of the AAF **(Doc. 1)** and reiterated in War Department Circular 138 **(Doc. 2)**. Executive Order 9877 **(Doc. 5)**, which stated the services' functions, did not specifically enumerate air defense as a function, but called for sustained defensive as well as offensive operations and directed the Air Force to coordinate air defense efforts. The Key West Agreement **(Doc. 7)** explicitly stated air defense of the United States as an Air Force function, in addition to its coordination effort. By 1950, the mission's importance had grown, largely as the result of the explosion of a Russian atomic device. ADC -- which had been reduced to an operational command reporting to the Continental Air Command -- was reestablished as an Air Force major command, and the Army formed an Antiaircraft Command.

The rise of these two air defense commands was punctuated by the signing of an Army-Air Force agreement on air defense doctrine, known as the Vandenberg-Collins Agreement in August 1950 **(Doc. 14)**. This agreement began the integration of air defense efforts and the collocation of Army and Air Force air defense headquarters at many echelons. By mid-1953, the magnitude of the air defense effort prompted the JCS to approve formation of a joint Continental Air Defense Command (CONAD), effective 1 September 1954 **(Doc. 20)**. The Air Force portion included ADC, while the Army contingent was composed of its Antiaircraft Command. The Navy contributed radar ships and would augment CONAD's forces in wartime with Marine and Navy fighter aircraft, all under the executive agency of the Air Force.

Within the air defense mission, Secretary of Defense Wilson divided responsibility between two services in his 1956 Roles and Missions Memorandum **(Doc. 21)**, with the Army assigned point defense and the Air Force assigned area defense. At the same time, each service received developmental responsibility for the surface-to-air missile suited to its functional area. While each service developed weapon systems to carry out the air defense mission, much attention was spent on early warning radars and identification of attacking aerospace vehicles. By 1960, this grew to include objects in space, and in November 1960 the JCS assigned operational command of the space detection and tracking system to CONAD; operational control was assigned to the North American Air Defense Command (NORAD) -- a Canadian/American command formed in 1957 **(Doc. 26)**. The division of responsibility for air defense between the services made it essential that a single commander coordinate the effort, and that principle had been embodied in the Vandenberg-Collins Agreement. However, after the 1956 Roles and Missions Memorandum, the two services differed on whether an Army field commander would be responsible for air defense and control air operations over his combat area. Despite this difference, the overseas unified commanders had resolved command and control arrangements. Embodied in the LeMay-Decker Agreement of July 1962 **(Doc. 28)**, these arrangements called for the unified commander to appoint an area air defense commander, normally the air component commander.

AIR TRANSPORT

Air transport emerged from World War II with its prestige greatly enhanced by its effectiveness in furthering the war effort. The original plans for the air war in World War II had drastically understated air transport requirements since airlift of supplies, men, and equipment on a large scale had never before been attempted. When massive airlift efforts became necessary, the status, prestige, and overall size of the airlift force grew. As a result, when the War Department reorganized **(Doc. 2)** in 1946, the Air Transport Command was continued in the AAF. This command provided air transport, airways communication, and search and rescue for the Army. Under Executive Order 9877 **(Doc. 5)**, the new Air Force received as one of its primary functions the mission of providing airlift and support for airborne operations and air transport for the armed forces, except for certain Navy transport routes.

The Navy had been in the air transport business almost as long as the Air Force and had used airlift heavily during the war. The Navy had wanted to retain its own air transport service after the war, but it retained only certain routes. However, given the large size of the Navy's aircraft fleet, and the fact that only a single organization for air transport was really required, Secretary of Defense Forrestal created the joint Military Air Transport Service (MATS) **(Doc. 9)** in May 1948. MATS was not assigned the function of airlift for airborne operations, nor did it fly on routes solely of Navy interest.

The Air Force retained the mission of ferrying airborne troops into combat. This mission was reinforced by the terms of the two Pace-Finletter Agreements **(Docs. 16 and 17)**, when the Army was prohibited from providing aircraft for that purpose. Further reinforcement came from promulgation of DOD Directive 5100.1 **(Doc. 19)** in March 1954. Under the terms of Secretary of Defense Wilson's 1956 Roles and Missions Memorandum **(Doc. 21)**, the Army was allowed to provide small aircraft to airlift personnel and materiel within the combat zone, with ground transportation resources for the Army correspondingly reduced. The Army was also specifically prohibited from providing aircraft for strategic and tactical airlift.

In 1956, following implementation of DOD policies regarding missions assigned to various services, Secretary Wilson designated the Secretary of the Air Force as the single manager for airlift service within DOD in December 1956 **(Doc. 22)**. This assignment was to integrate into a single agency all transport aircraft involved in point-to-point scheduled service and was prompted by the proliferation of special purpose aircraft throughout DOD. As a result, MATS received most of the Navy's aircraft from its fleet logistics air wings and Tactical Air Command's (TAC) heavy troop carrier transports.

By 1957, Secretary Wilson again found it necessary to clarify roles and missions and reiterated the Air Force mission to provide air transport for Army needs in March 1957 **(Doc. 23)**. This was prompted by Army efforts to assume the role itself. This included airlift of Army men and supplies into the combat zone and air evacuation from the combat zone, including aeromedical evacuation.

By the early 1960s, MATS had begun to evolve from a scheduled air transport organization into a combat-oriented airlift service. At the behest of Congress,

BASIC DOCUMENTS

MATS was redesignated the Military Airlift Command (MAC) **(Doc. 29)** in October 1965, although earlier efforts to make the command a JCS specified command had lapsed. One year later, the reduced Navy portion of MAC was removed altogether as the Air Force took over airlift almost completely in April 1966 **(Doc. 30)**. In the 1970s, MAC received all military transport aircraft (except for Navy carrier onboard delivery and Marine KC-130 tanker aircraft) and became a JCS specified command on 1 February 1977 **(Doc. 33)**. It now finally appeared that all DOD transport aircraft, with rare exceptions, were under a single agency to enable that agency to oversee all military airlift in peace and war. This made MAC directly responsible to the JCS, and the command was provided with a combat mission.

SPACE

One area that was of little consequence at the end of World War II grew in importance through the 1950s and 60s and currently occupies a central role: the role of the military in space. Until the Russians launched Sputnik in 1957, American space efforts had moved along slowly. The acceleration in space efforts after 1957 came under the civilian auspices of the National Aeronautics and Space Administration (NASA). In the military, the Air Force (and to a certain extent, the Army) largely controlled space efforts. The Air Force was involved with going into space with a variety of launch vehicles, while also developing boosters for ICBMs which could contribute to the civilian space effort. Military efforts in space were deliberately kept small during the Eisenhower administration.

While both the Army and the Navy had space programs, the Air Force had assumed the lead through its space research and ballistic missile programs. In addition, the Air Force felt that it could lay claim to space as an extension of its responsibility for the air. However, in the early years of NASA and the civilianization of the space effort, the Air Force had lost its primacy, and space was open to all the services to some degree. In March 1961, however, with the change of administrations, Secretary of Defense Robert S. McNamara assigned responsibility for research, development, test, and engineering of space systems to the Air Force **(Doc. 27)**. One consequence of this decision was the formation of the Air Force Systems Command (AFSC) the following month, the result of functional realignments between the old Air Research and Development Command and the Air Materiel Command.

Throughout the decade the Air Force's role in space grew, as many warning and surveillance satellites were launched into orbit. By 1970, the Air Force was not the only service seeking access to space. Accordingly, Deputy Secretary of Defense David Packard issued a new DOD Directive in September 1970 **(Doc. 32)** on development of space systems. It did not change responsibility for existing systems, but allowed the other services to be responsible for execution of space programs. The Air Force retained responsibility for development, production, and deployment of warning and surveillance systems, as well as for all launch vehicles and support.

By 1980, the Air Force space effort had grown so much that it had become fragmented throughout a variety of commands and headquarters. For example, warning and surveillance systems were assigned to SAC, while air defense aircraft were assigned to TAC. Operational control for those items actually rested with NORAD. Many of the space systems were operated by the AFSC. Accordingly, the Air Force combined all of its space assets (except for the fighter aircraft which remained assigned to TAC), into the Air Force Space Command which was activated on 1 September 1982 **(Doc. 36)**. This was merely a prelude to a later action, the formation of a unified United States Space Command on 23 September 1985 which gave all of the services access to space through development of and planning for space systems for warning and surveillance, communications, navigation, and other functions.

JOINTNESS

This emphasis on unified action and joint organization was not new in the 1980s, but had been an objective ever since the formation of the Department of Defense. While the interservice bickering had prompted several DOD reorganizations (see below) and forced a concentration of power in the office of the Secretary of Defense, the services rarely reached agreement on significant issues. One of those times had been in April 1966, when the Army and Air Force agreed on tactical airlift, wherein the Air Force retained responsibility for fixed-wing tactical airlift, while allowing the Army responsibility for rotary-wing intra-theater movement of troops and supplies **(Doc. 31)**. In September 1975, the Chief of Naval Operations and the Air Force Chief of Staff signed an agreement on USAF collateral functions training **(Doc. 34)**, which allowed the Air Force to assist in activities hitherto almost entirely a naval preserve.

One of the most significant joint activities took place in May 1984 when the Army and Air Force Chiefs of Staff signed a memorandum of agreement on joint force development **(Doc. 37)**. The promise of this document, later dubbed the 31 Initiatives, loomed large as a number of outstanding issues were settled between the two services, not the least of which was the agreement to coordinate closely issues of concern to both services in the future.

ORGANIZATION

The integrated structure of the Department of Defense, provided for in the National Security Act, was designed to execute the policies determined by the statutory agencies formed by the act and by the President. The overall structure of the Defense Department underwent fundamental change three times between 1947 and the end of 1985: in 1949 with amendments to the act; under Reorganization Plan Number 6 of 1953; and through the Reorganization Act of 1958. Each change attempted to foster greater cohesion and unified effort to achieve Defense Department goals by concentrating power in the Office of the Secretary of Defense (OSD) at the expense of the military services. The 1949 amendments to the act **(Doc. 11)** designated the Department of Defense as an executive department, removing its original name and nebulous status (National Military Establishment) and relegated the three services to military departments. The Secretary of Defense received unqualified "direction, authority, and control" over the department and was named the President's principal assistant in defense matters. This act began the process of centralization in OSD, and removed the service secretaries as statutory members of the National Security Council.

Further centralization was accomplished under

Reorganization Plan Number 6 of 1953 **(Doc. 18)**, which abolished the Munitions Board and the Research and Development Board and replaced them with six Assistant Secretaries of Defense. This process was accelerated with the Reorganization Act of 6 August 1958 **(Doc. 24)**. The reorganization removed the service secretaries from the operational chain of command, replacing them with a chain which ran from the President and the Secretary of Defense through the JCS to the unified and specified commanders. In addition, the legislative authority for the service chiefs to command their services was repealed, and research and development was centralized in the Defense Secretary's office. The resultant organization provided for three military departments that were separately organized, rather than "separately administered."

Most of the changes brought greater responsibility and authority to the Secretary of Defense, at the expense of the service secretaries and chiefs of staff. Using this increased power, each of the Defense Secretaries attempted to settle interservice roles and missions controversies. In fact, the increased centralization of authority in OSD was due in large measure to an inability by that office to impose cohesion and unified effort on the services. This condition appeared most often in budget matters, since in austere eras the services have fought over priorities at each other's expense. However, interservice rivalries over mission areas masked fundamental agreement on ultimate aims and camouflaged vast areas of consensus. The areas most subject to controversy were: adequacy of close air support for Army troops; division of the strategic nuclear role; the role of naval aviation and the Marine Corps; division of responsibility for guided missiles; and responsibility for space systems development and use.

By the mid-1980s the areas of controversy dividing the services had diminished markedly. The 31 Initiatives **(Doc. 37)** demonstrated unprecedented agreement between the Army and the Air Force on mutual support and individual responsibilities. The strategic nuclear portion of the bombardment mission had endured more than twenty years of division between the Navy and the Air Force. Naval and Marine Corps aviation remained firmly entrenched as accepted elements of the Defense Department. Guided missile responsibility had been parcelled out to the services, in consonance with mission areas. The role of the military in space had finally been rationalized with the formation of the unified Space Command, and with hints at a new space policy for the United States (impelled by the loss of the space shuttle Challenger in January 1986). The major change impending at the time this narrative was written involved a major legislative reorganization of the Department of Defense, whose ultimate effects were unknown, but which signaled the first major change in DOD operations since the 1958 Eisenhower reorganization.

(1) **Army Adjutant General Letter Reorganizing the Army Air Forces, 21 March 1946**

Entering 1946, the Army Air Forces (AAF) was in the throes of accelerated demobilization from the war, with group strength less than half that of September 1945. The waning months of 1945 had witnessed the opening salvoes in the battle for a single department of national defense, which promised to be a protracted affair. Gen. Carl A. Spaatz, Commanding General of the AAF, ordered a reorganization to implement the lessons of World War II and provide an effective striking force in being. He faced the prospect of independence at some indeterminate future time and the immediate need to implement the markedly reduced post-war air force program.

The urgency to provide a post-war organization stemmed from a rapidly shrinking force structure and a provision of the First War Powers Act of 1941 which provided for the expiration of war-time organizations six months after the end of hostilities. This meant that without some reorganization, the AAF would revert from their coequal status with the Army Ground Forces (AGF) to their pre-war subordinate status. War Department post-war plans called for greater autonomy for the air arm, and consideration was given to request continuing legislation to preserve the organizational status quo until some form of unification occurred. This path was not followed since it would have frozen in place wartime organization which conferred only co-equal status on the AAF.

General Spaatz wanted to reorganize the AAF major commands, as well as the headquarters, hoping to form an organization that would last throughout the unification struggle and beyond. At the end of the war, overseas units were assigned to numbered air forces. Operational forces in the continental United States were assigned to Continental Air Force (CAF). CAF had been formed in 1944 to oversee redeployment, provide air defense of the country, and ultimately form and command the continental strategic reserve. Original ideas were to have just two commands in the United States -- CAF and a strategic strike force -- but Gen. Dwight D. Eisenhower's accession to the Army Chief of Staff position and his desire for tactical air units dedicated to support Army ground forces, prompted the inclusion of a tactical command. Spaatz and other AAF leaders hoped to have the Air Staff on a par with the War Department General Staff, and HQ CAF equal to

AGF. However, at the time that the AAF reorganized its major commands, AAF and AGF were co-equal under the Army Chief of Staff. With the issuance of this 21 March 1946 letter, the reorganization of the AAF desired by Spaatz was implemented.

This letter provided the direction to the AAF to establish and activate three commands -- Strategic Air Command (SAC), Tactical Air Command (TAC), and Air Defense Command (ADC) -- in order to carry out the three major combat missions described in War Department Field Manual 100-20, issued in 1943. (An earlier version of this 21 March letter, dated 11 March, was revoked in paragraph one and never distributed.) This grouping would provide for functional headquarters overseeing numbered air forces to oversee and train operational units. The fundamental significance of this organization was apparent from the fact that each of these commands has existed for the entire period since 1946 (except during 1948 to 1950 when TAC and ADC were reduced to operational commands under the Continental Air Command). SAC was charged with being prepared to conduct long range operations in any part of the world, conduct long range reconnaissance over land or sea, and provide combat units capable of sustained combat operations in any part of the world. TAC was required to cooperate with land and sea forces in ground and amphibious operations, train and equip tactical units for operations anywhere in the world, and develop air-ground doctrine. ADC received the mission of providing air defense of the United States, although assignment of tactical units to this command lagged due to budget and force structure limitations. This reorganization grouped the AAF along functional lines, with a major command for each mission, acting as an intermediate headquarters between HQ AAF and the operational wings or groups.

****

Robert F. Futrell, Ideas, Concepts and Doctrine: A History of Basic Thinking in the United States Air Force, 1907-1964, (Maxwell AFB, Ala: Air University, 2nd edition 1974), pp 104-105.

Herman S. Wolk, Planning and Organizing the Postwar Air Force, 1943-1947, (Washington, D.C.: Office of Air Force History, 1984), pp. 20-29, 100-12, and 114-38.

WAR DEPARTMENT
The Adjutant General's Office
Washington 25, D. C.

AG 322 (21 Mar 46)
OB-I-AFCOR-(971 (d))-M

SUBJECT: Establishment of Air Defense, Strategic Air and
Tactical Air Commands; Redesignation of the
Headquarters, Continental Air Forces and Certain
Other Army Air Forces Units; Activation,
Inactivation and Assignment of Certain Army Air
Forces Units.

TO: Commanding Generals,
            Army Air Forces
            Continental Air Forces

1. Letter, this office, AG 322 (11 Mar 46) OD-I-AFOOR-
(930(d))-M, 13 March 1946, subject as above, is revoked.
(Distribution withheld).
2. Effective this date:
a. The following Commands are established under
the Commanding General, Army Air Forces:
            Strategic Air Command
            Tactical Air Command
            Air Defense Command
b. The Headquarters, Continental Air Forces is
redesignated as the Headquarters, Strategic Air Command,
with station at Bolling Field, Washington, D. C. This
Headquarters will move from its present station to Andrews
Field, Maryland, on or about 1 July 1946, as directed by
the Commanding General, Army Air Forces.
c. The Headquarters, Tactical Air Command is constituted,
assigned to the Army Air Forces and will be activated at
Tampa, Florida, on or before 31 March 1946.
            (1) The Commanding General, Tactical Air
                  Command is authorized to designate,
                  organize and discontinue Army Air
                  Forces Base Units within the block
                  of numbers 300 to 399, inclusive,
                  and within the bulk allotment of
                  personnel authorized his command.
d. The Headquarters, Air Defense Command is constituted,
assigned to the Army Air Forces and will be activated at
Mitchel Field, New York, on or before 31 March 1946.
            (1) The Commanding General, Air Defense Command
                  is authorized to designate, organize and
                  discontinue Army Air Forces Base Units within

the block of numbers 100 to 199, inclusive, and within the bulk allotment of personnel authorized his command.

e. Personnel will be authorized in accordance with bulk allotment of personnel as published in Army Air Forces letters of the 150-series.

f. Administrative and housekeeping equipment is authorized in accordance with T/A 20-1, as amended.

g. The Headquarters, Ninth Air Force is assigned to the Tactical Air Command and will be activated by the Commanding General thereof at Biggs Field, El Paso, Texas, on or before 31 March 1946.

(1) Personnel for manning the Headquarters, Ninth Air Force will be furnished from the bulk allotment of personnel authorized the Tactical Air Command and as directed by the Commanding General thereof.

(2) Administrative and housekeeping equipment is authorized in accordance with T/A 20-1, as amended.

h. The Headquarters, Fifteenth Air Force is assigned to the Strategic Air Command and will be activated by the Commanding General thereof, at Colorado Springs, Colorado, on or before March 1946.

(1) Personnel for manning the Headquarters, Fifteenth Air Force will be furnished from the bulk allotment of personnel authorized the Strategic Air Command, and as directed by the Commanding General thereof.

(2) Administrative and housekeeping equipment is authorized in accordance with T/A 20-1, as amended.

3. Effective this date:

a. The Headquarters, Second Air Force is relieved from its present assignment, assigned without change of station to the Strategic Air Command, and will be inactivated by the Commanding General thereof on or before 31 March 1946. Concurrently with its inactivation, this unit is assigned in an inactive status to the Air Defense Command.

(1) Personnel and equipment will be utilized to the fullest extent practicable in manning and equipping the Headquarters, Fifteenth Air Force.

(2) Records of the inactivated unit will be disposed of and reported in

accordance with provisions of AR 15-15,
20 September 1945, and TM 12-259.
   b. The Headquarters and Headquarters Squadron,
XIX Tactical Air Command is relieved from its present assignment,
assigned without change of station to the Tactical Air
Command, and will be inactivated by the Commanding General
thereof on or before 31 March 1946.
   (1) Personnel and equipment will be utilized
       to the fullest extent practicable in
       manning and equipping the Headquarters,
       Ninth Air Force.
   (2) Records of the inactivated unit will be
       disposed of and reported in accordance
       with provisions of AR 15-15, dated 20
       September 1945, and TM 12-259.
   c. The Headquarters, Third Air Force is relieved
from its present assignment and assigned to the Tactical
Air Command, and will be transferred, less personnel and
equipment, from its present station to the Greenville Army
Air Base, Greenville, South Carolina, on or before 31 March
1946, as directed by the Commanding General, Tactical Air
Command.
   (1) Personnel for remanning the Headquarters
       Third Air Force will be furnished from
       the bulk allotment of personnel
       authorized the Tactical Air Command
       and as directed by the Commanding
       General thereof.
   (2) Administrative and housekeeping equipment
       is authorized in accordance with
       T/A 20-1, as amended.
   d. The Headquarters and Headquarters Squadron,
IX Troop Carrier Command is relieved from its present assignment,
assigned to the Tactical Air Command without change of
station, and will be inactivated by the Commanding General
thereof on or before 31 March 1946.
   (1) Personnel and equipment will be utilized
       to the fullest extent practicable in
       remanning and reequiping the Headquarters
       Third Air Force.
   (2) Records of the inactivated unit will be
       disposed of and reported in accordance
       with provisions of AR 15-15, 20 September
       1945, and TM 12-259.
4. Effective this date:
   a. The following units are relieved from the control

of the War Department and assigned in an inactive status
to the Commands indicated below:

Unit	Command
Hq & Hq Sq, Tenth Air Force	Air Defense Command
Hq & Hq Sq, Twelfth Air Force	Tactical Air Command
Hq & Hq Sq, Fourteenth Air Force	Air Defense Command
Hq & Hq Sq, 53d Troop Carrier Wing	Tactical Air Command (for further assignment to Third Air Force)

   b. The following units are relieved from their
present assignments and assigned without change of station
to the Commands indicated below:

Unit	Command
Hq, First Air Force	Air Defense Command
Hq, Fourth Air Force	Air Defense Command

   c. The units listed in the attached inclosure
are relieved from their present assignments and assigned
to the Tactical Air Command without change of station:
      (1) The current group assignments of the units
            listed in inclosure 1 are not affected by
            this action.
   d. All units currently assigned to the Continental
Air Forces and not specifically assigned by this letter
are assigned to the Strategic Air Command without change
of station.
   5. The funds of the Continental Air Forces will be assumed
by the Strategic Air Command until suitable distribution
between the Air Defense Command, Tactical Air Command and
the Strategic Air Command can be provided under the provisions
of AAF Letter 30-25, 4 August 1945.
   6. Twenty (20) copies of the order issued pursuant to
this letter will be forwarded to the Commanding General,
Army Air Forces (Attention: Publication Division, Air Adjutant
General); in addition to the distribution directed in paragraph
17c, AR 310-50. No other distribution will be made to
offices of Headquarters, Army Air Forces.
   7. When the actions directed herein have been accomplished
a report will be submitted to this office by letter and
copies furnished the Service Commander concerned.
   8. Obligate the appropriate allotment published in
Section III, Circular No 178, War Department, 1945, as
amended, to the extent necessary.
BY ORDER OF THE SECRETARY OF WAR:
                        /s/ Edward F. Witsell
                        Major General
                        The Adjutant General

(2) <u>War Department Circular 138, 14 May 1946</u>

Subsequent to the reorganization of the Army Air Forces (AAF) the War Department itself underwent reorganization. Under the authority of Executive Order 9722 of 13 May 1946, War Department Circular 138 promulgated reorganization of the War Department effective 11 June 1946. Once again the driving force behind this reorganization was the expiration of the Department's wartime organization under the terms of the First War Powers Act, increased by Gen. Dwight D. Eisenhower's desire to form a more functional organization to promote economy and efficiency. War Department Circular 138 formally reflected the AAF reorganization depicted in the 21 March 1946 letter.

In this reorganization, the AAF were made coordinate with the Army Ground Forces under the Army Chief of Staff and the War Department General Staff. The Circular recognized the 21 March reorganization, forming the three major combat air commands, and recognized continuation of several other commands, including the Air Materiel Command, Air Training Command, Air University, and the Air Transport Command. With the formation of six continental army areas went a requirement that the AAF form six air defense areas aligned geographically with the army areas. These were formed, and a numbered air force assigned to each area, though their forces existed mostly on paper given the emphasis on equipping Strategic Air Command (SAC) and Tactical Air Command (TAC) first. The object of this reorganization was to allow the AAF the maximum autonomy permitted by law without fostering unnecessary duplication of service. The Commanding General, AAF was assigned the functions, duties, and powers of the Commanding General, General Headquarters, Air Force (Air Force Combat Command), and of the Chief of the Air Corps. This Commanding General reported to the Army Chief of Staff.

Under the terms of the First War Powers Act of 18 December 1941, the wartime organization of the armed forces expired six months following the close of hostilities. As a result, it was necessary to transfer the functions of the Commanding General, GHQ Air Force and of the Chief of the Air Corps to the Commanding General, AAF. These functions were also transferred to the Chief of Staff of the Air Force when the functions of the Commanding General, AAF were transferred to that office.

Appendix II (Army Ground Forces) and Charts A (War

BASIC DOCUMENTS

Department) and C (Army Ground Forces) have been purposely omitted as not germane to Air Force roles and missions.

****
Herman S. Wolk, <u>Planning and Organizing the Postwar Air Force, 1943-1947</u>, (Washington, D.C.: Office of Air Force History, 1984), pp 107-10, 130-38, and 145-48.

Circular   WAR DEPARTMENT
No. 138   Washington 25, D.C., 14 May 1946

Effective until 14 November 1947 unless sooner rescinded or superseded

WAR DEPARTMENT REORGANIZATION

This circular is tentative and will be revised at the earliest practicable date after 1 Sept 1946. Not later than 1 Sept 1946 all War Department General and Special Staff Divisions, the Army Air Forces, the Army areas, and the technical and administrative services will submit to the Chief of Staff (Attention: Director of Organization and Training, War Department General Staff) comments and recommendations on this circular. These comments and recommendations should cover the efficiency and adequacy of the new organization, and suggestions for improvement of its structure and procedures.

BASIC DOCUMENTS

1. Authority.--Executive Order 9722, 13 May 1946, which amends Executive Order No. 9082, dated 28 Feb. 1942, authorizes a reorganization of the War Department and the Army, effective 11 June 1946. Pending changes in appropriate regulations, the following summary description of the new organization, together with directives for effecting the major changes required, is furnished for the information, guidance, and compliance of all concerned.

2. General.--a. The War Department and the Army are reorganized effective 0001, EST 11 June 1946 to provide under the Chief of Staff a War Department General and Special Staff; a ground force under a Commanding General, Army Ground Forces; and air force under a Commanding General, Army Air Forces; and Administrative and Technical Staffs and Service under their respective heads; all with headquarters in Washington, D.C. with the exception of the Army Ground Forces, which will as soon as practicable establish its headquarters at Fort Monroe, Virginia; and in addition thereto, six army areas, the Military District of Washington, and such overseas departments, task forces, base commands, defense commands, commands in theaters of operations, and other commands as the Secretary of War may find necessary. Charts A, B, and C illustrate the organization of the War Department, the Army Air Forces, and the Army Ground Forces.

b. The following principles have been applied in designing the organization of the War Department as illustrated on Chart A and described in this circular:

(1) The Army Air Forces must be provided with the maximum degree of autonomy permitted by law without permitting

24

the creation of unwarranted duplication in the functions of service, supply, and administration.

(2) A simple and flexible organization with clear-cut command is needed to satisfy the requirements of economy and efficiency.

(3) The top organization of the War Department must be capable of carrying out the Chief of Staff's orders quickly and effectively. At the peak of this top organization is the War Department General Staff which must be the agency to deal with matters of high policy and high-level planning and which must also direct and supervise, to the end that orders and directives are issued and supervised to the necessary degree in their execution.

(4) The structure of the staff organization supporting the Chief of Staff and the Deputy Chief of Staff must be as simple as possible with a minimum of individuals habitually reporting direct to the Chief of Staff or his Deputy.

(5) Adequate organizational means must be provided for carrying on the best possible research and development program and intelligence and counterintelligence activities, and for the elimination of unnecessary overlapping of activities of the War Department.

(6) The necessary degree of efficiency and vitality in the top echelons of the War Department can be attained only through the aggressive application of the principle of decentralization. Thus, no functions should be performed at the staff level of the War Department which can be decentralized to the major commands, the Army areas, or the administrative and technical services without loss of adequate control by the General and Special Staffs.

(7) There should be a single continuous command channel from top to bottom of the War Department organization.

(8) Direct contact and mutual arrangements within approved policies between major commands, staff divisions, and administrative and technical staffs and services are desirable and are authorized and encouraged.

3. Assignment of functions established by statute.-a. The functions, duties, and powers of the chiefs of the following arms are assigned to the Commanding General, Army Ground Forces: Infantry, Cavalry, Field Artillery, and Coast Artillery Corps (except those relating to procurement, storage, and issue).

b. The functions, duties, and powers of the Commanding General, General Headquarters, Air Force (Air Force Combat

Command) and of the Chief of the Air Corps are assigned to the Commanding General, Army Air Forces.

c. The functions, duties, and powers of the Quartermaster General relating to procurement, storage, and issue are assigned to the Chief of Ordnance.

d. The functions, duties, and powers of The Quartermaster General relating to water and commercial transportation are assigned to the Chief of Transportation. The functions, duties and powers of The Quartermaster General relating to the procurement supply, and 3d and 4th echelon maintenance of general and special motor vehicles are assigned to the Chief of Ordnance.

4. Transfer of functions and personnel from Special Planning Divisions, War Department Special Staff.-The Special Planning Division, War Department Special Staff is abolished. Its functions, and such parts or individuals of its staff as may be required, are transferred to the Organization and Training Division, War Department General Staff.

5. Transfer of functions and personnel from Headquarters, Army Service Forces.-Headquarters, Army Service Forces is abolished. The following functions and personnel are transferred:

a. The functions of the Military Personnel Division, Headquarters, Army Service Forces, and such parts or individuals of its staff as may be required, are transferred to the Personnel and Administration Division, War Department General Staff. The Director of Personnel and Administration will reassign such functions and individuals as he deems advisable to The Adjutant General.

b. The functions of the Personal Affairs Division, Headquarters, Army Service Forces, and such parts or individuals of its staff as may be required, are transferred to The Adjutant General.

c. The functions of the Director of Military Training, Headquarter, Army Service Forces, and such parts or individuals of his staff as may be required, are transferred to the Organization and Training will reassign such functions and individuals as he deems advisable to the Commanding General, Army Ground Forces.

d. The functions of the Intelligence Division, Headquarters, Army Service Forces, and such parts or individuals of its staff as may be required, are transferred to the Intelligence Division, War Department General Staff.

e. The labor supply and industrial relations functions of the former Industrial Personnel Division, Headquarters, Army Service Forces, and such parts or individuals of the Division as may be required, are transferred to the Service, Supply, and Procurement Division, War Department General Staff.

f. The civilian personnel functions of the former Industrial

Personnel Division, Headquarters, Army Service Forces, and such parts or individuals of the Division as may be required, are transferred to the Civilian Personnel Division, Office of the Secretary of War.

g. The functions of the former Research and Development Division, Headquarters, Army Service Forces, and such parts or individuals of its staff as may be required, are transferred to the Research and Development Division, War Department General Staff.

h. The position of the Fiscal Director, Headquarters, Army Service Forces, is abolished. Such functions and duties, parts, or individuals of that office as may be required are transferred to the Chief of Finance.

i. The Special Services Division, Headquarters, Army Service Forces, is established as an administrative service of the War Department.

j. Functions of Headquarters Army Service Forces Space Control, and such parts or individuals of its staff as may be required, are transferred to the Commanding General, Military District of Washington.

k. Headquarters, Army Service Forces office supply functions, and such individuals concerned with these functions as may be required, are transferred to the Procurement and Accounting Division, Office of the Secretary of War.

l. The functions of the Recurring Reports Control System, Headquarters, Army Service Forces, and such individuals connected with this system as may be required, are transferred to the Strength Accounting and Statistics Office, Office, Chief of Staff.

m. The command functions of Headquarters, Army Service Forces with respect to service, supply, and procurement activities are abolished. General Staff responsibility in these fields, to include responsibility for functions presently charged to the Logistics Group, Operations Division, is charged to the Director of Service, Supply, and Procurement, War Department General Staff. Such parts or individuals of Headquarters, Army Service Forces, of Logistics Group, OPD, and of the Office of the Assistant Chief of Staff, G-4, War Department General Staff, as may be required are transferred to the Service, Supply , and Procurement Division, War Department General Staff.

n. The functions of The Adjutant General pertaining to civilian personnel of Headquarters, Army Service Forces, so far as they concern civilian personnel transferred from Headquarters, Army Service Forces, to the War Department General and Special Staffs, are transferred to the Personnel and Administrative Branch, Office, Chief of Staff.

6. Organization of continental United States.---a. For command

of all activities except activities of the Army Air Forces and exempted installations, the continental United States is divided as follows:

First Army Area--------------------States presently included in the First and Second Service Commands

Second Army Area------------------States presently included in the Third and Fifth Service Commands

Third Army Area-------------------States presently included in the Fourth Service Command

Fourth Army Area------------------States presently included in the Eighth Service Command

Fifth Army Area-------------------States presently included in the Sixth and Seventh Service Command

Sixth Army Area-------------------States presently included in the Ninth Service Command

Military District of Washington---District of Columbia, and such adjacent territory as may be prescribed from time to time.

 b. All functions of command (except with respect to Army Air Forces activities and exempted installations) within these areas are assigned as follows:

To Commanding General, First Army--First Army Area
To Commanding General, Second Army--Second Army Area
To Commanding General, Seventh Army--Third Army Area
To Commanding General, Fourth Army --Fourth Army Area
To Commanding General, Fifth Army* --Fifth Army Area
To Commanding General, Sixth Army--Sixth Army Area
To Commanding General, Military District of Washington--
 Military District of Washington

 c. Army headquarters will be established at or in the vicinity of the following location:

Headquarters, First Army--New York City, New York
Headquarters, Second Army--Baltimore, Maryland
Headquarters, Seventh Army--Atlanta, Georgia
Headquarters, Fourth Army--San Antonio, Texas

---

* To be activated by the Commanding General, Army Ground Forces. Upon return of the Third Army from overseas, the Seventh Army will be inactivated and replaced by the Third Army.

Headquarters, Sixth Army--San Francisco, California

d. Service command headquarters listed below are abolished, effective as of the date of the reorganization. Their functions, together with such parts and individuals of these headquarters as may be required, are transferred as follows:

From Headquarters, Second Service Command to Headquarters, First Army.

From Headquarters, Third Service Command to Headquarters, Second Army.

From Headquarters, Fourth Service Command to Headquarters, Seventh Army.

From Headquarters, Eighth Service Command to Headquarters, Fourth Army.

From Headquarters, Sixth Service Command to Headquarters, Fifth Army.

e. Headquarters, First Service Command will remain at Boston, Massachusetts, as an area command under the Commanding General, First Army, with functions and duties as prescribed by him.

f. Headquarters, Fifth Service Command, will remain at Columbus, Ohio, as an area command under the Commanding General, Second Army, with functions and duties as prescribed by him.

g. Headquarters, Seventh Service Command, will remain at Omaha, Nebraska, as an area command under the Commanding General, Fifth Army, with functions and duties as prescribed by him.

h. Headquarters, Ninth Service Command, will remain at Salt Lake City, Utah, as an area command under the Commanding General, Sixth Army, with functions and duties as prescribed by him.

7. Army Air Forces commands.--For command of Army Air Forces activities, the Commanding General, Army Air Forces, will establish--

a. A Tactical Air Command with headquarters at Langley Field, Virginia.

b. A Strategic Air Command with headquarters at Andrews Field, Maryland.

c. An Air Defense Command with headquarters at Mitchel Field, New York.

d. Six air defense areas with headquarters in the vicinity of the army headquarters set forth above.

e. Such other commands as he deems necessary.

8. Chief of Staff.--The Chief of Staff is the principal military adviser to the President and to the Secretary of War on the conduct of war and the principal military adviser and executive to the Secretary of War on the activities of the Military establishment. The Chief of Staff has command of all components of the Army of the United States and of the operating forces comprising the Army Ground forces, the Army Air forces, the army areas,

oversea departments, task forces, base commands, defense commands, commands in theaters of operations, and all other commands, and the related supply and service establishments of the Army, and is responsible to the Secretary of War for their use in war and plans and preparations for their readiness for war. The Chief of Staff, under the direction of the Secretary of War, is responsible for the coordination and direction of the War Department General and Special Staffs and the administrative and technical services.

9. Chief of Public Information.--The Chief of Public Information advises the Secretary of War and the Chief of Staff on matters of policy relating to public relations and information and coordinates the operations of the Public Relations Division, the Legislative and Liaison Division, and the Information and Education Division, War Department Special Staff.

10. War Department General Staff.--The War Department General Staff, under the direction of the Chief of Staff, will be responsible for the development of the Army and will insure the existence of a well-balanced and efficient military team. It is specifically charged with the duty of providing such broad basic policies and plans as will enable the Commanding Generals of the Army Ground Forces, the Army Air Forces, task forces, theaters of operations, oversea commands, and such other commands as may be established, and the heads of the administrative and technical services, to prepare and execute detailed programs. In addition, the General Staff assists the Chief of Staff by issuing in the name of the Secretary of War and the Chief of Staff, necessary directives to implement such plans and policies and supervises the execution of these directives. In performing its duties the General Staff follow the principle of decentralization to the fullest degree. No function will be performed at the general or special staff level of the War Department which can be decentralized to the fullest degree. No function will be performed at the general or special staff level of the War Department which can be decentralized to the major commands, the army areas, or the administrative and technical services without loss of adequate control of operations by the General and Special Staffs. The War Department General Staff will include six divisions, each under the immediate control of a director. Each director will plan, direct, and supervise the execution of operations within the confines of his sphere of action. In carrying out their duties, the Directors of the six General Staff Divisions will be guided by the following general principles:

a. They will plan, direct, coordinate, and supervise. They will assist the Chief of Staff in getting things done, in addition to coordinating, planning, and policymaking on an Army-wide level.

b. They will, by means of direct contact with troops, determine

30

that orders, instructions, and directions are being carried out as the Chief of Staff intended.

c. They will follow the principle of decentralization to the fullest degree. The War Department General Staff will concern itself primarily only with matters which must be considered on a War Department or Army-wide level. All other matters will be decentralized down to the proper echelons of command for action or decision. In order for this to be done properly, adequate authority will be delegated to responsible commanders and the heads of the administrative and technical services. Each director will take necessary action to indoctrinate each officer of his division with a thorough understanding of the duties, functions, responsibility, and authority of the various echelons of command in the Army.

d. They must act to minimize duplication. While observing the principle of decentralization, all general staff directors will take appropriate action to minimize duplication and overlapping between the commands and services. This subject becomes of increasing importance as procedures are approved providing for greater autonomy for the Army Air Forces within the War Department structure.

The aim will be to provide the Army Air Forces with the maximum degree of autonomy permitted by law without permitting the creation of unwarranted duplication in the functions of service, supply, and administration. The only workable procedure for removing and preventing duplications lies in the good faith and friendly collaboration of using commands and services, under the monitorship of the appropriate general staff director.

11. Director of Personnel and Administration.--The Director of Personnel and Administration, War Department General Staff, is the military personnel manager of the War Department. He has the primary general staff interest in manpower. He is the adviser to and assistant to the Chief of Staff for administrative matters and for matters relating to manpower as a whole and to military personnel as individuals throughout the Army. He has overall War Department responsibility for the procurement, allocation,* and reallocation of personnel in bulk in accordance with established requirements and priorities, and for the separation of individuals from the military service.

12. Director of Intelligence.--The Director of Intelligence, War Department General Staff, is the responsible War Department inst[r]umentality for the collection and evaluation of information and for the dissemination of intelligence pertaining to foreign

---

* Until otherwise directed, the War Department Manpower Board will continue its present procedures for the control of zone of interior operating personnel.

countries, their war potential and military forces. He is responsible for the procurement of information and intelligence relating to the activities of individuals or agencies potentially or actually dangerous to the preservation of the military establishment within the zone of interior of foreign positive intelligence. He is responsible for meeting intelligence requirements of the Army Ground Forces, the Army Air Forces, continental and oversea commands, and the administrative and technical services. As intelligence is a vital function of command, the commanding generals of the major commands and their subordinate units must have intelligence agencies adequate to meet their intelligence requirements. Operating under general coordination of the War Department, all intelligence agencies must mutually support and collaborate with each other to form a team serving their own, subordinate, and higher echelons. The Director of Intelligence is responsible for representing the War Department on intelligence and counterintelligence matters with other departments of the Government and with foreign governments.

13. Director of Organization and Training.--The Director of Organization and Training, War Department General Staff, will exercise General Staff direction of the organization, mobilization, demobilization, and training of all components of the Army of the United States. Except for individual training, he is primarily concerned with matters relating to units as distinguished from the primary interest of the Director of Personnel and Administration in matters relating to individuals.

14. Director of Service, Supply, and Procurement.--The Director of Service, Supply, and Procurement, War Department General Staff, will exercise General Staff responsibility for all matters of service, supply, and procurement pertaining to the Army. The Director of Service, Supply, and procurement reports to the Chief of Staff on matters pertaining to service and supply. On procurement and related matters, he is under the direction of the Under Secretary of War. The Director of Service, Supply, and Procurement is responsible for.--

	(Operational and strategic planning--in collaboration with the Director of Plans and Operations)
Logistical Planning	

Service activities.

Supply control.

Distribution, storage, and maintenance of supplies and equipment.

	As to development contracts, the determination of the contractor to be employed, the scope of the contract, and the main features as to price and other particulars, is a staff function of the Director of Research and Development. The drafting, execution, and administration of the contracts is a part of the procurement program.
Purchasing Production	

Disposal of surplus military and industrial property, including real estate, salvage, and scrap.

15.   Director of Plans and Operations.--The Director of Plans and Operations, War Department General Staff, is responsible for the formulation, development, direction, supervision, and coordination of strategic and operational plans, current and future, for the Army. He exercises General Staff supervision and direction of strategic and operational matters relating to overseas and major commands, including activities concerning locations and armament of coast and land fortifications and of emergency plans and operations for the use of Army troops in domestic disturbances. Without vitiating the primary interests of other general staff directors in their respective fields of responsibility, he coordinates all policies and directives and changes thereto, including allocation of resources, affecting strategic, operational, and political matters relating to oversea and major commands. He estimates the current situation to determine military policy, objectives, and major elements of requirements and means. He provides representation on various boards and committees concerned with strategic and operational planning. As Senior Army Planner, he supervises and coordinates the war planning activities of the general staff directors and the major commands and furnishes guidance on current and future plans and operations. He

develops and keeps current the future and operational plans involving the Army in conjunction with appropriate joint agencies. He reviews and recommends action to the Chief of Staff on joint and combined papers and initiates War Department execution of approved papers of joint and combined agencies, the State-War-Navy Coordinating Committee, the Air Coordinating Committee, and other similar agencies.

16. Director of Research and Development.--The Director of Research and Development, War Department General Staff, has primary War Department interest in the application of national scientific resources to the solution of military problems. He is the adviser to the Secretary of War and the Chief of Staff on all War Department matters relating to research and development. He has over-all War Department responsibility for the initiation, allocation, coordination, and progress of research and development programs. He is also charged with bringing about the expeditious demonstration of new or improved weapons, military equipment, and techniques of their employment to the using services. The Director is responsible that adequate provision is made for the mobilization of the scientific effort for carrying forward the research and development program of the War Department.

17. War Department Special Staff.--The following divisions, because of their fields of activity, report direct to the Deputy Chief of Staff and are designated as Special Staff Divisions:

   Public Relations Division
   Legislative and Liaison Division
   Information and Education Division
   National Guard Bureau
   Executive for Reserve and ROTC Affairs
   Office of the Inspector General
   Historical Division
   War Department Manpower Board
   Budget Division
   Civil Affairs Division

18. Public Relations Division.--The Chief, Public Relations Division, War Department Special Staff, will coordinate, process, and release all War Department announcements of public interest, including photographs and motion pictures, to news-gathering agencies, radio stations and networks, film producers, and other public and private organizations in the field of public information; will supervise War Department contacts with these agencies; and will assist outside writers by gathering material and arranging interviews with officials within and outside the War Department.

19. Legislative and Liaison Division.--The Chief, Legislative and Liaison Division, War Department Special Staff, will for-

mulate, coordinate, and accomplish the War Department legislative program, except appropriations bills; will participate in official War Department contacts with the Congress and its individual Members, except in matters pertaining to appropriations; and will coordinate contacts of other War Department agencies with the Congress.

20. Information and Education Division.--The Chief, Information and Education Division, War Department Special Staff, is charged with developing basic plans and policies for information and education activities for military personnel. He supervises the execution of information and education programs, but in so doing does not engage in operations or administrative duties where an agency exists for that purpose.

21. National Guard Bureau.--The National Guard Bureau, War Department Special Staff, is the agency through which the War Department maintains relations with the National Guard in the 48 States, the District of Columbia, Hawaii, Alaska, and Puerto Rico, and is charged with the administration of approved War Department policies, other than those relative to training, for the National Guard not in the service of the United States, and the promulgation of War Department directives and regulations applicable to the National Guard, including those relating to training.

22. Office of the Executive for Reserve and ROTC Affairs.--The Executive for Reserve and ROTC Affairs, War Department Special Staff, will advise and assist the Chief of Staff in the exercise of his supervision and control of the Organized Reserves and the Reserve Officers' Training Corps, including liaison therewith, and in keeping the Secretary of War informed on Reserve and ROTC affairs. He will be responsible for maintaining close contact, mutual understanding, and effective cooperation between the War Department and the Reserve component and ROTC, and for necessary staff functions involved in this mission, except those functions assigned to other agencies of the War Department.

23. Office of The Inspector General.--The Office of The Inspector General, War Department Special Staff, is charged with inquiring into and reporting upon matters which affect the efficiency and economy of the Army of the United States, making such inspections, investigations, surveys, and studies as may be prescribed by law or regulations, as may be directed by the Secretary of War, the Under Secretary of War, the Assistant Secretaries of War, or the Chief of Staff, or as may be requested by the Commanding Generals, Army Ground Forces or Army Air Forces.

24. Historical Division.--The Chief, Historical Division, War Department Special Staff, is responsible for preparing plans and policies for, and exercising supervision and direction over, War Department and Army historical activities other than current

reports.

25. War Department Manpower Board.--The War Department Manpower Board, War Department Special Staff, is charged with continuous survey of the military and civilian personnel employed in operating the zone of interior installations, with the objective of recommending to the Chief of Staff measures for the most effective and economical use of such personnel. Until otherwise directed, the War Department Manpower Board will continue its present procedures for the control of zone of interior operating personnel.

26. Budget Division.--The Chief, Budget Division, War Department Special Staff, will be responsible for preparing plans and policies and exercising general supervision and control over all War Department and Army budgetary matters, and for formulating and coordinating basic fiscal policy for the War Department. The Chief is also Budget Officer for the War Department and Chairman of the Budget Advisory Committee.

27. Civil Affairs Division.--The Chief, Civil Affairs Division, War Department Special Staff, formulates policy, prepares plans, and takes action in coordination with other War Department agencies, other agencies of the Government, and international or voluntary relief and welfare agencies on civil affairs/military government matters, including war crimes. He insures that the Secretary of War, the Chief of Staff, and interested staff divisions are properly advised on civil affairs/military government matters.

28. Administrative staffs and services.--a. The administrative services are as follows:

    Adjutant General's Department
    Judge Advocate General's Department
    Corps of Chaplains
    Office of the provost Marshal General
    Special Services Division

b. The heads of the administrative services are also administrative staff officers of the War Department. As such, they function according to the principles referred to in paragraph 29b. The War Department General and Special Staffs will decentralize appropriate functions to the administrative services to the maximum extent practicable. Direct communication and instruction between the appropriate staff divisions and the administrative services is directed as provided in paragraph 29c.

c. The administrative services are supervised and coordinated in their activities relating to personnel and administration by the Director of Personnel and Administration, except that with respect to courts-martial and certain legal matters. The Judge Advocate General will report direct to the Secretary of War for the Under Secretary of War. Activities of the above services, other than those connected with personnel and administration will, with the exception mentioned above, be under the supervision and coordination of appropriate staff divisions, and direct communication for the purpose is authorized. These arrangements are not intended to preclude the furnishing of services and advice to other agencies of the War Department. Such procedure is authorized and encouraged.

29. Technical staffs and services.--a. The technical services are as follows:

> Ordnance Department
> Signal Corps
> Quartermaster Corps
> Corps of Engineers
> Transportation Corps
> Medical Department
> Chemical Warfare Service
> Finance Department

b. The heads of the technical services are also technical staff officers of the War Department. As such their general functions (see par. 18, FM 101-5) include-

(1) Technical and administrative advice and recommendations to the Secretary of War, the Chief of Staff, and the War Department General and Special Staffs.

(2) Preparation of plans, estimates, and orders in order to relieve these staffs of routine duties.

(3) Coordination with these staffs of their operational, administrative, and technical plans and activities.

In their capacities as heads of technical services, they are commanders of troops or activities assigned to their control and heads of technical an supply services, and as such have the usual functions of command or control over troops, activities, or services. These two functions of staff and command, although vested in a single individual, are separate and distinct in that each involves different responsibilities and duties, and the exercise of one is not to be confused with nor permitted to interfere with the exercise of the other.

c. The technical services are supervised and coordinated in their activities relating to service, supply, and procurement by the Director of Service, Supply, and Procurement. All other activities of the technical services are supervised and coordinated by the appropriate staff divisions in accordance with the principles governing the relationship between general staff and technical staff as laid down in paragraph 5, FM 101-5. The War Department General and Special Staffs will decentralize appropriate functions to the technical services to the maximum extent practicable.

Direct communication and instruction between the appropriate staff divisions and the technical services is directed as follows:

(1) Personnel and administration--Personnel and Administration Division.

(2) Intelligence--Intelligence Division.

(3) Training of technical and supply troops under their command and the operation of schools for the training of officers and of technical specialists for the Army as a whole and organizational matters pertaining to the technical services--Organization and Training Division.

(4) Technical aspects of operational and strategic plans and of operations--Plans and Operations Division.

(5) Service, supply, and procurement activities--Service, Supply, and Procurement Division.

(6) Research and development--Research and Development Division.

(7) Budgetary activities--Budget Division.

(8) Public relations--Public Relations Division.

(9) Legislative matters (other than appropriations) --Legislative and Liaison Division.

d. Relations with subordinate commands of the major commands.--Directions or instructions will be issued to subordinate commands of the major commands through appropriate channels of command and not directly from one technical staff officer to the corresponding staff officer in the subordinate command. However, the duties of the heads of the technical services, acting in their capacities as technical staff officers of the War Department, will include such Army-wide technical supervision and inspections of activities as the Chief of Staff may prescribe.

30. Army Air Forces.--a. The Commanding General, Army Air Forces, is charged with the functions, responsibilities, and authorities of command authorized by law, Army Regulations, and custom over individuals and units assigned to the Army Air Forces.

b. The subordinate commands of the Army Air Forces are as follows:

Strategic Air Command
Air Defense Command
Tactical Air Command
Air Materiel Command
Air Training Command
Air University
Air Proving Ground Command
Air Transport Command

c. For a description of the detailed functions and responsibilities of the Commanding General, Army Air Forces, and the subordinate commands of the Army Air Forces, see appendix I.

31. Army Ground Forces.--The Commanding General, Army Ground Forces, commands the six armies within the continental United States and is charged with the functions, responsibilities, and authorities of command authorized by law, Army Regulations, and custom over individuals and units assigned to the Army Ground Forces.

32. Army areas.--The commanding general of each of the armies and of the Military District of Washington will command all units, posts, camps, stations, and except units, posts, camps, stations, or installations commanded by the Army Air Forces. The commanding general of each of the armies is responsible for the operations, training, administration, services, and supply of all units, posts, camps, stations, and installations of his command. He is responsible for certain activities at exempted stations, as set forth in appendix II.

Note.--For a description of the detailed functions and responsibilities of the Army Ground Forces and the army areas as well as channels of command and communication, see appendix II.

33. Classification of installations.--a. Installations are classified as follows:

(1) Class I installations.--Installations under the command of the commanding general of an army or of the Military District of Washington.

(2) Class II installations.--Installations under the command of the head of an administrative or technical service or other War Department official. Stations presently classified as Class IV are hereby reclassified as Class II with exceptions and additions as noted below.

(3) Class III installations.--Installations under the command of the Commanding General, Army Air Forces.

b. Installations of the types listed below are included in Class II:

(1) Government-owned manufacturing plans of all supply services.

(2) Research testing laboratories, proving grounds, and technical service boards.

(3) Storage depots, supply arsenals, remount depots, and motor bases, including maintenance and repair of equipment thereat.

(4) Transportation zones and transportation districts.

(5) Ports of embarkation within the continental United States, including subports of embarkation, staging areas, and oversea discharge and replacement depots.

(6) Signal Corps Photographic Center.
(7) Procurement districts.
(8) General Hospitals.
(9) Finance Offices, United States Army.
(10) Alaska Communication System.
(11) Branch offices of the Information and Education
     Division, War Department Special Staff.
(12) Schools and replacement training centers operated by
     the heads of the administrative and technical
     services and by the Commanding General, Army Ground
     Forces.
(13) United States Military Academy.
(14) Command and General Staff School.
(15) General service schools that may be established from
     time to time.
(16) Quartermaster market centers.
(17) Technical service repair shops.
(18) Other installations that may be designated by the
     War Department from time to time

   c. For statement of services performed by army commanders for
Class II and Class III installations, see Appendix II.

   34. Administrative procedure for addressing, identifying, and
custody of communications.--a. Effective as of 11 June 1946,
other than those matters requiring the attention of the Secretary
of War, the Under Secretary of War, the Assistant Secretary of
War, or the Assistant Secretary of War for Air, or as otherwise
authorized by current instructions of the Secretary of War, all
communications and dispatches, including wire, radio, cable, and
teletype, intended for the consideration of the War Department
General or Special Staffs will be addressed to the Chief of Staff,
United States Army, Washington 25, D.C. All others, as well as
all doubtful cases, will be addressed to The Adjutant General, War
Department, Washington 25, D.C.

   b. Where special instructions direct it, mail addressed to The
Adjutant General will include the specific subdivisions of The
Adjutant General's Office, the street address and the building.

   c. It is not intended to prevent direct communication whenever
advisable between the various agencies of the War Department and
the major commands. In the interests of decentralization, direct
communication is encouraged. Major commands may address communications directly to the War Department General and Special
Staff Divisions, the administrative and technical services, and
other agencies of the War Department, which pertain solely to the
activities of those War Department agencies.

   d. Major commands and oversea departments and
commands.--Communications intended for Headquarters, Army Air

Forces; Headquarters, Army Ground Forces; the army areas; the Military District of Washington; or oversea departments and commands will be addressed in accordance with AR 340-15, or instructions of the commanding general thereof.

e. Communications intended for boards, exempted stations, exempted activities, including the Manhattan District, military missions, and commissions will be addressed to the president, commander, chairman, or head of the activity according to his title and not to him by name.

f. Custody of communications.

(1) The Adjutant General will maintain current files of communications received by or referred to him for action and of directives authenticated or published and distributed by him to elements of the Military Establishment. Supporting papers essential to an understanding of the background of a communication or directive (or in lieu of such papers, a full memo for record) will in all cases be routed to The Adjutant General's Office for file with the related communication or directive. The Adjutant General will also maintain current military personnel records of the Army, current civilian personnel records of specified staff elements, and other files incident to the administration of his office.

(2) Divisions of the War Department General and Special Staffs will each maintain an office of record for its current correspondence. Such current files will be cut off at regular intervals to facilitate transfer, when noncurrent, to the War Department Records Branch, The Adjutant General's Office. In organizing current files, the guidance of records administrators designated under the provisions of AR 15-15, will be fully utilized. The Adjutant General will provide such additional assistance as may be necessary.

(3) Files of staff elements and activities affected by the reorganization will not be merged when activities are consolidated. Existing files will be broken off as of the effected date of consolidation or other major internal reorganization and new files will be established. The old files will be held by the successor office or activity for a period normally not exceeding one year, during which time incomplete cases may be brought forward to the new files. The noncurrent files will then be transferred to the War Department Records Branch, The Adjutant General's Office. Activities which are discontinued will close

out their files and retire them at the earliest practicable date.

g. Identification of communications.

    (1) All War Department telegrams, radiograms, and cables will include an identifying office symbol of five letters, the first two or three of which will identify the subdivision of the War Department or of the Army and the last two or three of which will identify the sending agency.

    (2) Basic symbol letters will be as follows:

        (a) War Department General Staff--------------WDG
        (b) War Department Special Staff--------------WDS
        (c) Army Air Forces---------------------------AF
        (d) Army Ground Forces------------------------GN
        (e) First Army Area--------------------------AH
        (f) Second Army Area-------------------------AI
        (g) Third Army Area--------------------------AJ
        (h) Fourth Army Area-------------------------AK
        (i) Fifth Army Area--------------------------AL
        (j) Sixth Army Area--------------------------AM
        (k) Military District of Washington------------AN

    (3) Each agency in (2) above will assign appropriate additional letters to identify subdivisions of their command.

    (4) War Department General and Special Staff symbols are assigned as follows:

        (a) Chief of Staff, U. S. Army--------------WDCSA
        (b) Chief of Public Information-------------WDCPI
        (c) Director of Personnel and
            Administration------------------------WDGPA
        (d) Director of Intelligence---------------WDGID
        (e) Director of Organization and Training---WDGOT
        (f) Director of Service, Supply, and
            Procurement---------------------------WDGSP
        (g) Director of Plans and Operations--------WDGPO
        (h) Director of Research and Development----WDGRD
        (i) Public Relations Division--------------WDSPR
        (j) Legislative and Liaison Division--------WDSLL
        (k) Information and Education Division------WDSIE
        (l) National Guard Bureau------------------WDSNG
        (m) Executive for Reserve and ROTC Affairs--WDSRR
        (n) Office of The Inspector General---------WDSIG
        (o) Historical Division--------------------WDSHD
        (p) War Department Manpower Board----------WDSMB
        (q) Budget Division------------------------WDSBU
        (r) Civil Affairs Division-----------------WDSCA

(5) The Adjutant General will be responsible for the revision of War Department Memorandum 850-45, Basic Office Symbols, 10 February 1945, in order to establish office symbols for the administrative and technical services and other War Department agencies.

h. Identification of correspondence.--Office symbols will be used to identify correspondence in accordance with the provisions of TM 12-253 and other War Department instructions.

35. Revision of publications.--Revisions of the organization statements of the War Department General and Special Staffs and the administrative and technical services as presently contained in War Department General Staff circulars and Army Service Forces Manual M301 respectively, will be prepared by the appropriate agencies and forwarded to the Deputy Chief of Staff. Organization statements for the General and Special Staffs will be published as War Department General Staff circulars. Organization statements for the administrative and technical services will be published as War Department Memorandums. Both will be prepared in the format of the War Department General Staff Circular, Organization Series. Necessary concurrences will be secured by the agencies preparing the statements and will be indicated clearly in the Summary Sheet accompanying this material to the Deputy Chief of Staff.

36. Rescission.--WD Circular 59, 1942, as amended by section I, WD Circular 107, 1942; section IV, WD Circular 183; section X WD Circular 368, 1944; and section V, WD Circular 281, 1945, is rescinded.

CHART B

ORGANIZATION OF THE ARMY AIR FORCES

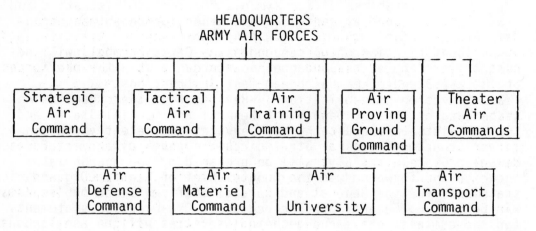

11 June 1946

Appendix I

ARMY AIR FORCES

1. Functions and responsibilities.--The Commanding General, Army Air Forces, is charged with functions, responsibilities, and authorities of command authorized by law, Army Regulations, and custom over individuals and units assigned to the Army Air Forces. Specifically, the Commanding General, Army Air Forces, will-

a. Direct the operations and training of the Air Commands within the continental United States.

b. Exercise control over administrative matters bearing directly on operations and training and in such other matters as delegated by the War Department.

c. Determine the organization, composition, equipment, and training of all air combat and service units assigned to the Army Air Forces.

d. Be responsible for repair and utility functions at all Class III installations.

e. Prepare estimates of funds necessary to operate the activities under Army Air Forces control for presentation to the Budget Officer for the War Department. The Army Air Forces will be represented on the Budget Advisory Committee.

f. Conduct those intelligence activities which pertain to his field of primary responsibility.

g. Initiate requirements for the research and development of items of equipment in which the Army Air Forces has a primary interest.

h. Determine, in conformance with the broad directives of the War Department, Army Air Forces materiel and personnel requirements, both quantitative and qualitative.

i. Conduct the Army Air Forces part of the Universal Military Training Program under such directives as are issued by the War Department.

j. Operate schools and replacement facilities as directed by War Department.

k. Supervise and inspect the training of air components of the ROTC, the National Guard, and the Organized Reserves as instructed by the War Department. Direct and supervise National Guard inspections by inspectors general.

l. Verify that all Army Air Forces units and installations are supplied, equipped, housed, hospitalized, and furnished transportation for the performance of their missions and maintain logistical efficiency within the Army Air Forces.

m. Conduct research, develop, procure, and distribute those items of equipment which are peculiar to the Air Force and such other items as may be prescribed by the Secretary of War.

n. Cooperate with the Commanding General, Army Ground Forces, in the development and determination of such special tactics as are necessary to support the Army Ground Forces and for the use of arms by the Army Air Forces, especially antiaircraft artillery.

o. Cooperate with the Commanding General, Army Ground Forces, in the development and determination of the technique of fire at aerial targets, in prescribing military characteristics of weapons and equipment, and in preparation of Tables of Organization and Equipment for units of antiaircraft artillery.

p. Recommend to the War Department the means, including the necessary antiaircraft artillery units, required for air defense.

2. Subordinate commands and functions.--Under the command of the Commanding general, Army Air Forces, the subordinate commands of the Army Air Forces perform the following functions:

a. Strategic Air Command.

(1) Organizes, trains, and maintains a global air striking force to be employed and sustained as directed by the Commanding General, Army Air Forces.

(2) Trains very heavy bombardment crews and units for the performance of global bombardment operations.

(3) Trains very long range reconnaissance and photographic and mapping crews and units for the performance of global reconnaissance operations.

(4) Trains long range fighter crews and units for the performance of fighter, fighter escort, and joint Army and Navy operations.

(5) Maintains assigned units in a state of readiness to permit immediate operations, either alone or jointly with other forces, against enemies of the United States.

(6) Conducts such UMT unit training as may be appropriate and directed by the Commanding General, Army Air Forces.

(7) Controls installations and pursues activities required for the conduct of its functions.

b. Air Defense Command.

(1) Provides for the air defense of the United States.

(2) Organizes, administers, trains and maintains combat and service units as may be assigned by the Commanding General, Army Air Forces.

(3) Organizes, administers, trains, and maintains the Air National Guard and the Air Reserve.

(4) Conducts UMT unit training as may be directed by the Commanding General Army Air Forces.

   (5) Organizes, administers, trains, and maintains
     aircraft warning and control units.
   (6) Controls and trains antiaircraft units as may be
     assigned to this command.
   (7) Control such installations and pursues activities
     required for the conduct of its functions

c. Tactical Air Command.
   (1) Organizes, administers, trains, and maintains combat
     units skilled in the art of joint operations with
     ground and sea forces.
   (2) Promotes progressive development of air-ground coor-
     dination techniques and doctrines.
   (3) Participates in such land and sea operations and
     field exercises as may be directed by the
     Commanding General, Army Air Forces.
   (4) Controls and trains such antiaircraft units as may
     be assigned.
   (5) Controls installations and pursues activities
     required for the conduct of its functions.
   (6) Conducts such UMT unit training as may be directed
     by the Commanding General, Army Air Forces.

d. Air Materiel Command.
   (1) Conducts research and development of aeronautical
     materials, associated equipment, accessories, and
     supplies procured by the Army Air Forces, and of
     such other materials as may be allocated to the
     Army Air Forces for research and development.
   (2) Conducts all experimental, static, and flight tests
     necessary to the development of such material.
   (3) Procures aircraft, spare parts, equipment, supplies,
     and services peculiar to the Army Air Forces and
     such other materials and services as may be allo-
     cated to the Army Air Forces for procurement.
   (4) Performs the operating functions relating to
     contract termination and the salvage and disposal
     of all Army Air Forces aircraft, accessories,
     equipment, and supplies, and for such other
     material as may be allocated to the Army Air
     Forces for procurement.
   (5) Performs the operating functions for the Army Air
     Forces with respect to production resources, sche-
     duling of production, allocation of production by
     plants, and production control, in facilities
     under Army Air Forces control.
   (6) Quality control and acceptance of aircraft,
     accessories, equipment, and supplies procured by

the Army Air Forces.

(7) Modifies materiel procured by the Army Air Forces and such other materiel as is authorized for modification.

(8) Computes requirements for equipment and supplies procured by the Army Air Forces and such others as are assigned to the Army Air Forces for determination of requirements, and administers funds pertaining thereto.

(9) Administers the distribution of aircraft equipment and supplies procured by the Army Air Forces and for which storage and issue are assigned and performs depot supply operating functions to accomplish the receipt, shipment, storage, issue, salvage, and disposal of approved Army Air Forces equipment and supplies procured by the Army Air Forces, and for such other materiel as is assigned to the Army Air Forces.

(10) Establishes a system of stock control and reports to insure the most efficient distribution of supplies and equipment procured by the Army Air Forces, wherever located, and for such other materiel as is assigned for storage and issue.

(11) Maintains, repairs, and restores all supplies and equipment procured by the Army Air Forces, when beyond the facilities of the Army Air Forces base and using organization, and other equipment when so directed.

(12) Issues technical and operating instructions, directive upon the Army Air Forces, for all responsibilities assigned the Army Air Forces and assists in the compliance therewith.

(13) Maintains technical supervision, through liaison representatives, over all Army Air Forces supplies and equipment shipped through ports of embarkation.

(14) Keeps the Commanding General, Army Air Forces, informed on the progress or delays in carrying out the foregoing programs and recommends action to insure that Army Air Forces supplies and equipment are developed, procured, supplied, and maintained as expeditiously as possible to fulfill the requirements of commands in the zone of interior and in theaters of operations.

(15) Organizes, processes, and prepares for dispatch all air depot groups and air service units, on the

48

depot level, required by the Army Air Forces and provides technical training peculiar to the requirements of the missions of these organizations.

(16) As directed by the Commanding General, Army Air Forces, provides other specialized maintenance training for aircraft and items of communications equipment allocated to the Army Air Forces.

(17) Provides personnel and facilities as directed for assisting development of air forces of certain friendly nations.

(18) Accumulates, evaluates, disseminates, and maintains reference material relative to technical data for research and development and historical study of all aircraft and related equipment and other equipment procured by the Army Air Forces.

(19) Exercises command control over the Army Air Forces Institute of Technology.

(20) Performs such other services as may be assigned by the Commanding General, Army Air Forces.

(21) Operates the technical intelligence services of the Army Air Forces.

e. Air Training Command.

(1) Provides format basic military training for all selectees and enlistees not having previous military training.

(2) Provides all air crew training of individuals leading to initial ratings.

(3) Provides certain graduate flying training courses.

(4) Provides formal training leading to original military occupational specialties by SSN for officers and enlisted personnel. This includes the operation of officer candidate schools.

(5) Provides advanced formal training for enlisted personnel.

(6) Provides certain advanced administrative and technical training courses for officers. This includes basic training in the intelligence techniques necessary to combat reporting, photographic intelligence, prisoner of war interrogation, briefing and interrogation of combat crews, and such other techniques as are peculiar or pertinent to the operation of intelligence activities in the field.

(7) Provides formal training for foreign personnel in accordance with the Training Command mission for

United States personnel.

    (8) Conducts Universal Military Training, Air Reserve Officers Training Courses, and Army Air Forces Extension Courses.

    (9) Maintains standards of proficiency in all phases of training and conducts training research leading toward improvement of individual proficiencies and methods of selection.

f. Air University.

    (1) Operates as an exempted activity under the Commanding General, Army Air Forces.

    (2) Supervises Army Air Forces schools and colleges.

    (3) Exercises broad supervision over the curricula of the Army Air Forces Institute of Technology.

    (4) Supervises continuing study of facilities of civilian educational institutions for the higher education of selected officers in scientific and technical and in other appropriate fields.

    (5) Submits to the Commanding General, Army Air Forces, plans and recommendations for organization and operation of the over-all Army Air Forces school system.

g. Air Proving Ground Command.--The Army Air Forces Proving Ground Command consists of the Army Air Forces Board and the Army Air Forces Proving Ground.

    (1) Army Air Forces Board.

        (a) Reviews, evaluates, and makes recommendations on the materiel and equipment used by the Army Air Forces, the results of tests of new developments and the action to be followed in future developments.

        (b) Develops and recommends the doctrines and techniques to be used in the training and employment of the Army Air Forces.

        (c) Determines the lessons learned from combat operations.

        (d) Advises the Commanding General, Army Air Forces, on all general policies affecting personnel, training, equipment, and organization.

        (e) Plans and supervises the development and testing, under simulated combat conditions, of new and different tactics and techniques of aerial warfare, including air defense; reviews and evaluates such tests, and makes recommendation based thereon.

        (f) Prepares, or collaborates in the preparation,

and recommends revisions to Headquarters, Army Air Forces, of all Field Service Regulations and War Department Field Manuals affecting the Army Air Forces, and such other War Department publications as contain Air Forces tactical doctrine.

(g) Collects, evaluates, and disseminates information pertaining to Army Air Forces activities in Arctic, desert, and tropic regions.

(2) Army Air Forces Proving Ground.

(a) Conducts tests of new and different tactics and techniques of aerial warfare under simulated combat conditions, and develops improved operational techniques.

(b) Conducts tests of materiel and equipment and appropriate organizations proposed for use by the Army Air Forces for operational and tactical suitability, under simulated combat conditions, as a basis for establishing military requirements.

(c) Provides such services, facilities, and assistance to the Air Materiel Command, and to other agencies designated by higher authority, as may be necessary to complete engineering and development tests.

(d) Provides detachments at proving grounds of other arms and services, as requested, to facilitate the establishment of Army Air Forces qualitative requirements and standards as approved by the Commanding General, Army Air Forces.

h. Air Transport Command.--Provides and operates for the Army on a global scale the following services:

Air Transport, airways communications, weather, aircraft accident prevention, air search and rescue, and aeronautical charts for the Air Forces and for such other Government agencies as may be directed by higher authority.

(3) Outline Command Plan, 14 December 1946

The successful adoption and use of unified commands in World War II predisposed the American military towards their use in the post-war period. Accordingly, on 12 December 1946 the Joint Chiefs of Staff (JCS) forwarded to President Harry S. Truman an outline command plan, which he approved on 14 December 1946. The immediate impetus for the formation of unified commands grew out of Navy dissatisfaction with command arrangements in the Pacific. During World War II, unified commands had been used in Europe with little difficulty. But in the Pacific, command had been divided between Gen. Douglas MacArthur, and Adm. Chester W. Nimitz, both of whom held five star rank and would not willingly be subordinate to the other.

The Navy wanted to establish commands based on geographic areas, while the Army and Army Air Forces (AAF) favored unity of command based on assignment of mission and forces. Both the Army and the AAF feared the Navy's plan for a unified Pacific command would deprive General MacArthur of control of air and ground forces needed to complete his mission. From February to December of 1946, the two sides discussed the issue, and settled on a compromise position which left two commands in the Pacific, although based on geographic area rather than function. The two commands, the Far East and Pacific commands were only two of the seven authorized. The other five were, Alaskan, Northeast, Caribbean, and European commands, and the Atlantic Fleet.

The JCS exercised strategic direction over the armed forces, assigning forces to the unified commands as well as missions and tasks. All forces not specifically assigned by the JCS remained under control of the individual service. Each unified command operated under a designated service chief acting as executive agent for the JCS. In a separate provision of the plan, the JCS recognized the existence of the Strategic Air Command (SAC), as a command of the AAF, composed of AAF strategic air forces not otherwise assigned and not normally based overseas, yet responsible to the JCS. The JCS did not formally assign a mission to SAC at that time, in fact not until 13 April 1948, but this was SAC's beginning as a JCS specified command, although it was not formally labelled as such until 1951.

Unified commands' forces consisted of two or more components from different services, each component commanded by an officer of that component. Each unified commander had a joint staff with membership from the various components under his command. On administrative, training, and construction matters, the components communicated directly with their own service headquarters, but operationally were commanded by the unified commander acting under the direction of the JCS, acting through an executive agent. Force assignments were determined by the JCS. The ultimate outcome for the services was to limit their role to mainly one of organizing, training, and equipping forces for operational employment within the unified command structure.

****

Herman S. Wolk, <u>Planning and Organizing the Postwar Air Force, 1943-1947</u>, (Washington, D.C.: Office of Air Force History, 1984), pp 158-60.

JCS Special Historical Study, "History of the Unified Command Plan," (Washington, D.C.: Historical Division, Joint Secretariat, JCS, 1977), pp 1-6.

THE JOINT CHIEFS OF STAFF
Washington 25, D.C.

12 December 1946

MEMORANDUM FOR THE PRESIDENT:

The Joint Chiefs of Staff have prepared an over-all plan for command of U. S. forces outside the continental United States. The objective is to attain a greater degree of unified command than now exists. They have reached agreement on all points.

You will note a significant change in connection with the Marianas Islands and the Bonins. The enclosed over-all plan makes General MacArthur responsible for their security, and their local forces and facilities will be assigned to his operational control to facilitate his discharging the responsibilities of his present mission. The Joint Chiefs of Staff agree that eventually operational control should revert to the Pacific command.

Attention is invited to divergent views of General MacArthur which are being submitted to you separately.

The enclosure is recommended for your approval.

For the Joint Chiefs of Staff:

William D. Leahy
Fleet Admiral, U. S. Navy,
Chief of Staff to the
Commander in Chief of the Army and Navy

Enclosure.

OUTLINE COMMAND PLAN

1. As an interim measure for the immediate postwar period, with particular consideration to the requirements for occupation of former enemy areas, the following commands will be established under the Joint Chiefs of Staff:

    a. Far East Command. Including U. S. forces in Japan, Korea, the Ryukyus, the Philippines, the Marianas Islands, and the Bonins.

        (1) The Commander in Chief, Far East, will exercise unified command over all forces allocated to him by the Joint Chiefs of Staff or other authority.

        (2) Missions:

            (a) Discharge U.S. occupation responsibilities in Japan and Southern Korea.

            (b) Discharge U.S. military responsibilities in the Philippines.

            (c) Maintain the security of the Far East Command including the protection of sea and air communications.

            (d) Support U.S. policy within the scope of his command responsibility.

            (e) Support the Commander in Chief, Pacific, in his mission.

            (f) Make plans and preparations within the resources assigned to him and prospectively available to him in case of a general emergency to:

                1. Provide for the safety of U.S. forces in Korea and China.

                2. Oppose enemy advances.

                3. Secure Japan, the Ryukyus, the Marianas, and the Bonins and discharge U.S. military responsibilities in the Philippines.

        (3) In case of an emergency declared by the Commander in Chief, Far East, command of U.S. armed forces in or affecting China will be exercised by him.

        (4) The Commander in Chief, Far East, shall have operational control of the facilities and local forces in the Marianas Islands and the Bonins Islands. This operational control does not include responsibility for the military and civil government of these islands, nor any responsibility for naval administration and naval logistics in these islands.

b. Pacific Command.

        (1) The Commander in Chief, Pacific, will exercise unified command over all forces allocated to him by the

Joint Chiefs of Staff or other authority.

(2) Missions:

(a) Defend the U.S. against attack through the Pacific Ocean.

(b) Support the Far East and Alaskan commanders in their missions.

(c) Conduct operations in the Pacific including the protection of sea and air communications, except as otherwise assigned.

(d) Maintain the security of U.S. island positions in the Pacific except as otherwise assigned.

(e) Provide naval forces as directed to discharge U.S. military commitments in China. The Joint Chiefs of Staff will retain under their own direction activities of the armed forces in or affecting China. In case of an emergency, declared by the Commander in Chief, Far East, these responsibilities pass to him.

(f) Support U.S. policy within the scope of his command responsibility.

(g) Make plans for accomplishing these missions in case of a general emergency.

c. Alaskan Command. Including forces assigned to the Aleutians.

(1) The Commander in Chief, Alaska, will exercise unified command over all forces allocated to him by the Joint Chiefs of Staff or other authority.

(2) Missions:

(a) Maintain the security of Alaska and the Aleutians, including the protection of sea and air communications, and protect the United States from attack through that area and the Arctic regions within his command.

(b) Support the Far East, Pacific, and Strategic Air commanders in their missions.

(c) Control the airways through the Arctic, except as that responsibility is otherwise assigned.

(d) Make plans for accomplishing these missions in case of a general emergency.

d. Northeast Command. Including forces assigned to Newfoundland, Labrador, and Greenland.

(1) The commander will exercise unified command over all forces allocated to him by the Joint Chiefs of Staff or other authority.

(2) Missions:

(a) Maintain the security of the Northeast Command including the protection of sea and air communications and defend the United States from attack through the Arctic regions within his command.

(b) Support the European, Atlantic Fleet and Strategic Air commanders in their missions.

(c) Control airways through the Arctic regions, except as that responsibility is otherwise assigned.

(d) Support U.S. policy within the scope of his command responsibility.

(e) Make plans for accomplishing these missions in case of a general emergency.

e. The Atlantic Fleet.

(1) The Commander in Chief, Atlantic Fleet, will:

(a) Defend the United States against attack through the Atlantic Ocean.

(b) Control the sea and secure the airways through the Atlantic except as otherwise assigned.

(c) Support the U.S. forces in Europe and in the Mediterranean.

(d) Support the forces of the Northeast and Caribbean Commands.

(e) Support U.S. policy within the scope of his command responsibility.

(f) Make plans for accomplishing these missions in case of a general emergency.

f. Caribbean Command. Including forces in Panama and the Antilles.

(1) The Commander in Chief, Caribbean, will exercise unified command over all forces allocated to him by the Joint Chiefs of Staff or other authority.

(2) Missions:

(a) Defend the United States against attack through the Caribbean, including protection of sea and air communications. (Within the Caribbean Command the routing and control of shipping will be the responsibility of the appropriate naval sea frontier commander. The Chief of Naval Operations will be responsible for coordinating these activities between the naval component command in the Caribbean, the adjacent continental sea frontiers, and the Atlantic Fleet.)

(b) Maintain the security of the Panama Canal and of U.S. bases in Panama and the Caribbean.

(c) Support the Atlantic Fleet commander in his missions.

(d) Support United States policy within the scope of his command responsibility.

(e) Make plans for accomplishing these missions in

case of a general emergency.

(3) Certain designated naval bases in the Caribbean area will be reserved to the operational control of the Atlantic Fleet. The security of these bases, to include plans for the use of appropriate units of the Atlantic Fleet in the area in time of emergency, will be a responsibility of the Caribbean Command.

g. European Command.

(1) The Commander in Chief, U.S. Forces European Theater, will exercise unified command over all forces allocated to him by the Joint Chiefs of Staff or other authority.

(2) Missions:

(a) Support United States policy in Europe within the scope of his command responsibility.

(b) Occupation of Germany.

(c) Make plans and preparations, with the resources available to him, and prospectively available to him for meeting a general emergency. He will be responsible for supervising and coordinating all plans and actions of U.S. forces in Europe made available for meeting an emergency involving the forces under his command.

2. The relationships of the Joint Chiefs of Staff to the U.S. commands in Italy and Austria and to the U.S. representatives on the Allied Councils for Germany, Austria, and the Balkans, and to the U.S. Naval Forces in Europe and the Mediterranean remain unchanged.

3. In making plans for accomplishing their missions the Northeast and Alaskan commanders will be guided by such special international arrangements as may be made between the United States and Canada and Newfoundland in the planning and conduct of pertinent operations.

4. There is established a Strategic Air Command comprised of strategic air forces not otherwise assigned. These forces are normally based in the United States. The commander of the Strategic Air Command is responsible to the Joint Chiefs of Staff as are other commanders provided for in this plan.

5. Unified command in each command will be established in accordance, in so far as practicable, with Chapter 2, paragraph 12, of Joint Action of the Army and Navy, component forces consisting of Army, Army Air, and Naval forces. Forces assigned to a command will normally consist of two or more components and each will be commanded directly by an officer of that component. Each commander will have a joint staff with appropriate members from the various components of the Services under his command in key positions of responsibility. Commanders of component forces will

communicate directly with appropriate headquarters on matters such as administration, training, supply, expenditure of appropriated funds, and authorization of construction, which are not a responsibility of unified command. The assignment of forces and the significant changes therein will be as determined by the Joint Chiefs of Staff.

6. The Joint Chiefs of Staff will exercise strategic direction over all elements of the armed forces. Missions and tasks of all independent commands will be prescribed by the Joint Chiefs of Staff. Forces not specifically assigned by the Joint Chiefs of Staff will remain under the operational control of the respective Services. However, all action of strategic significance will be referred to the Joint Chiefs of Staff. For each command operating under missions prescribed by the Joint Chiefs of Staff, the Chief of Staff, U.S. Army, the Chief of Naval Operations, or the Commanding General, Army Air Forces, as appropriate, will be designated to act as the executive agent for the Joint Chiefs of Staff.

7. The assignment of an area of responsibility to one commander will not be construed as restricting the forces of another command from temporarily extending appropriate operations into that area, or forces operating under the strategic direction of the Joint Chiefs of Staff from conducting operations from or within that area, as may be required for the accomplishment of assigned tasks as mutually agreed by the commanders concerned or as directed by the Joint Chiefs of Staff.

8. Within each major command there shall be established an adequate system of control under the principle of unified command, for purposes of local defense.

9. The command structure envisioned herein will not operate to cancel or delay construction and development projects which have been approved and/or for which funds are already available. On the other hand, nothing in this paper will be construed as authorizing construction or modifying existing controls or directives concerning construction.

10. All previous conflicting directives will be cancelled.

Approved Dec 14, 1946
(signed)
Harry S Truman

(4) National Security Act, 26 July 1947

The National Security Act of 1947 grew out of the lessons learned in World War II, and the near universal belief that a consolidated military establishment would lead to greater efficiency and cost savings. The Navy objected, arguing it could become more inefficient under unification. Army Ground Forces (AGF) and Army Air Forces (AAF) officers understood very clearly that their war effort had been aided immeasurably by the formation of unified theater commands. High ranking officers in both branches of the Army wanted to translate this experience into the peacetime military establishment. Their efforts at unification were rewarded in 1947 with the passage of the National Security Act, over the objections of many Navy officers, who wanted an organization which coordinated the three branches, rather than administered them. President Harry S. Truman's support was essential to the unification effort when he forced the Secretary of War and the Secretary of the Navy to reach agreement on unification. President Truman ultimately decided the most contentious issues upon which the two secretaries were unable to reach agreement.

The National Security Act of 1947 established the national security framework for the United States government. The act created the National Military Establishment (NME) headed by a civilian Secretary of Defense, who was responsible for establishing "general policies and programs for the National Military Establishment and for all the departments and agencies therein" and exercising "general direction, authority, and control over such departments and agencies." The NME consisted of three executive departments -- the Department of the Army, Department of the Navy, and Department of the Air Force -- each headed by a civilian secretary. The act established the United States Air Force (USAF) under the Department of the Air Force. It transferred to the USAF the AAF, the Army Air Corps, and the General Headquarters (GHQ) Air Force (Air Force Combat Command), as well as all of the personnel assigned to those units. Throughout the war, officers had continued to be commissioned in the Air Corps. The Office of the Chief of the Air Corps and the GHQ Air Force had been absorbed by the AAF in 1942 under terms of the First War Powers Act of 1941, whose provisions required the wartime organization to expire six months after the war ended and caused reversion to the pre-war organizational structure. As a result, official transfers had to reflect the existence of these non-operational units until the formation of the USAF and its own organizational structure.

The terms of the act specified an appointed Chief of Staff, of general officer rank, to exercise command over the Air Force. The Air Force received aviation forces, both combat and service not otherwise assigned, and was charged with preparing air forces necessary for effective prosecution of war in sustained offensive and defensive air operations.

Under the compromises embodied in the act, the Navy explicitly retained its naval aviation, and "such aviation as may be organic therein." The Army retained "such aviation and water transport as may be organic therein." The act further specified that the Navy was allowed land-based naval aviation, while the Marine Corps was authorized to retain its supporting air components. The precise language of this act differed from the original legislation proposed, as a result of congressional compromise. As a result, the act and Executive Order 9877, which delineated the functions of the armed forces, contained inconsistencies. These would later provide areas of disagreement between the services.

****
Public Law 253, 61 Stat., Chap. 343, 80th Congress, 1st Session, "The National Security Act of 1947." 26 July 1947.

Herman S. Wolk, <u>Planning and Organizing the Postwar Air Force, 1943-1947</u>, (Washington, D.C.: Office of Air Force History, 1984), p 29.

Steven L. Rearden, <u>History of the Office of the Secretary of Defense, The Formative Years 1947-1950</u>, (Washington, D.C.: OSD History Office, 1984, pp 1-27.

PUBLIC LAW 253--July 26, 1947

Public Law 253   Chapter 343

AN ACT

To promote the national security by providing for a
Secretary of Defense; for a National Military Establishment;
for a Department of the Army, a Department of the Navy, and
a Department of the Air Force; and for the coordination of
the activities of the National Military Establishment with
other departments and agencies of the Government concerned
with the national security.

BE IT ENACTED BY THE SENATE AND HOUSE OF REPRESENTATIVES
OF THE UNITED STATES OF AMERICA IN CONGRESS ASSEMBLED,

Short Title

That this Act may be cited as the "National Security Act
of 1947".

Table of Contents

Title III - Miscellaneous

Declaration of Policy

Sec. 2. In enacting this legislation, it is the intent of Congress to provide a comprehensive program for the future security of the United States; to provide for the establishment of integrated policies and procedures for the departments, agencies, and functions of the Government relating to the national security; to provide three military departments for the operation and administration of the Army, the Navy (including naval aviation and the United States Marine Corps), and the Air Force, with their assigned combat and service components; to provide for their authoritative coordination and unified direction under civilian control but not to merge them; to provide for the effective strategic direction of the armed forces and for their operation under unified control and for their integration into an efficient team of land, naval, and air forces.

TITLE I - COORDINATION FOR NATIONAL SECURITY

National Security Council

Sec. 101. (a) There is hereby established a council to be known as the National Security Council (hereinafter in this section referred to as the "Council").

The President of the United States shall preside over meetings of the Council: PROVIDED, That in his absence he may designate a member of the Council to preside in his place.

The function of the Council shall be to advise the President with respect to the integration of domestic, foreign, and military policies relating to the national security so as to enable the military services and the other departments and agencies of the Government to cooperate more effectively in matters involving the national security.

The Council shall be composed of the President; the Secretary of State; the Secretary of Defense, appointed under section 202; the Secretary of the Army, referred to in section 205; the Secretary of the Navy; the Secretary of the Air Force, appointed under section 207; the Chairman of the National Security Resources Board, appointed under section 103; and such of the following named officers as the President may designate from time to time: The Secretaries of the executive departments, the Chairman of the Munitions Board appointed under section 213, and the Chairman of the Research and Development Board appointed under section 214; but no such additional member shall be designated until the advice and consent of the Senate has been given to his appointment to the office the holding of which authorizes his designation as a member of the Council.

(b) In addition to performing such other functions as the President may direct, for the purpose of more effectively coordinating the policies and functions of the departments and agencies of the Government relating to the national security, it shall, subject to the direction of the President, be the duty of the Council--

(1) to assess and appraise the objectives, commitments, and risks of the United States in relation to our actual and potential military power, in the interest of national security, for the purpose of making recommendations to the President in connection therewith; and

(2) to consider policies on matters of common interest to the departments and agencies of the Government concerned with the national security, and to make recommendations to the President in connection therewith.

(c) The Council shall have a staff to be headed by a civilian executive secretary who shall be appointed by the President, and who shall receive compensation at the rate of $10,000 a year. The executive secretary, subject to the direction of the Council, is hereby authorized, subject to the civil-service laws and the Classification Act of 1923, as amended, to appoint and fix the compensation of such personnel as may be necessary to perform such duties as may be prescribed by the Council in connection with the performance of its functions.

(d) The Council shall, from time to time, make such recommendations, and such other reports to the President as it deems appropriate or as the President may require.

Central Intelligence Agency

Sec. 102. (a) There is hereby established under the
National Security Council a Central Intelligence Agency with
a Director of Central Intelligence, who shall be the head
thereof. The Director shall be appointed by the President,
by and with the advice and consent of the Senate, from among
the commissioned officers of the armed services or from among
individuals in civilian life. The Director shall receive
compensation at the rate of $14,000 a year.

(b) (1) If a commissioned officer of the armed services
is appointed as Director then --

(A) in the performance of his duties as Director, he shall
be subject to no supervision, control, restriction, or prohi-
bition (military or otherwise) other than would be operative
with respect to him if he were a civilian in no way connected
with the Department of the Army, the Department of the Navy,
the Department of the Air Force, or the armed services or any
component thereof; and

(B) he shall not possess or exercise any supervision,
control, powers, or functions(other than such as he possesses,
or is authorized or directed to exercise, as Director) with
respect to the armed services or any component thereof, the
Department of the Army, the Department of the Navy, or the
Department of the Air Force, or any branch, bureau, unit or
division thereof, or with respect to any of the personnel
(military or civilian) of any of the foregoing.

(2) Except as provided in paragraph (1), the appointment
to the office of Director of a commissioned officer of the
armed services, and his acceptance of and service in such
office, shall in no way affect any status, office, rank, or
grade he may occupy or hold in the armed services, or any
emolument, perquisite, right, privilege, or benefit incident
to or arising out of any such status, office, rank, or grade.
Any such commissioned officer shall, while serving in the office
of Director, receive the military pay and allowances (active
or retired, as the case may be) payable to a commissioned
officer of his grade and length of service and shall be paid,
from any funds available to defray the expenses of the Agency,
annual compensation at a rate equal to the amount by which
$14,000 exceeds the amount of his annual military pay and
allowances.

(c) Notwithstanding the provisions of section 6 of the
Act of August 24, 1912 (37 Stat. 555), or the provisions of any
other law, the Director of Central Intelligence may, in his
discretion, terminate the employment of any officer or employee

of the Agency whenever he shall deem such termination necessary or advisable in the interests of the United States, but such termination shall not affect the right of such officer or employee to seek or accept employment in any other department or agency of the Government if declared eligible for such employment by the United States Civil Service Commission.

(d) For the purpose of coordinating the intelligence activities of the several Government departments and agencies in the interest of national security, it shall be the duty of the Agency, under the direction of the National Security Council--

(1) to advise the National Security Council in matters concerning such intelligence activities of the Government departments and agencies as relate to the national security;

(2) to make recommendations to the National Security Council for the coordination of such intelligence activities of the departments and agencies of the Government as relate to the national security;

(3) To correlate and evaluate intelligence relating to the national security, and provide for the appropriate dissemination of such intelligence within the Government using where appropriate existing agencies and facilities: PROVIDED, That the Agency shall have no police, subp[o]ena, law-enforcement powers, or internal-security functions: PROVIDED FURTHER, That the departments and other agencies of the Government shall continue to collect, evaluate, correlate, and disseminate departmental intelligence: AND PROVIDED FURTHER, That the Director of Central Intelligence shall be responsible for protecting intelligence sources and methods from unauthorized disclosure;

(4) to perform, for the benefit of the existing intelligence agencies, such additional services of common concern as the National Security Council determines can be more efficiently accomplished centrally;

(5) to perform such other functions and duties related to intelligence affecting the national security as the National Security Council may from time to time direct.

(e) To the extent recommended by the National Security Council and approved by the President, such intelligence of the departments and agencies of the Government, except as hereinafter provided, relating to the national security shall be open to the inspection of the Director of Central Intelligence, and such intelligence as relates to the national security and is possessed by such departments and other agencies of the Government, except as hereinafter provided, shall be made available to the Director of Central Intelligence for correlation, evaluation, and dissemination: PROVIDED, HOWEVER, That upon the written request of the Director of Central Intelligence, the Director of the Federal Bureau of Investigation shall make available to the Director of Central Intelligence such information for correlation, evaluation, and dissemination as may be essential to the national security.

(f) Effective when the Director first appointed under subsection (a) has taken office--

(1) the National Intelligence Authority (11 Fed. Reg. 1337,1339, February 5, 1946) shall cease to exist; and

(2) the personnel, property and records of the Central Intelligence Group are transferred to the Central Intelligence Agency, and such Group shall cease to exist. Any unexpended balances of appropriations, allocations, or other funds available or authorized to be made available for such Group shall be available and shall be authorized to be made available in like manner for expenditure by the Agency.

National Security Resources Board

Sec. 103. (a) There is hereby established a National Security Resources Board (hereinafter in this section referred to as the "Board") to be composed of the Chairman of the Board and such heads or representatives of the various executive departments and independent agencies as may from time to time be designated by the President to be members of the Board. The Chairman of the Board shall be appointed from civilian life by the President, by and with the advice and consent of the Senate, and shall receive compensation at the rate of $14,000 a year.

(b) The Chairman of the Board, subject to the direction of the President, is authorized, subject to the civil-service laws and the Classification Act of 1923, as amended, to appoint and fix the compensation of such personnel as may be necessary to assist the Board in carrying out its functions.

(c) It shall be the function of the Board to advise the President concerning the coordination of military, industrial, and civilian mobilization, including--

(1) policies concerning industrial and civilian mobilization in order to assure the most effective mobilization and maximum utilization of the Nation's manpower in the event of war;

(2) programs for the effective use in time of war of the Nation's natural and industrial resources for military and civilian needs, for the maintenance and stabilization of the civilian economy in time of war, and for the adjustment of such economy to war needs and conditions;

(3) policies for unifying, in time of war, the activities of Federal agencies and departments engaged in or concerned with production, procurement, distribution, or transportation of military or civilian supplies, materials, and products;

(4) the relationship between potential supplies of, and potential requirements for, manpower, resources, and productive facilities in time of war;

(5) policies for establishing adequate reserves of strategic and critical material, and for the conservation of these reserves;

(6) the strategic relocation of industries, services, government, and economic activities, the continuous operation of which is essential to the Nation's security.

(d) In performing its functions, the Board shall utilize to the maximum extent the facilities and resources of the departments and agencies of the Government.

TITLE II-THE NATIONAL MILITARY ESTABLISHMENT

Establishment of the National Military Establishment

Sec. 201. (a) There is hereby established the National Military Establishment, and the Secretary of Defense shall be the head thereof.

(b) The National Military Establishment shall consist of the Department of the Army, the Department of the Navy, and the Department of the Air Force, together with all other agencies created under title II of this Act.

Secretary of Defense

Sec. 202 (a) There shall be a Secretary of Defense, who shall be appointed from civilian life by the President, by and with the advice and consent of the Senate: PROVIDED, That a person who has within ten years been on active duty as a commissioned officer in a Regular component of the armed services shall not be eligible for appointment as Secretary of Defense. The Secretary of Defense shall be the principal assistant to the President in all matters relating to the national security. Under the direction of the President and subject to the provisions of this Act he shall perform the following duties:

(1) Establish general policies and programs for the National Military Establishment and for all of the departments and agencies therein;

(2) Exercise general direction, authority, and control over

such departments and agencies;

(3) Take appropriate steps to eliminate unnecessary duplication or overlapping in the fields of procurement, supply, transportation, storage, health, and research;

(4) Supervise and coordinate the preparation of the budget estimates of the departments and agencies comprising the National Military Establishment; formulate and determine the budget estimates for submittal to the Bureau of the Budget; and supervise the budget programs of such departments and agencies under the applicable appropriation Act:
PROVIDED, That nothing herein contained shall prevent the Secretary of the Army, the Secretary of the Navy, or the Secretary of the Air Force from presenting to the President or to the Director of the Budget, after first so informing the Secretary of Defense, any report or recommendation relating to his department which he may deem necessary: AND PROVIDED FURTHER, That the Department of the Army, the Department of the Navy, and the Department of the Air Force shall be administered as individual executive departments by their respective Secretaries and all powers and duties relating to such departments not specifically conferred upon the Secretary of Defense by this Act shall be retained by each of their respective Secretaries.

(b) The Secretary of Defense shall submit annual written reports to the President and the Congress covering expenditures, work, and accomplishments of the National Military Establishment, together with such recommendations as he shall deem appropriate.

(c) The Secretary of Defense shall cause a seal of office to be made for the National Military Establishment, of such design as the President shall approve, and judicial notice shall be taken thereof.

Military Assistants to the Secretary

Sec. 203. Officers of the armed services may be detailed to duty as assistants and personal aides to the Secretary of Defense, but he shall not establish a military staff.

Civilian Personnel

Sec. 204. (a) The Secretary of Defense is authorized to appoint from civilian life not to exceed three special assistants to advise and assist him in the performance of his duties. Each such special assistant shall receive compensation at the rate of $10,000 a year.

(b) The Secretary of Defense is authorized, subject to

the civil-service laws and the Classification Act of 1923, as amended, to appoint and fix the compensation of such other civilian personnel as may be necessary for the performance of the functions of the National Military Establishment other than those of the Departments of the Army, Navy, and Air Force.

Department of the Army

Sec. 205. (a) The Department of War shall hereafter be designated the Department of the Army, and the title of the Secretary of War shall be changed to Secretary of the Army. Changes shall be made in the titles of other officers and activities of the Department of the Army as the Secretary of the Army may determine.

(b) All laws, orders, regulations, and other actions relating to the Department of War or to any officer or activity whose title is changed under this section shall, insofar as they are not inconsistent with the provisions of this Act, be deemed to relate to the Department of the Army within the National Military Establishment or to such officer or activity designated by his or its new title.

(c) The term "Department of the Army" as used in this Act shall be construed to mean the Department of the Army at the seat of government and all field headquarters, forces, reserve components, installations, activities, and functions under the control or supervision of the Department of the Army.

(d) The Secretary of the Army shall cause a seal of office to be made for the Department of the Army, of such design as the President may approve, and judicial notice shall be taken thereof.

(e) In general the United States Army, within the Department of the Army, shall include land combat and service forces and such aviation and water transport as may be organic therein. It shall be organized, trained, and equipped primarily for prompt and sustained combat incident to operations on land. It shall be responsible for the preparation of land forces necessary for the effective prosecution of war except as otherwise assigned and, in accordance with integrated joint mobilization plans, for the expansion of peacetime components of the Army to meet the needs of war.

Department of the Navy

Sec. 206. (a) The term "Department of the Navy" as used in this Act shall be construed to mean the Department of the

Navy at the seat of government; the headquarters, United States
Marine Corps; the entire operating force of the United States
Navy, including naval aviation, and of the United States Marine
Corps, including the reserve components of such forces; all
field activities, headquarters, forces, bases, installations,
activities, and functions under the control or supervision of
the Department of the Navy; and the United States Coast Guard
when operating as a part of the Navy pursuant to law.

(b) In general the United States Navy, within the
Department of the Navy, shall include naval combat and services
forces and such aviation as may be organic therein. It shall
be organized, trained, and equipped primarily for prompt and
sustained combat incident to operations at sea. It shall be
responsible for the preparation of naval forces necessary
for the effective prosecution of war except as otherwise assigned,
and, in accordance with integrated joint mobilization plans,
for the expansion of the peacetime components of the Navy
to meet the needs of war.

All naval aviation shall be integrated with the naval
service as part thereof within the Department of the Navy.
Naval aviation shall consist of combat and service and training
forces, and shall include land-based naval aviation, air transport
essential for naval operations, all air weapons and air techniques
involved in the operations and activities of the United States
Navy, and the entire remainder of the aeronautical organization
of the United States Navy, together with the personnel necessary
therefor.

The Navy shall be generally responsible for naval reconnaissance, antisubmarine warfare, and protection of shipping.

The Navy shall develop aircraft, weapons, tactics, technique, organization and equipment of naval combat and service
elements; matters of joint concern as to these functions shall be
coordinated between the Army, the Air Force, and the Navy.

(c) The United States Marine Corps, within the Department
of the Navy, shall include land combat and service forces and
such aviation as may be organic therein. The Marine Corps
shall be organized, trained, and equipped to provide fleet
marine forces of combined arms, together with supporting air
components, for service with the fleet in the seizure or
defense of advanced naval bases and for the conduct of such
land operations as may be essential to the prosecution of a
naval campaign. It shall be the duty of the Marine Corps to
develop, in coordination with the Army and the Air Force, those
phases of amphibious operations which pertain to the tactics,
technique, and equipment employed by landing forces. In
addition, the Marine Corps shall provide detachments and

organizations for service on armed vessels of the Navy, shall provide security detachments for the protection of naval property at naval stations and bases, and shall perform such other duties as the President may direct: PROVIDED, That such additional duties shall not detract from or interfere with the operations for which the Marine Corps is primarily organized. The Marine Corps shall be responsible, in accordance with integrated joint mobilization plans, for the expansion of peacetime components of the Marine Corps to meet the needs of war.

Department of the Air Force

Sec. 207. (a) Within the National Military Establishment there is hereby established an executive department to be known as the Department of the Air Force, and a Secretary of the Air Force, who shall be the head thereof. The Secretary of the Air Force shall be appointed from civilian life by the President, by and with the advice and consent of the Senate.

(b) Section 158 of the Revised Statutes is amended to include the Department of the Air Force and the provisions of so much of Title IV of the Revised Statutes as now or hereafter amended as is not inconsistent with the Act shall be applicable to the Department of the Air Force.

(c) The term "Department of the Air Force" as used in this Act shall be construed to mean the Department of the Air Force at the seat of government and all field headquarters, forces, reserve components, installations, activities, and functions under the control or supervision of the Department of the Air Force.

(d) There shall be in the Department of the Air Force an Under Secretary of the Air Force and two Assistant Secretaries of the Air Force, who shall be appointed from civilian life by the President by and with the advice and consent of the Senate.

(e) The several officers of the Department of the Air Force shall perform such functions as the Secretary of the Air Force may prescribe.

(f) So much of the functions of the Secretary of the Army and of the Department of the Army, including those of any officer of such Department, as are assigned to or under the control of the Commanding General, Army Air Forces, or as are deemed by the Secretary of Defense to be necessary or desirable for the operations of the Department of the Air Force or the United States Air Force, shall be transferred to and vested in the Secretary of the Air Force and the Department of the Air Force: PROVIDED, That the National Guard Bureau shall, in addition to the functions and duties performed by it for the Department of the Army, be charged with similar functions and duties for the Department of the Air Force, and shall be the channel of communication between the Department of the Air Force and the several States on all matters pertaining to the Air National Guard: AND PROVIDED FURTHER, That in order to permit an orderly transfer, the Secretary of Defense may, during the transfer period hereinafter prescribed, direct that the Department of the Army shall continue for appropriate periods to exercise any of such functions, insofar as they relate to the Department of the Air Force, or the United States Air Force or their property and personnel. Such of the property, personnel, and records of the Department of the Army used in the exercise of functions transferred under this subsection as the Secretary of Defense shall determine shall be transferred or assigned to the Department of the Air Force.

(g) The Secretary of the Air Force shall cause a seal of office to be made for the Department of the Air Force, of such device as the President shall approve, and judicial notice shall be taken thereof.

United States Air Force

Sec. 208. (a) The United States Air Force is hereby established under the Department of the Air Force. The Army Air Forces, the Air Corps, United States Army, and the General Headquarters Air Force (Air Force Combat Command), shall be transferred to the United States Air Force.

(b) There shall be a Chief of Staff, United States Air Force, who shall be appointed by the President, by and with the advice and consent of the Senate, for a term of four years from among the officers of general rank who are assigned to or commissioned in the United States Air Force. Under the direction of the Secretary of the Air Force, the Chief of Staff, United States Air Force, shall exercise command over the United States Air Force and shall be charged with the duty of carrying into execution all lawful orders and directions which may be transmitted to him. The functions of the Commanding General, General Headquarters Air Force (Air Force Combat Command), and of the Chief of the Air Corps and of the Commanding General, Army Air Forces, shall be transferred to the Chief of Staff, United States Air Force. When such transfer becomes effective, the offices of the Chief of the Air Corps, United States Army, and Assistants to the Chief of the Air Corps, United States Army, provided for by the Act of June 4, 1920, as amended (41 Stat. 768), and Commanding General,

General Headquarters Air Force, provided for by section 5 of the Act of June 16, 1936 (49 Stat. 1525), shall cease to exist. While holding office as Chief of Staff, United States Air Force, the incumbent shall hold a grade and receive allowances equivalent to those prescribed by law for the Chief of Staff, United States Army. The Chief of Staff, United States Army, the Chief of Naval Operations, and the Chief of Staff, United States Air Force, shall take rank among themselves according to their relative dates of appointment as such, and shall each take rank above all other officers on the active list of the Army, Navy, and Air Force: PROVIDED, That nothing in this Act shall have the effect of changing the relative rank of the present Chief of Staff, United States Army, and the present Chief of Naval Operations.

(c) All commissioned officers, warrant officers, and enlisted men, commissioned, holding warrants, or enlisted, in the Air Corps, United States Army, or the Army Air Forces, shall be transferred in branch to the United States Air Force. All other commissioned officers, warrant officers, and enlisted men, who are commissioned, hold warrants, or are enlisted, in any component of the Army of the United States and who are under the authority or command of the Commanding General, Army Air Forces, shall be continued under the authority or command of the Chief of Staff, United States Air Force, and under the jurisdiction of the Department of the Air Force. Personnel whose status is affected by this subsection shall retain their existing commissions, warrants, or enlisted status in existing components of the armed forces unless otherwise altered or terminated in accordance with existing law; and they shall not be deemed to have been appointed to a new or different office or grade, or to have vacated their permanent or temporary appointments in an existing component of the armed forces, solely by virtue of any change in status under this subsection. No such change in status shall alter or prejudice the status of any individual so assigned, so as to deprive him of any right, benefit, or privilege to which he may be entitled under existing law.

(d) Except as otherwise directed by the Secretary of the Air Force, all property, records, installations, agencies, activities, projects, and civilian personnel under the jurisdiction, control, authority, or command of the Commanding General, Army Air Forces, shall be continued to the same extent under the jurisdiction, control, authority, or command, respectively, of the Chief of Staff, United States Air Force, in the Department of the Air Force.

(e) For a period of two years from the date of enactment

of this Act, personnel (both military and civilian), property, records, installations, agencies, activities, and projects may be transferred between the Department of the Army and the Department of the Air Force by direction of the Secretary of Defense.

(f) In general the United States Air Force shall include aviation forces both combat and service not otherwise assigned. It shall be organized, trained, and equipped primarily for prompt and sustained offensive and defensive air operations. The Air Force shall be responsible for the preparation of the air forces necessary for the effective prosecution of war except as otherwise assigned and, in accordance with integrated joint mobilization plans, for the expansion of the peacetime components of the Air Force to meet the needs of war.

Effective Date of Transfers

Sec. 209. Each transfer, assignment, or change in status under section 207 or section 208 shall take effect upon such date or dates as may be prescribed by the Secretary of Defense.

War Council

Sec. 210. There shall be within the National Military Establishment a War Council composed of the Secretary of Defense, as Chairman, who shall have power of decision; the Secretary of the Army; the Secretary of the Navy; the Secretary of the Air Force; the Chief of Staff, United States Army; the Chief of Naval Operations; and the Chief of Staff, United States Air Force. The War Council shall advise the Secretary of Defense on matters of broad policy relating to the armed forces, and shall consider and report on such other matters as the Secretary of Defense may direct.

Joint Chiefs of Staff

Sec. 211. (a) There is hereby established within the National Military Establishment the Joint Chiefs of Staff, which shall consist of the Chief of Staff, United States Army; the Chief of Naval Operations; the Chief of Staff, United States Air Force; and the Chief of Staff to the Commander in Chief, if there be one.

(b) Subject to the authority and direction of the President and the Secretary of Defense, it shall be the duty of the Joint Chiefs of Staff--

(1) to prepare strategic plans and to provide for the stra-

tegic direction of the military forces;

(2) to prepare joint logistic plans and to assign to the military services logistic responsibilities in accordance with such plans;

(3) to establish unified commands in strategic areas when such unified commands are in the interest of national security;

(4) to formulate policies for joint training of the military forces;

(5) to formulate policies for coordinating the education of members of the military forces;

(6) to review major material and personnel requirements of the military forces, in accordance with strategic and logistic plans; and

(7) to provide United States representation on the Military Staff Committee of the United Nations in accordance with the provisions of the Charter of the United Nations.

(c) The Joint Chiefs of Staff shall act as the principal military advisers to the President and the Secretary of Defense and shall perform such other duties as the President and the Secretary of Defense may direct or as may be prescribed by law.

Joint Staff

Sec. 212. There shall be, under the Joint Chiefs of Staff, a Joint Staff to consist of not to exceed one hundred officers and to be composed of approximately equal numbers of officers from each of the three armed services. The Joint Staff, operating under a Director thereof appointed by the Joint Chiefs of Staff, shall perform such duties as may be directed by the Joint Chiefs of Staff. The Director shall be an officer junior in grade to all members of the Joint Chiefs of Staff.

Munitions Board

Sec. 213. (a) There is hereby established in the National Military Establishment a Munitions Board (hereinafter in this section referred to as the "Board").

(b) The Board shall be composed of a Chairman, who shall be the head thereof, and an Under Secretary or Assistant Secretary from each of the three military departments, to be designated in each case by the Secretaries of their respective departments. The Chairman shall be appointed from civilian life by the President, by and with the advice and consent of the Senate, and shall receive compensation at the rate of

$14,000 a year.

(c) It shall be the duty of the Board under the direction of the Secretary of Defense and in support of strategic and logistic plans prepared by the Joint Chiefs of Staff--

(1) to coordinate the appropriate activities within the National Military Establishment with regard to industrial matters, including the procurement, production, and distribution plans of the departments and agencies comprising the Establishment;

(2) to plan for the military aspects of industrial mobilization;

(3) to recommend assignment of procurement responsibilities among the several military services and to plan for standardization of specifications and for the greatest practicable allocation of purchase authority of technical equipment and common use items on the basis of single procurement;

(4) to prepare estimates of potential production, procurement, and personnel for use in evaluation of the logistic feasibility of strategic operations;

(5) to determine relative priorities of the various segments of the military procurement programs;

(6) to supervise such subordinate agencies as are or may be created to consider the subjects falling within the scope of the Board's responsibilities;

(7) to make recommendations to regroup, combine, or dissolve existing interservice agencies operating in the fields of procurement, production, and distribution in such manner as to promote efficiency and economy;

(8) to maintain liaison with other departments and agencies for the proper correlation of military requirements with the civilian economy, particularly in regard to the procurement or disposition of strategic and critical material and the maintenance of adequate reserves of such material, and to make recommendations as to policies in connection therewith;

(9) to assemble and review material and personnel requirements presented by the Joint Chiefs of Staff and those presented by the production, procurement, and distribution agencies assigned to meet military needs, and to make recommendations thereon to the Secretary of Defense; and

(10) to perform such duties as the Secretary of Defense may direct.

(d) When the Chairman of the Board first appointed has taken office, the Joint Army and Navy Munitions Board shall cease to exist and all its records and personnel shall be transferred to the Munitions Board.

(e) The Secretary of Defense shall provide the Board with

such personnel and facilities as the Secretary may determine to be required by the Board for the performance of its functions.

Research and Development Board

Sec. 214. (a) There is hereby established in the National Military Establishment a Research and Development Board (hereinafter in this section referred to as the "Board"). The Board shall be composed of a Chairman, who shall be the head thereof, and two representatives from each of the Departments of the Army, Navy, and Air Force, to be designated by the Secretaries of their respective Departments. The Chairman shall be appointed from civilian life by the President, by and with the advice and consent of the Senate, and shall receive compensation at the rate of $14,000 a year. The purpose of the Board shall be to advise the Secretary of Defense as to the status of scientific research relative to the national security, and to assist him in assuring adequate provision for research and development on scientific problems relating to the national security.

(b) it shall be the duty of the Board, under the direction of the Secretary of Defense--

(1) to prepare a complete and integrated program of research and development for military purposes;

(2) to advise with regard to trends in scientific research relating to national security and the measures necessary to assure continued and increasing progress;

(3) to recommend measures of coordination of research and development among the military departments and allocation among them of responsibilities for specific programs of joint interest;

(4) to formulate policy for the National Military Establishment in connection with research and development matters involving agencies outside the National Military Establishment;

(5) to consider the interaction of research and development and strategy, and to advise the Joint Chiefs of Staff in connection therewith; and

(6) to perform such other duties as the Secretary of Defense may direct.

(c) When the Chairman of the Board first appointed has taken office the Joint Research and Development Board shall cease to exist and all its records and personnel shall be transferred to the Research and Development Board.

(d) The Secretary of Defense shall provide the Board with such personnel and facilities as the Secretary may determine to be required by the Board for the performance of its functions.

TITLE III-MISCELLANEOUS

Compensation of Secretaries

Sec. 301. (a) The Secretary of Defense shall receive the compensation prescribed by law for heads of executive departments.

(b) The Secretary of the Army, the Secretary of the Navy, and the Secretary of the Air Force shall each receive the compensation prescribed by law for heads of executive departments.

Under Secretaries and Assistant Secretaries

Sec. 302. The Under Secretaries and Assistant Secretaries of the Army, the Navy, and the Air Force shall each receive compensation at the rate of $10,000 a year and shall perform such duties as the Secretaries of their respective departments may prescribe.

Advisory Committees and Personnel

Sec. 303. (a) The Secretary of Defense, the Chairman of the National Security Resources Board, and the Director of Central Intelligence are authorized to appoint such advisory committees and to employ, consistent with other provisions of this Act, such part-time advisory personnel as they may deem necessary in carrying out their respective functions and the functions of agencies under their control. Persons holding other offices or positions under the United States for which they receive compensation while serving as members of such committees shall receive no additional compensation for such service. Other members of such committees and other part-time advisory personnel so employed may serve without compensation or may receive compensation at a rate not to exceed $35 for each day of service, as determined by the appointing authority.

(b) Service of an individual as a member of any such advisory committee, or in any other part-time capacity for a department or agency hereunder, shall not be considered as service bringing such individual within the provisions of section 109 or 113 of the Criminal Code (U.S.C., 1940 edition, title 18, secs. 198 and 203), or section 19 (e) of the Contract Settlement Act of 1944, unless the act of such individual, which by such section is made unlawful when performed by an individual referred to in such section, is with respect to any particular matter which directly involves a department or agency which such person is advising or in which such department or agency is directly interested.

Status of Transferred Civilian Personnel

Sec. 304. All transfers of civilian personnel under this Act shall be without change in classification or compensation, but the head of any department or agency to which such a transfer is made is authorized to make such changes in the titles and designations and prescribe such changes in the duties of such personnel commensurate with their classification as he may deem necessary and appropriate.

Saving Provisions

Sec. 305 (a) All laws, orders, regulations, and other actions applicable with respect to any function, activity, personnel, property, records, or other thing transferred under this Act, or with respect to any officer, department, or agency, from which such transfer is made, shall, except to the extent rescinded, modified, superseded, terminated, or made inapplicable by or under authority of law, have the same effect as if such transfer had not been made; but, after any such transfer, any such law, order, regulation, or other action which vested functions in or otherwise related to any officer, department, or agency from which such transfers was made shall, insofar as applicable with respect to the function, activity, personnel, property, records or other thing transferred and to the extent not inconsistent with other provisions of this Act, be deemed to have vested such function in or relate to the officer, department, or agency to which the transfer was made.

(b) No suit, action, or other proceeding lawfully commenced by or against the head of any department or agency or other officer of the United States, in his official capacity or in relation to the discharge of his official duties, shall abate by reason of the taking effect of any transfer or change in title under the provisions of this Act; and, in the case of any such transfer, such suit, action, or other proceeding may be maintained by or against the successor of such head or other officer under the transfer, but only if the court shall allow the same to be maintained on motion or supplemental petition filed within twelve months after such transfer takes effect, showing a necessity for the survival of such suit, action, or other proceeding to obtain settlement of the questions involved.

(c) Notwithstanding the provisions of the second paragraph of section 5 of title I of the First War Powers Act, 1941, the existing organization of the War Department under the provisions of Executive Order Numbered 9082 of February 28, 1942, as modified by Executive Order Numbered 9722 of May 13, 1946, and the existing organization of the Department of the Navy under the provisions of Executive Order Numbered 9635 of September 29, 1945, including the assignment of functions to organizational units within the War and Navy Departments, may, to the extent determined by the Secretary of Defense, continue in force for two years following the date of enactment of this Act except to the extent modified by the provisions of this Act or under the authority of law.

Transfer of Funds

Sec. 306. All unexpended balances of appropriations, allocations, nonappropriated funds, or other funds available or hereafter made available for use by or on behalf of the Army Air Forces or officers thereof, shall be transferred to the Department of the Air Force for use in connection with the exercise of its functions. Such other unexpended balances of appropriations, allocations, nonappropriated funds, or other funds available or hereafter made available for use by the Department of War or the Department of the Army in exercise of functions transferred to the Department of the Air Force under this Act, as the Secretary of Defense shall determine, shall be transferred to the Department of the Air Force for use in connection with the exercise of its functions. Unexpended balances transferred under this section may be used for the purposes for which the appropriations, allocations, or other funds were originally made available, or for new expenditures occasioned by the enactment of this Act. The transfers herein authorized may be made with or without warrant action as may be appropriate from time to time from any appropriation covered by this section to any other such appropriation or to such new accounts established on the books of the Treasury as may be determined to be necessary to carry into effect provisions of this Act.

Authorization for Appropriations

Sec. 307. There are hereby authorized to be appropriated such sums as may be necessary and appropriate to carry out the provisions and purpose of this Act.

Definitions

Sec. 308 (a) As used in this Act, the term "function" includes functions, powers and duties.

(b) As used in this Act, the term "budget program" refers to recommendations as to the apportionment, to the allocation and to the review of allotments of appropriate funds.

Separability

Sec. 309 If any provisions of this Act or the application thereof to any person or circumstances is held invalid, the validity of the remainder of the Act and of the application of such provision to other persons and circumstances shall not be affected thereby.

Effective Date

Sec. 310. (a) The first sentence of section 202 (a) and sections 1, 2, 307, 308, 309, and 310 shall take effect immediately upon the enactment of this Act.

(b) Except as provided in subsection (a), the provisions of this Act shall take effect on whichever of the following days is the earlier: The day after the day upon which the Secretary of Defense first appointed takes office, or the sixtieth day after the date of the enactment of this Act.

Succession to the Presidency

Sec. 311. Paragraph (1) of subsection (d) of section 1 of the Act entitled "An Act to provide for the performance of the duties of the office of President in case of the removal, resignation, death, or inability both of the President and Vice President", approved July 18, 1947, is amended by striking out "Secretary of War" and inserting in lieu thereof "Secretary of Defense", and by striking out "Secretary of the Navy,"

Approved July 26, 1947.

(5) **Executive Order 9877, 26 July 1947**

President Harry S. Truman signed Executive Order 9877 on the same day as the National Security Act. The order, a complement to the act, explicitly spelled out the functions of the armed forces, most of which had not been stated previously. Within the common mission of defense of the United States, the Air Force received the functions to: organize, train, and equip forces for a variety of air operations. Unfortunately, congressional amendments to the act had introduced inconsistencies between the order and the act.

The order limited the Navy to aircraft for reconnaissance, antisubmarine warfare, and protection of shipping, though not restricting the Navy to particular aircraft types. The act allowed "such aviation as may be organic therein," and specified naval aviation consisting of combat, service and training forces, and included land-based aviation. In terms of air transport, the order limited it to that necessary for administration and "over routes of sole interest to the naval forces," while the act allowed "air transport essential for naval operations." These differences left each service able to interpret the conflicting directives to its own best advantage.

The order spelled out the specific functions of the Air Force more completely than the act. The Air Force received its four major mission areas of strategic bombardment, air support to land forces, air defense, and air transport (the latter limited by the provision of certain transport exclusively to the Navy). This newest of services was generally responsible for the preparation of air forces for the effective prosecution of war.

The original drafts of the act and the order had been written at the same time, but after passage of the amended act, President Truman wished to sign both the act and the order at the same time, and there was no time in which to make the order consistent with the act. This set the stage for some conflicts over roles and missions between the Navy and the Air Force, each of which interpreted conflicting guidance to best suit its own purposes.

****
Steven L. Rearden, History of the Office of the Secretary of Defense, The Formative Years, 1947-1950, (Washington, D.C.: OSD Historical Office, 1984), pp 392-93.

BASIC DOCUMENTS

Robert F. Futrell, <u>Ideas, Concepts, and Doctrine: A History of Basic Thinking in the United States Air Force, 1907-1964</u>, (Maxwell AFB, Ala: Air University, 2nd. edition 1974), pp 97-98.

EXECUTIVE ORDER 9877

FUNCTIONS OF THE ARMED FORCES

By virtue of the authority vested in me by the Constitution and laws of the United States, and as President of the United States and Commander in Chief of the Armed Forces of the United States, I hereby prescribe the following assignment of primary functions and responsibilities to the three armed services.

Section I - The Common Missions of the Armed Forces of the United States are:

1. To support and defend the Constitution of the United States against all enemies, foreign or domestic.

2. To maintain, by timely and effective military action, the security of the United States, its possessions and areas vital to its interest.

3. To uphold and advance the national policies and interests of the United States.

4. To safeguard the internal security of the United States as directed by higher authority.

5. To conduct integrated operations on the land, on the sea, and in the air necessary for these purposes.

In order to facilitate the accomplishment of the foregoing missions the armed forces shall formulate integrated plans and make coordinated preparations. Each service shall observe the general principles and fulfill the specific functions outlined below, and shall make use of the personnel, equipment and facilities of the other services in all cases where economy and effectiveness will thereby be increased.

Section II - Functions of the United States Army

General

The United States Army includes land combat and service forces and such aviation and water transport as may be organic therein. It is organized, trained and equipped primarily for prompt and sustained combat incident to operations on land. The Army is responsible for the preparation of land forces necessary for the effective prosecution of war, and, in accordance with integrated joint mobilization plans, for the expansion of peacetime components of the Army to meet the needs of war.

The specific functions of the United States Army are:

1. To organize, train and equip land forces for:

    a. Operations on land, including joint operations.

    b. The seizure or defense of land areas, including airborne and joint amphibious operations.

    c. The occupation of land areas.

    2. To develop weapons, tactics, technique, organization and equipment of Army combat and service elements, coordinating with the Navy and the Air Force in all aspects of joint concern, including those which pertain to amphibious and airborne operations.

    3. To provide, as directed by proper authority, such missions and detachments for service in foreign countries as may be required to support the national policies and interests of the United States.

    4. To assist the Navy and Air Forces in the accomplishment of their missions, including the provision of common services and supplies as determined by proper authority.

Section III-Functions of the United States Navy

General

    The United States Navy includes naval combat and service forces, naval aviation, and the United States Marine Corps. It is organized, trained and equipped primarily for prompt and sustained combat at sea. The Navy is responsible for the preparation of naval forces necessary for the effective prosecution of war, and in accordance with integrated joint mobilization plans, for the expansion of the peacetime components of the Navy to meet the needs of war.

    The specific functions of the United States Navy are:

    1. To organize, train and equip naval forces for:

    a. Operations at sea, including joint operations.

    b. The control of vital sea areas, the protection of vital sea lanes, and the suppression of enemy sea commerce.

    c. The support of occupation forces as required.

    d. The seizure of minor enemy shore positions capable of reduction by such landing forces as may be comprised within the fleet organization.

    e. Naval reconnaissance, antisubmarine warfare, and protection of shipping. The air aspects of those functions shall be coordinated with the Air Force, including the development and procurement of aircraft, and air installations located on shore, and use shall be made of Air Force personnel, equipment and facilities in all cases where economy and effectiveness

will thereby be increased. Subject to the above
provision, the Navy will not be restricted as to types
of aircraft maintained and operated for these purposes.

    f. The air transport necessary for essential internal
administration and for air transport over routes of
sole interest to naval forces where the requirements
cannot be met by normal air transport facilities.

    2. To develop weapons, tactics, technique, organization
and equipment of naval combat and service elements,
coordinating with the Army and the Air Force in all aspects of
joint concern, including those which pertain to amphibious
operations.

    3. To provide, as directed by proper authority, such
missions and detachments for service in foreign countries as
may be required to support the national policies and interests
of the United States.

    4. To maintain the U.S. Marine Corps whose specific
functions are:

    a. To provide Marine Forces together with supporting
air components, for service with the Fleet in the
seizure or defense of advanced naval bases and for
the conduct of limited land operations in connection
therewith.

    b. To develop, in coordination with the Army and the
Air Force those phases of amphibious operations which
pertain to the tactics, technique and equipment employed
by landing forces.

    c. To provide detachments and organizations for service
on armed vessels of the Navy.

    d. To provide security detachments for protection of naval
property at naval stations and bases.

    e. To provide, as directed by proper authority, such
missions and detachments for service in foreign
countries as may be required to support the national
policies and interests of the United States.

    5. To assist the Army and the Air Force in the
accomplishment of their missions, including the provision of
common services and supplies as determined by proper authority.

Section IV-Functions of the United States Air Force

General

    The United States Air Force includes all military aviation
forces, both combat and service, not otherwise specifically
assigned. It is organized, trained, and equipped primarily for

prompt and sustained air offensive and defensive operations. The Air Force is responsible for the preparation of the air forces necessary for the effective prosecution of war except as otherwise assigned and, in accordance with integrated joint mobilization plans, for the expansion of the peacetime components of the Air Force to meet the needs of war.

The specific functions of the United States Air Force are:

1. To organize, train and equip air forces for:

a. Air operations including joint operations.

b. Gaining and maintaining general air supremacy.

c. Establishing local air superiority where and as required.

d. The strategic air force of the United States and strategic air reconnaissance.

e. Air lift and support for airborne operations.

f. Air support to land forces and naval forces, including support of occupation forces.

g. Air transport for the armed forces, except as provided by the Navy in accordance with paragraph 1f of Section III.

2. To develop weapons, tactics, technique, organization and equipment of Air Force combat and service elements, coordinating with the Army and Navy on all aspects of joint concern, including those which pertain to amphibious and airborne operations.

3. To provide, as directed by proper authority, such missions and detachments for service in foreign countries as may be required to support the national policies and interests of the United States.

4. To provide the means for coordination of air defense among all services.

5. To assist the Army and Navy in accomplishment of their missions, including the provision of common services and supplies as determined by proper authority.

HARRY S. TRUMAN

THE WHITE HOUSE
  July 26, 1947

(6) Army-Air Force Implementation Agreements, 15 September 1947

Under the terms of the National Security Act, the Secretary of Defense was authorized to transfer personnel, property, agencies, activities, and a variety of functions from the Army to the Air Force. Two years were alloted for the orderly transfer of functions and equipment. In order to provide a logical framework in which to effect the transfers, the Army's Deputy Chief of Staff, Lt. Gen. J. Lawton Collins, and the Deputy Commander and Chief of Air Staff, Lt. Gen. Hoyt S. Vandenberg, met with their staffs and worked out a series of agreements on which functions would be transferred, and how quickly.

The Army-Air Force Implementation Agreements began the process of separating the newly formed U.S. Air Force from the U.S. Army. The agreements included understandings on all of the major and minor functions which the Army and Air Force performed in common, including service support, troop allotments, and various special services. All commissioned officers in the Air Corps (Regular Army), Air Corps (Reserve), and Air Corps (AUS) were transferred to the Department of the Air Force, as were all warrant officers and enlisted personnel under the command, authority, or jurisdiction of the Commanding General, Army Air Forces. The agreements included understandings on the transfer of certain intelligence functions to the Air Force, assignment of strategic missile responsibility to the Air Force, assignment of air defense antiaircraft artillery units to the Air Force, and Air Force responsibility for research and development of guided missiles. In essence, these agreements settled which functions would transfer to the Air Force, while leaving the timing open, pending full establishment of a Headquarters USAF capable of handling the functions transferred.

Some of the more important agreements concerned control and employment of weapon systems. The Army retained control over tactical missiles, while the Air Force received responsibility for strategic systems. Surface-to-air missiles for area air defense went to the Air Force, as did antiaircraft artillery for air defense. Despite the seeming finality of these assignments, responsibility for guided missiles remained an issue between the services well into the 1950s. The Air Force received responsibility for organizing, equipping, and operating liaison squadrons, as well as for providing air transport (except that which was considered organic to the Army).

Forty transfer orders implementing the Army-Air Force agreements were issued between 26 September 1947 and 12 October 1949. The first order provided for the transfer of functions from the Secretary of the Army to the Secretary of the Air Force, the transfer of units from the Army Air Forces (including the Air Corps United States Army, and the GHQ Air Force (Air Force Combat Command), and the transfer of functions from the Commanding General, Army Air Forces, to the Chief of Staff of the Air Force. Also included in this initial order were all of the commissioned officers of the Air Corps, warrant officers, and enlisted personnel under the jurisdiction of the Commanding General, Army Air Forces, and installations likewise under the Commanding General's jurisdiction.

Subsequent transfer orders were less sweeping in nature, providing for the transfer of functions and personnel as agreed to in the Army-Air Force agreements. Many of the supporting functions which the Army provided for the Army Air Forces, and vice versa, remained intact pending promulgation of further transfer orders. Ultimately, the Air Force received responsibility for the full range of functions, including procurement, budget authority, and research and development.

****

Army-Air Force Agreements as to the Initial Implementation of the National Security Act of 1947, 15 September 1947 (document above); OSD Transfer Orders, published as Joint Army Air Force Bulletins between 26 September 1947 and 12 October 1949.

ARMY - AIR FORCE

AGREEMENTS

as to the

INITIAL

IMPLEMENTATION

OF

THE NATIONAL SECURITY ACT

OF 1947

(Subject to Approval of the Secretary of Defense)

Compiled by
The Offices of
The Deputy Chief of Staff
and
The Deputy Commander Army Air Forces

WAR DEPARTMENT

Washington

15 September 1947

MEMORANDUM FOR THE SECRETARY DESIGNATE OF DEFENSE:

Subject: Separation of the Air Force from the U.S. Army.

Reference is made to the enclosed letter to the Secretary of War from the Chief of Staff, United States Army, with the enclosure thereto which contains a report of agreements reached between the War Department and the Army Air Forces relative to the initial establishment of the United States Air Force separate from the United States Army.

At my request, Mr. Symington, the Secretary Designate of the Department of the Air Force, has reviewed jointly with me the report submitted by the Chief of Staff, United States Army. We are both in full accord with the agreements contained therein. We believe that the agreements solve in a practical manner the initial problems attendant upon separation, and that experience will prove that they are fundamentally sound and sufficiently flexible to meet changing conditions that may develop in the future.

We recommend jointly that you, as Secretary of Defense, approve these agreements upon the assumption of the duties of that office and that you direct their implementation by the Department of the Army and the Department of the Air Force in such manner as is indicated in the agreements.

In accordance with our recent conversation, I am forwarding informational copies to components of the Army and Air Force and am releasing the contents to the press, making it clear, however, that none of the agreements are effective except to the extent approved by you as Secretary of Defense.

(signed)
Kenneth C. Royall
Secretary of War

War Department
THE CHIEF OF STAFF
Washington

15 September 1947

MEMORANDUM FOR THE SECRETARY OF WAR:

SUBJECT: Separation of the Air Force from the U. S. Army.

The attached report of agreements is submitted in accordance with the oral instructions of the Secretary of War issued upon the ratification of The National Security Act of 1947, Public Law 253, 80th Congress.

These agreements are based upon preliminary studies instituted by the War Department such as the report of a Board of Officers, Major General William Hall as senior member, and upon later studies made in the office of the then Under Secretary (the present Secretary) of War. The agreements are in consonance with the testimony given before the Congress in support of The National Security Act of 1947 by Mr. Patterson, Mr. Royall, Mr. Symington, General Spaatz and myself.

Upon receipt of the Secretary of War's oral instructions, General Spaatz and I directed our staffs to prepare jointly, in the form of agreements, the basic policies upon which the United States Air Force would be established separate from the Army and that if any disagreements occurred, they would be presented jointly to us for resolution. I am happy to report that through the able executive direction of my Deputy Chief of Staff, Lieutenant General J. Lawton Collins and the Deputy Commander and Chief of Air Staff, Lieutenant General H. S. Vandenberg and through the spirit of cooperation existing between all elements of the War Department and Air Staffs, agreements have been reached on all basic policies.

General Spaatz and I are in complete accord and recommend that these agreements be forwarded to the Secretary Designate of Defense with the recommendation that he approve them upon the assumption of his duties as Secretary of Defense and that he direct their implementation by the Department of the Army and the Department of the Air Force at such times and dates as are mutually agreed upon between the Chief of Staff, U. S. Army and Chief of Staff U. S. Air Force.

(signed)
Dwight D. Eisenhower

FOREWORD

At the direction of General Eisenhower and General Spaatz, the agreements on the pages which follow have been reached between the major War Department and Air Staffs. Upon specific notification to implementing agencies they will be used as the basic policies which will govern the establishment of the Department of the Air Force separate from the Department of the Army.

TABLE OF CONTENTS

BASIC DOCUMENTS

SECTION I

BASIC POLICY AGREEMENTS

1. Service Support

Service support of the Air Force by the Army will continue substantially as now constituted. Each department will make use of the means and facilities of the other department in all cases where economy consistent with operational efficiency will result. Except as otherwise mutually agreed upon, cross-servicing and cross-procurement as now in effect will continue until modified by the Secretary of Defense.

2. Organic Services

Where service units are an organic part of an Air Force group or wing, they will, in general, be Air Force units; service units not an organic part of an Air Force group or wing and which perform a service essentially common to the Air Force and to the Army, such as engineer battalions or signal companies, will, in general, be Army units attached for duty to the Air Force. Application of this policy to specific units can only be determined by full consideration of the particular composition and function of the unit and its relationship to the organizational structure of the Air Force. A unit such as the Air Force Band, because of its peculiar relationship to the U. S. Air Force will be an Air Force unit. Chaplains and medical personnel will remain with the Army. These same principles, with a detailed analysis of the particular field of service activity involved, will determine which individual positions should be filled by Air Force officers and which should be filled by Army officers attached for duty.

3. Regular Army Officers

A total of 20,000 Regular Army commissions will be allotted to the Air Force for Regular Air Force officers. Regular commissions for officer personnel whose basic branch is other than Air Force, and who are attached for duty with the Air Force as individuals, or with Army units providing services to the Air Force, will be included in the 30,000 allotted to the Army.

4. Troop Basis

a. The United States Air Force will carry personnel of the United States Army attached as individuals or as units providing services solely to the Air Force, in the Air Force Troop Basis. The Army and the Air Force Troop Bases will be mutually adjusted to accomplish this objective.

b. The United States Air Force will include in its budget, funds for the personnel and units included in the Air Force Troop Basis, in accordance with paragraph a above.

c. The United States Army will carry the U. S. Army personnel and units described in paragraph a above in a separate section of the Army Troop Basis as a matter of information. However, to prevent duplication, they will not be included within the Army Troop Basis for budget estimating purposes.

d. Organization and Training Division, War Department General Staff, and the Assistant Chief of Air Staff-3 will adjust troop spaces between the Army and the Air Force promptly as agreements for the separation of functions are resolved with the view of the publication of Army and Air Force Troop Programs and Troop Bases simultaneously at the earliest practicable date.

BASIC DOCUMENTS

SECTION II

AGREEMENTS ON PERSONNEL

AND ADMINISTRATIVE FUNCTIONS

1.   Policies, Regulations, Circulars, etc.

Pending establishment of an agency within the Office of the Secretary of Defense or the Joint Staff of the Joint Chiefs of Staff for the promulgation of personnel policies, new policies and changes to existing policies concerning personnel will be coordinated between the two Departments by the initiating Department. Until changed in accordance with this procedure, present policies, regulations, circulars, etc. will remain in effect and be implemented individually by the respective Departments.

2.   Central Examining Stations and Induction Stations

The United States Army will operate these installations. The United States Air Force will furnish a proportional share of the personnel needed for their operation in accordance with space allocations as determined by the Department of the Army and the Department of the Air Force.

3.   Career Guidance Plan for Warrant Officers and Enlisted Men

a. The Army (The Adjutant General) will complete the job analysis program. To handle the analysis of purely Air Force type jobs the Air Force will furnish the necessary personnel.

b. The Army, in conjunction with the Air Force, will complete the Enlisted Efficiency Report Project.

c. The Army, in conjunction with the Air Force, will complete the Enlisted Qualification Record Project.

d. The Army will complete the MOS Proficiency Tests for all jobs not strictly Air Corps type jobs. The Air Force will complete the Tests for strictly Air Corps type jobs.

e. The Army and the Air Corps will each develop their own promotion and assignment procedures.

4.   Central Welfare Fund

The Air Force will receive a proportionate share of the Central Welfare Fund. The recommended share to be determined by the Central Welfare Board and presented to the Chiefs of Staff, United States Army and United States Air Force for approval.

5. Safety

Pending the establishment of a Safety Agency by the Secretary of Defense, the Safety Branch, Personnel and Administration Division, War Department General Staff will continue as the coordinating agency for ground safety in the two Departments.

6. Decorations

Pending the establishment of a Joint Army-Navy-Air Force Decorations Board, the War Department Decorations Board will continue to pass on all awards, except the Distinguished Flying Cross and the Air Medal, for members of both Departments. Air Force officers will continue to serve on the War Department Decorations Board as long as it acts for both Departments.

7. Dependent Schools

From money appropriated for the operation of such schools in the United States, the United States Air Force will receive a proportionate share, based on the number of students, for the operation of schools on Air Force installations. Overseas theater commander will handle such funds for all personnel within his theater.

8. Graduates of the United States Military Academy

Until an Air Force Academy is established, the United States Air Force will receive a proportion of each graduating class of the Military Academy. These graduates will be transferred to the United States Air Force upon graduation and will remain assigned to the Air Force regardless of their ability to complete flying training. The percentage of each class to be so transferred will be determined by the Director of Organization and Training and the Assistant Chief of Air Staff-3.

9. Special Services

The United States Air Force will furnish qualified officers for duty with the Special Service Division and those Special Service agencies which furnish common services in accordance with space allocations as determined by the Department of the Army and the Department of the Air Force.

a. The Army Motion Picture Service will continue to service both Departments as at present.

b. The Army Exchange Service will continue to service both Departments as at present.

c. The United States Air Force will promulgate its own policies with regard to recreational athletics and other recreational activities.

d. The United States Air Force will establish their own procedures pertaining to non-appropriated funds, including disposition and expenditures of dividends from the Motion Picture Service and the Exchange Service.

e. The Army will procure, store, and distribute to both Departments all Special Service supplies purchased from appropriated funds.

f. Special Service Division will continue to be the agency for liaison with outside welfare agencies, such as USO, Red Cross, etc.

g. The United States Air Force will utilize Army Special Service training facilities, such as the Special Service School.

h. The United States Air Force will supply their own Special Service officers.

10. Transfer and Detail of Personnel

a. All officers who hold commissions in the Air Corps, Regular Army; Air Corps, Reserve; and Air Corps, AUS, are transferred to the Department of the Air Force. All warrant officers and enlisted men now under the command, authority or jurisdiction of the Commanding General, Army Air Forces, are transferred to the United States Air Force except those:

(1) Assigned to units listed in inclosure 1. (deleted, but consisting of common service type units).

(2) Assigned to units, organizations or installations organized from bulk authorizations which furnish medical service.

(3) Assigned to medical duties in Air Force units.

b. Any individual, assigned to the Army, in accordance with paragraph 10 a, (1), (2) and (3) above, whose original enlistment was for assignment to the Air Corps or Army Air Forces may submit a written request to the Chief of Staff, U. S. Air Forces, prior to 1 July 1949, requesting transfer to the Department of the Air Force.

c. Any individual transferred as a result of 10a above who does not desire such transfer shall submit a written request, prior to 1 July 1949, through channels to the Chief of Staff, United States Army, asking for transfer to the Department of the Army.

d. Any individual, other than those specified in 10a above, who desires transfer to the United States Air Force may submit a request through channels, prior to 1 July 1949, to the Chief of Staff, United States Air Force.

e. After the separation of the United States Air Force from the United States Army, personnel of each Department may be "attached for duty with" the other Department. Such personnel will be attached for a specific length of time for a specific purpose, but while so attached for duty will be under the command and jurisdiction of the Chief of Staff of the Department to which attached.

f. Until 1 July 1948 officers of the Army may be detailed in the United States Air Force to undergo flight training. After this date no such details will be permitted. For personnel of the Army now detailed to the Army Air Force or Air Corps, except those undergoing flight training, and personnel of the Air Corps detailed in another branch, one of the following actions will be taken:

(1) The detail terminated and the individual "attached for duty with" the appropriate Department.

(2) The detail terminated and the individual returned to his basic Department.

(3) The detail terminated and the individual transferred to the appropriate Department.

g. Air Force personnel now on duty with the Army will be relieved from such duty over a two-year period ending 30 June

1949, until the number remaining on such duty is equal to the number agreed upon by the two Departments. Similar action will be taken for Army personnel now on duty with the Army Air Force.

h. Personnel engaged in joint Army-Air Force missions or activities will remain assigned to their parent Department notwithstanding the fact either Department may be charged with the accomplishment or supervision or the joint mission or activity. Each Department will furnish a proportionate share of the operating personnel for joint or common installations or activities in accordance with space allocation as determined by the Department of the Army and Department of the Air Force.

i. Personnel of the Women's Army Corps, both officer and enlisted, on duty with the Army Air Force will remain assigned to the United States Army pending the enactment of appropriate legislation establishing procedures for the appointment and enlistment of women in the United States Air Force.

SECTION III

AGREEMENTS ON INTELLIGENCE FUNCTIONS

The following functions will be assumed by the Air Force at mutually agreeable dates:

1. Mapping and Photography

a. Maintenance of liaison with all map and photo producing agencies of the U. S. Government.

b. Maintenance in accessible form of general information on map, chart, photographic and geodetic activities for the Air Force.

c. Receive requests for and prepare directives for and supervise the execution of programs for the procurement of all reconnaissance photography, required by Air Force and other agencies for photo interpretation. Maintain centralized file of photographic reconnaissance requests.

d. Receive requests for, prepare directives for and supervise the execution of programs for the procurement of all aerial photographic, aerial charting and geodetic control material required by the Air Force.

e. Recommend degree of classification and monitor release of aerial mapping and intelligence photographic material under prescribed security regulations.

f. Procure for the Air Force from foreign sources aerial photographic charts and chart information, utilizing the Air Attache system.

2. Foreign Liaison

Provide official liaison between military representatives of foreign governments and the Department of the Air Force.

3. Counter Intelligence Corps

The function of the Counter Intelligence Corps as it applies to the Department of the Air Force will be assumed by the Air

BASIC DOCUMENTS

Force prior to 31 December 1947 in the Z/I and on 1 July 1948 overseas. The transfer of functions will be as follows:

    a.   <u>Within the Z/I</u>:

        (1) <u>Officer Personnel</u> - Air Force officers on duty with the Army CIC and Army CIC officers on duty with Air Force or Air Force CIC units will be relieved of present assignment and be reassigned within their own departments on a schedule mutually agreeable to the CIC and the Department of the Air Force.

        (2) <u>Enlisted Personnel</u> - Enlisted personnel, subject to their consent, will be transferred to the department with which serving. In the event that individual consent is not obtained, personnel will be reassigned within their proper departments forthwith.

        (3) <u>Procurement</u> - Effective immediately the Air Force will procure its personnel under its own specific standards.

        (4) <u>Training</u>

        (a) The CIC Center, Camp Holabird, will continue to train personnel for the Air Force until further orders. In order for the Air Force to participate in this training, the Air Force will furnish a share of the staff and instructional and civilian personnel commensurate with the proportion of Air Force trainees to the total number of trainees. Space authorizations for officers, enlisted men and civilians will be transferred to the Air Force and personnel will remain on duty at Camp Holabird in accordance with the above proportion.

        (b) In the event that the Air Force decides to separate the training function from the Army, one year's notice will be given.

        (5) The control, administration, supply and policy direction of the 700th CIC Detachment will pass to the Air Force prior to 31 December 1947.

        (6) <u>Supply</u>

        (a) Items of equipment and supply authorized in T/O&E 30-500, Counter Intelligence Corps Detachment, will be procured, stored, and issued in a manner established for T/O&E supply.

(b) The procurement and storage of items of special investigative equipment and supply not included in T/O&E 30-500 will continue to be a function of CIC Supply Depot, Camp Holabird, until further orders.

(c) Basic annual requirements will be submitted separately by CIC of the Departments of the Army and Air Force effective for the Fiscal Year 1950.

(d) Research and development of special investigative equipment and techniques will continue to be a function of CIC, Department of the Army, until further orders.

b. <u>Overseas</u> - Plans will be issued at a later date concerning the separation of CIC overseas.

c. <u>General</u>

(1) Present credentials, issued in block will be used until further notice.

(2) CIC property in the possession of Air Force units will be transferred to the Air Force.

4. Command Functions - Security and Counter Intelligence

The command functions pertaining to Security and Counter Intelligence will be assumed by the Air Force as follows:

a. The assumption of responsibility for the following type investigations will be completed by Air Force prior to 31 December 1947.

(1) Air Force civilian personnel (does not include special investigations of civilian personnel required by Executive Order 9835 nor distribution of investigative personnel to be provided therefor. This to be covered at a later date).

(2) Review of Public Law 808 cases.

b. The assumption of responsibility for the following type investigations will be completed by the Air Force prior to 1 July 1948.

(1) Newly integrated AF officers and USMA graduates.

        (2)   Clearance of commercial facilities:

            (a)   Plants

            (b)   Personnel

        (3)   Maintenance of records of Air Force cases.

        (4)   All phases of safeguarding military information.

        (5)   Control of the release of classified and unclassified information to foreign governments.

    c.   To assist the Air Force in assuming the above functions, the Intelligence Division, WDGS, will endeavor to make available a cadre of trained personnel.

5. Training

    a.   The Intelligence Division will continue to train Air Force personnel in strategic intelligence and attache orientation at the Strategic Intelligence School. The Air Force will participate in this training commensurate with the ratio between the total number of officer positions in the Air Attache system, plus the intelligence officer positions in the Office of AC/AS-2 and similar positions in the Army.

    b.   The Intelligence Division Language Schools will continue to train Air Force students on a reimbursable basis until further orders. At such time as there may be a separate Air Force Appropriation Act, reimbursement will be made to the Army for the actual additional expense caused by Air Force students.

6. Attache System

    a.   The Department of Army and Department of the Air Force will operate, maintain, supervise and control separate attache systems.

    b.   These separate systems will be complementary and mutually supporting.

    c.   The stations composing the separate systems will have been assigned to one or the other system by mutual consent of the two departments based on relative interest.

d. At each station in either system, the department maintaining the station will provide all the services and facilities to personnel on duty thereat of the other department that is provided for assigned personnel.

e. The Air Force will furnish Air support for intelligence purposes.

f. Personnel at stations of the opposite department will conform to all orders issued by the senior officer assigned to the station with the following exceptions:

(1) Personnel will be responsible to their parent headquarters in Washington for intelligence reporting.

(2) The senior officer of each department will render efficiency reports on and command the personnel of his department and will be charged with insuring their payment.

7. Funds

a. In FY 1948, and in all probability in FY 1949, Air Force funds will be in same Appropriation Act as Army. Therefore, ID Fiscal Branch will, until there is a separate Air Appropriation Act, allot funds to Air Attache Offices. Funds will be allotted as now programmed.

b. With reference to the entertainment function now carried on by ID Foreign Liaison for AAF, funds will be allocated to the Air Force to cover the necessary assumption of Air Force foreign liaison functions. (Note: Latin American tours should be paid from "Inter-American Relations, War Department" funds, $17,000 of which have been programmed by Budget Division for CG, AAF.)

SECTION IV

AGREEMENTS ON ORGANIZATION,

MOBILIZATION AND TRAINING FUNCTIONS

1. Planning Responsibility

Over-all planning responsibilities for organization, mobilization, demobilization, and training of all components of the Army
of the United States are now vested in Organization and Training
Division, War Department General Staff. It is agreed that over-
all planning for these functions as they apply to the Air Force
will be now transferred to the Air Force.

2. Universal Military Training

The Army will continue to support universal military training
before Congress. Such changes as are necessary in the Universal
Military Training Bill will be proposed to the Congress to
recognize the United States Air Force.

3. Command and Operational Employment of Ground-launched Guided
Missiles and Units; No Change in Present Agreements Which Are:

a. Surface-to-surface Missiles (exclusive of pilotless
aircraft).

(1) Tactical Missiles will be assigned to the United
States Army. Missiles within this category are those capable of
employment in support of land operation and capable of employment
against targets, the destruction or neutralization of which will
have a direct effect on current Army tactical operations. Such
missiles include those which supplement the fires of and require
coordination with artillery and/or tactical aircraft operating on
close support missions incident to Army tactical operations.

(2) Strategic missiles will be assigned to the U. S. Air
Force. Missiles within this category are those designed for
employment against targets, the destruction or neutralization of
which does not have a direct effect on current Army tactical
operations and which are normally the targets of bombers, other
than those operating on close-support missions incident to Army
tactical operations and which require coordination with the operations of such bombers.

b. <u>Surface-to-air Missiles.</u>

(1) Security-missiles designed for employment in support of Army tactical operations will be assigned to the U. S. Army.

(2) Missiles designed for employment in area air defense will be assigned to the U. S. Air Force.

4. Joint Use of Installations

The scope and nature of this problem requires that the determination for each such installation be handled separately, based on the required degree of common and specialized participation.

5. United States Military Academy and United States Military Academy Preparatory School

a. <u>The following constitutes an interim agreement:</u>

(1) The Air Force will continue to participate in the operation of the United States Military Academy and United States Military Academy Preparatory School in the present proportion.

(2) The troop spaces occupied by U. S. Air Force personnel as of 1 September 1947 will be transferred to the U. S. Air Force in accordance with paragraph 9 b.

(3) The present budgetary procedure will continue.

(4) The present system of allocation of graduate cadets and students will continue in force.

b. Final resolution of the above paragraphs (1) to (4) will be made at a later date.

6. Responsibility for Antiaircraft Artillery; No Change in Present Agreements Which Are:

a. The U. S. Army is responsible for the activation, training, and control of all antiaircraft artillery units and individuals assigned thereto, except as provided in paragraphs b and c below.

b. The U. S. Air Force will train and control all antiaircraft artillery units and individuals assigned or attached for air defense purposes.

c. The U. S. Army will provide sufficient antiaircraft artillery units personnel to accomplish the antiaircraft artillery requirements of air defense to the U. S. Air Force; and further, provide sufficient antiaircraft units and personnel for integrated air defense training.

7. Employment of Antiaircraft Artillery in the Zone of Interior

It is agreed that the joint agreement signed by General Spaatz and General Devers should continue for the present.

8. Responsibilities for Civilian Components

The Army will retain responsibility for Army units. The Air Force will assume responsibility for Air Force units.

9. Allocation of Troop Spaces

a. Of the 1,070,000 military troop space requirements of War Department, the initial U. S. Air Force troop space allotment will be 401,362 (generally composed as indicated for 30 June 1947 in the War Department Troop Program of 1 December 1946).

b. The initial U. S. Air Force troop space allotment will be adjusted as functions and responsibilities are transferred between U. S. Air Force and U. S. Army.

10. Allocation of Civilian Personnel

a. The U. S. Air Force will assume the function of authorizing and allocating its civilian personnel world wide. Further negotiation is necessary to determine the final allocation of graded civilian positions authorized by and subject to provisions of Section 14 Public Law 390 (176,000) to be transferred to Air Force control.

b. It is agreed that no effort should be made, at this time, to divide the 40,000 civilians available to the Army and Air Forces over and above Public Law 390 and Public Law 106.

11. Processing, Reviewing and Approval of Tables of Organization and Equipment and Tables of Allowances

Each department will process, review, and approve its own Tables of Organization and Equipment, EMLs and Tables of Allowances. The procedures for procurement of equipment and coordination between the Army and the Air Force must be worked out by Assistant Chief of Air Staff-4 and the Director, Service, Supply, and Procurement Division, WDGS.

12. Preparation, Processing and Approval of Tables of Allowances for Joint Air-Ground Activities.

Either department will be authorized to initiate joint tables of allowances. The initiating department must coordinate such tables with the other department and secure joint approval for publication.

13. Separation of Mobilization and Demobilization Planning

Each department will perform mobilization and demobilization planning for its respective Department as directed and coordinated by higher authority.

14. Allocation of Mobilization Responsibilities

The United States Air Force will have the responsibility for mobilizing all units and personnel which make up the Air Force command structure world wide. The fact that units are common is coincidental. Units which will perform common functions to be accomplished through cross service will be mobilized by the department supplying the cross service.

15. Weather Service

United States Air Forces will be responsible for maintenance of meteorological service for operation of the Air Forces and provision of meteorological service for the Army, except Army meteorological ballistics data which will remain in the Army.

16. Responsibility for Airborne Training

a. The U.S. Army, acting in coordination with the U.S. Navy and the U.S. Air Force, is responsible for the airborne training of the U.S. Army.

b. The U.S. Air Force, acting in coordination with the U.S. Navy and the U.S. Army, is responsible for the airborne training of the U.S. Air Force.

c. The U. S. Air Force is responsible that sufficient troop carrier units are maintained and made available to the U. S. Army to provide for the integrated training of such units with elements of the United States Army.

d. The U. S. Air Force is further responsible that adequate troop carrier units are maintained and made available to the U. S. Army to support air-borne operations incident to land operations.

17. Responsibility for Amphibious Training

Amphibious training will be conducted in two phases; that conducted individually by each department and that conducted jointly. The training conducted individually will be preparatory to joint participation and will be conducted individually by each department.

a. Matters requiring Joint (Army, Navy and Air Force) coordination controlled from a higher level than the Departments will be considered at a later date.

18. Responsibility for Foreign Training

Unless modified by higher authority it is agreed that the procedure to be followed in foreign training is that foreign nationals will be trained by the counterpart in the United States of the foreign military or Air Force of which the foreign national is a representative.

19. Procedure for Education in Civilian Schools

The requirements for education in civilian schools will be determined by each department individually. These requirements will be submitted to higher authority for approval or adjustment consistent with the total requirements of all departments and within the capabilities of civilian institutions. The program will be controlled by each department individually.

20. Control and Operation of Joint Schools

The operation of the Joint Schools will continue to be controlled from a higher level of authority than the departments.

21. Exchange of Officers for Training and Indoctrination

A free exchange of officers for training and indoctrination will be provided to include the school systems, commands and headquarters of the departments.

22. Training of Common Type Specialists

A common type specialist is defined as an individual whose training qualifies him to perform an identical function in either service. These specialists cannot necessarily be identified by Specification Serial Number common to both services. Common type specialists should be trained by the department having predominate interest in that specialty. The predominately interested department should be determined by mutual agreement or where agreement cannot be reached, by direction from higher authority. After this determination is made, both departments (The Navy to be included later) should participate in the training by assignment of personnel for the school overhead. The necessary troop basis should be allocated to each department to meet the requirements for participation.

23. Responsibility of Army and Air Force with Respect to Liaison Squadrons and Training of Liaison Aircraft Specialists of Ground Units

a. The United States Air Force is responsible that liaison squadrons are organized, equipped and operated in accordance with the requirements of the United States Army for such squadrons.

b. The United States Air Force is responsible for providing the necessary individual training of specialists, including pilots, to operate and maintain liaison aircraft and related equipment assigned as organic equipment to tactical ground Table of Organization and Equipment units.

c. The Chief of Staff, U. S. Army, is responsible for the training in tactical employment of pilots of ground units equipped with Table of Organization and Equipment liaison aircraft.

SECTION V

AGREEMENTS ON SERVICE, SUPPLY

AND PROCUREMENT (LOGISTICS) FUNCTIONS

GENERAL

Each department shall make use of the means and facilities of the other departments in all cases where economy consistent with operational efficiency will result. Except as otherwise mutually agreed upon, cross-servicing and cross-procurement as now in effect will continue until modified by the Secretary of Defense.

SERVICE ACTIVITIES

1. Real Estate and Construction

a. The Army and the Air Force will individually determine their separate requirements for real estate and construction and defend those requirements in their individual budget estimates.

b. The Army will acquire and dispose of real estate for itself and act as agent in the acquisition and disposal of real estate for the Air Force.

c. The Army will continue to act as custodian of all legal records pertaining to real estate for the Army and the Air Force, as now in effect, unless other arrangements are directed by the Secretary of Defense.

d. The Army is designated as the contract construction agent for the Air Force. The Air Force will provide funds for such construction, will collaborate in the preparation of specifications, including layout and architectural design, and will review and approve contracts prior to awards. Design of specialized technical facilities for Air Force use will be the responsibility of the Air Force.

2. Repairs and Utilities

a. The Army and the Air Force will individually determine their separate requirements, qualitative and quantitative, for all personnel, materiel, and services, and defend these requirements within their separate budget estimates. Each department will administer, direct, and supervise repairs and utilities activities at its own installations.

b. Repairs and utilities technical standards and general policies will be developed by joint agreement wherever possible and promulgated by each department, otherwise by direction of the Secretary of Defense.

b. Contracts for the purchase of utilities services (gas, water, electricity, etc.) will be negotiated and executed by the respective departments, governed by established joint policies. Where economy and efficiency, consistent with operational requirements, would result, one department will include provision for utility contract services for all other departments in a specified locality.

3. Hospitalization

a. General hospitals for the Army and the Air Force will be operated by the Army.

b. Station hospitals will be operated both by the Army and the Air Forces. In those areas where one department can provide services to the other Department, the Department with predominant interest as determined by agreement or direction will provide station hospital accommodations for both Army and Air Force Personnel.

4. Transportation

a. The Army will provide surface transportation (rail,highway and water, except organic transportation) including the operation of water ports for both the Army and the Air Force.

b. The Air Force will provide air transportation (except organic) including the operation of aerial ports for both the Army and the Air Force.

c. Until otherwise directed by the Secretary of Defense the Army will conduct rate negotiations with surface carriers and the Air Force will conduct rate negotiations with air carriers. Close coordination will be established and maintained between the Army and the Air Force in this regard in order to protect the best interests of the National Military Establishment.

d. Nothing in the foregoing will preclude the routine utilization of carriers by either department in accordance with existing procedures and practices and established rates.

5. Movement Control

The movement control function presently performed by the War Department will continue in operation insofar as movement operations of the Army and the Air Force are concerned until the function is assumed by a Joint Movement Control Agency organized for this purpose by direction of the Secretary of Defense.

6. Communications

Pending completion of negotiations between the Signal Corps, U. S. Army and the U. S. Air Force (based on principles for joint integrated communications established by the Joint Communications Board) and decision by the Secretary of Defense, the Signal Corps, U. S. Army will continue to provide the communications service (Army Command and Administrative net and commercial leased line contractual arrangements) which it now provides for the Army Air Forces, for the United States Air Force.

7. Personnel Ceilings

It was agreed that personnel ceilings between the Army and the Air Force should be adjusted to meet requirements of agreements reached herein.

8. Disbursing and Auditing

a. The Army Audit Agency, with suitable Air Force representation, will perform contract and industrial auditing, and military property account audits pertaining to supplies or property for the Departments of Army and Air Force until otherwise directed.

b. The Air Force will continue to operate its present disbursing network and make payments to its own military and civilian personnel through Air Force command channels in accordance with accounting directives of the Army Chief of Finance, or such higher authority as may be designated later.

c. AAF disbursing network will continue to furnish cross disbursing services to the Army and the Army disbursing network will continue to furnish cross disbursing services to the Air Force.

d. The Office of the Chief of Finance and the Army Finance Center, St. Louis, Missouri, with suitable proportional Air Force representation, and the Finance Offices, U. S. Army, and Finance Offices, U. S. Air Force, to be established by transfer, will continue to furnish common overhead finance service, necessary in sustenance of the Army and the Air Force disbursing networks. Such common service will continue pending a further study of the possibilities of furnishing such services within a joint office with a view of attaining economy, retention of an equal autonomous status within each Department and at the same time provide cadres of trained personnel within each Department for decentralization in time of war.

MAINTENANCE AND SUPPLY ACTIVITIES

9. Distribution of Supplies

    a. The distribution system now serving the Army and the Air Forces will remain in effect until modified by mutual agreement or by the Secretary of Defense, except that supplies and equipment now in the actual possession of the Army Air Forces will be released to Air Force control under the provisions of Public Law 253.

    b. Supplies and equipment procured by one Department for the other will be earmarked for the using Service and carried in stock as credits, subject to user demand. Through the Fiscal Year 1949, the Army will continue to provide the Air Force with supplies and equipment from existing stocks in accordance with current policies and practices except as modified by mutual agreement.

    c. Prior to the preparation of the Fiscal Year 1950 budget the Air Force and the Army will collaborate in the analysis of stock control accounts, of stocks on hand or under procurement, including war reserve materiel, which were procured for or in support of the Army and/or Air Force, in order that such stocks can be equitably allocated to the Army and Air Force and taken into proper consideration in preparation of the budget. After appropriate allocation these stocks will be earmarked for the using service and carried in storage as credits to user demand.

10. Maintenance

    a. Organization maintenance and field maintenance at and below installation level will be performed by each Department.

    b. Base maintenance (depot maintenance in Army Air Forces) of all items (peculiar and common) will normally be performed by the Department having <u>procurement</u> responsibility except that base maintenance responsibility in specific areas and for specific items may be otherwise assigned by mutual agreement or by direction of the Secretary of Defense in the interest of economy and efficiency.

PROCUREMENT ACTIVITIES

11. Procurement Responsibility

    a. There will be transferred to the Department of the Air Force complete procurement responsibility for all items of materiel and supply now assigned to the Air Force for procurement.

    b. From time to time there may be assigned to the Department of the Air Force procurement responsibility for specific items and/or categories as may be determined by the Munitions Board.

12. Field Purchasing Offices

    Purchasing offices and/or contract administration offices will be progressively consolidated and/or joint use of the physical locations and administration overheads effected as now directed in War Department Memorandum 734-5-7.

13. Procurement Regulations

    Interim joint regulations are now in preparation with target date of 1 October 1947 for promulgation and use. Certain changes will have to be effected subsequently as necessitated in accordance with final enactment of the Procurement Bill.

14. Readjustment

    a. <u>Contract Settlement including disposal of termination inventories.</u>

    (1) Settlement falling under the Contract Settlement Act of 1944, until that Act is no longer effective, will continue to be a joint responsibility of the Department of the Army and the Department of the Air Force, using the machinery now set up for the purpose.

    (2) The Department of the Air Force will assume responsibility for contract settlement of Air Force contracts not falling under the provisions of the Contract Settlement Act of 1944.

120

b. <u>Renegotiation.</u>

The Air Force renegotiation cases remaining will be transferred to the Department of the Army at an early date estimated prior to January 1948.

c. Government Furnished Property -- Activities under War Department Memorandum 734-5-5, 6 November 1946, will continue as joint effort under direction of Secretary of the Army, to completion.

d. The responsibility for disposition of Army-owned, Air Force controlled, and RFC-owned Air Force-sponsored, complete industrial facilities, and the industrial personal property connected therewith when not termination inventory, when determined excess to Air Force needs will be assumed by U. S. Air Force as soon as authorized by the Secretary of Defense.

15. Procurement Planning

Responsibility for procurement planning will be assigned to the Army and the Air Force in accordance with the assignment of procurement responsibilities.

16. Standards

a. Responsibility for packaging and inspection activities will be assigned to the Army and the Air Force in accordance with the assignment of procurement responsibility.

b. Preparation of specifications covering items of sole interest to one service will be the responsibility of that service. Specifications for items of common interest will be inaugurated by the service requiring such items and completely coordinated with each service prior to publication. Generally, custodianship of specifications will be vested in the procuring service.

17. Contract Approvals

The approval of all Air Force contracts will be assumed by the Air Force at a time to be determined by mutual agreement between the Secretary of the Army and the Secretary of the Air Force.

18. Matters Concerning Air Force Contract Fraud

The Air Force will assume these together with responsibility for the necessary direct contacts with the Department of Justice, at a time to be determined by mutual agreement between the Secretary of the Army and the Secretary of the Air Force.

19. Use of Government-Owned Production Facilities

Responsibility for approvals of use by the Air Force of government-owned production facilities belonging to RFC or other government agencies will be assumed by the Air Force as soon as authorized by the Secretary of Defense.

20. Industrial Mobilization Planning

a. Responsibility for Air Force Industrial Mobilization Planning will be assumed by the Air Force, subject to direction of the Munitions Board and coordination through it with Departments of the Army and of the Navy, as soon as authorized by the Secretary of Defense.

b. (1) Determination of all material and supply requirements for common items envisioned under industrial planning will be the responsibility of the using departments.

(2) The procuring department will be responsible for industrial planning for all items which it procures.

SECTION VI

AGREEMENTS ON PLANNING

AND OPERATIONAL FUNCTIONS

1. Planning and Policy

Complete responsibility for such planning and policy recommending functions as have been performed for the Army Air Force by the War Department will be assumed by the United States Air Force.

2. State, War, Navy Coordinating Committee

Responsibility for recommending action on appropriate State, War, Navy Coordinating Committee matters (the extent of this responsibility will be determined by the reorganization of State, War, Navy Coordinating Committee now under study), will be assumed by the Air Force.

3. Departmental Air Functions

Complete responsibility for departmental Air matters, (which have largely been discharged by the Air Forces in the past through the Air Coordinating Committee), such as liaison with coordinate government agencies on military Air matters, military aviation with regard to foreign countries, air agreements, etc. will be assumed by the Air Force.

4. Command Post

Responsibility for operating a Command Post for the Chief of the Air Force will be assumed by the Air Force.

5. Joint Advisory Board on American Republics

Responsibility for providing Department of the Air Force membership on Joint Advisory Board on American Republics (JABAR) will be assumed by that department.

6. Aviation Training Foreign Nationals

Aviation training of foreign nationals will be a responsibility of the Air Force.

7. Foreign Aid Programs

Responsibility for the implementation of aviation aspects of aid programs for foreign countries will be assumed by the Air Force.

8. Western Hemisphere Program

Responsibility for formulation of plans and policies pertaining to aviation aspects of the Western Hemisphere program will be assumed by the Air Force.

9. Latin American Air Missions and Commissions

Responsibility for administrative supervision of military air missions and commissions in Latin America to include execution of contracts and procurement of personnel and supplies will be assumed by the Air Force.

10. Politico-Military

Politico-military responsibilities as determined by subsequent division of responsibility within the National Security Organization and at such a date as may be mutually agreed upon will be assumed by the Air Force.

11. Military Survey Branch

The Military Survey Branch will function in a joint capacity during the interim period pending final resolution of politico-military responsibilities as between the three departments, the Secretary of Defense, and the Joint Staff.

12. State Department Liaison

State Department liaison activities now performed by Plans and Operations Division will continue to be performed by them for both the Army and the Air Force.

SECTION VII

AGREEMENTS ON RESEARCH

AND DEVELOPMENT FUNCTIONS

The following list of proposed actions will provide the groundwork for future cooperation:

1. Functions

The following functions of the Commanding General, Army Air Forces will no longer require War Department approval:

a. The preparation and conduct of a research and development program covering materiel, methods, and techniques for which he has research and development responsibility.

b. The establishment of the military characteristics for materiel used exclusively by the Army Air Forces, and the preparation of recommended military characteristics for other materiel used or intended for use by units of his command.

c. The coordination with the Chiefs of Technical Services concerned and the Commanding General, Army Ground Forces, of the military characteristics of materiel used by units of those agencies which are assigned to the Army Air Forces.

d. Coordination with the Commanding General, Army Ground Forces, and the Chiefs of Technical Services, of the military characteristics of the Army Air Forces materiel required to meet the needs of the Army Ground Forces and the technical services, respectively.

e. The initiation of requests for research and development of those items which are the responsibility of other developing agencies, but which support his own development activities.

f. The conduct and supervision of service tests of types of materiel used exclusively by the Army Air Forces, and for joint or separate supervision of service tests of materiel used jointly with other agencies.

g. The classification of materiel used exclusively by the Army Air Forces, and the preparation of classification actions on other materiel for which he has research and development responsibility.

h. The initiation of requests to the Chiefs of Technical Services, for the classification as to type of materiel developed by those services for use by the Army Air Forces.

i. The establishment of a basis of issue for units assigned to Army Air Forces.

j. The maintenance of a record (Status of Equipment Reports or similar lists) in which are listed all adopted items, by type classification, of materiel procured by the Army Air Forces.

k. The insurance that specifications for adopted items of materiel conform to approved military characteristics.

2. Projects

a. General.

Initial assignment of projects will be as shown in the War Department list of projects as of 30 June 1947. Thereafter it appears inevitable that each specific project will have to be resolved on its particular merits. For example, in the field of aircraft armament, the Ordnance Department will probably continue research and development work, even though the Air Force might understandably desire to perform some of this work themselves.

b. Meteorological Equipment Research and Development.

Responsibilities for meteorological equipment research and development will continue as at present subject to further coordination and later determination.

c. Guided Missile Program.

The Air Force will continue their responsibility for the research and development activities pertaining to guided missiles in the Army and the Air Force as prescribed. The duties of the Director of Research and Development, WDGS, will be continued by the Director of Research and Development, GS, USA, until such time as they may be taken over by the Research and Development Board of the National Military Establishment.

3. Inter-Service Coordination

In order to provide a better medium at the Department level for insuring coordination as between the Army, Navy and Air Force, it is proposed to broaden the operational concept of the War Department Research Council. The functions and responsibilities under this concept should be so defined as to ensure that there exists in each the Army, Navy and Air Forces an organization performing similar function concerning those Research and Development matters within the primary cognizance of the Department concerned as is consistent with the differences with the command structure of the three Departments. Clearly, for example, the Air Force and Navy should be represented on the Army council with authority to ensure that, where necessary, disputed matters would be referred to Research and Development Board for resolution. It is not contemplated, however, that a change would be required in the authority currently assigned to this Council. The existing technical committees of the technical services would continue to function as prescribed in War Department Circular 126, 17 May 1947. In addition, they would inform this Council of their action.

4. Personnel

a. The number of officers from Air Force to be assigned to Army research and development and vice versa will be worked out by mutual agreement.

b. Air Force officers now on duty with Research and Development Division will be released in accordance with an agreed table.

5. Budget

On Air Force projects included in appropriation titles Air Corps - Army and being or to be accomplished by the technical services, the Air Force should continue to prepare and defend the estimates, receive the funds, and allot to the technical services the amount involved for services rendered. Similar action will be taken on Army projects being accomplished by the Air Force.

6. Responsibility Change

The Research and Development Division, WDGS, loses no functions or responsibility except the review and approval of those functions listed in paragraph 1 above.

SECTION VII

AGREEMENTS ON BUDGETARY FUNCTIONS

1. Fiscal Year 1949 Budget

Formulation of policies to govern submission of the Fiscal Year 1949 Budget has been the subject of correspondence between Mr. Forrestal and Mr. Royall, and between the latter and Mr. Symington. Mr. Royall, with the concurrence of Mr. Symington, has recommended the following with respect to the Fiscal Year 1949 Budget:

a. A single budget will be submitted for the War Department (Department of the Army), this budget to include estimates of funds required for the support of the Air Force.

b. Each budget program making up the total budget will indicate the amounts which are included for the support of the Air Force.

c. This budget will be reviewed by the existing Budget Advisory Committee. Recommendations of the Committee to be submitted to both the Chief of Staff and the Commanding General, Army Air Force. Disagreements, if any, will be worked out between Mr. Royall and Mr. Symington.

d. Representatives of the War Department and the Air Force will appear jointly at the hearings planned by the Bureau of the Budget and before Committees of the Congress, as appropriate.

e. Funds which may be appropriated for the support of the Air Force in the War Department Fiscal Year 1949 Budget will be administered in a manner recommended by the two departments, and approved by the Secretary of Defense, after evaluation of organizational and functional changes arising out of the pending reorganization.

Indication of Mr. Forrestal's approval of these proposals will complete the solution of this problem.

2. Transfer of Current Funds

With respect to the transfer of current funds, it is believed that action should be taken to comply with the provisions of Section 306, Public Law 253, as expeditiously as possible. It is recognized, however, that it is to the mutual interest of the War Department and the Air Force to accomplish this transfer in a sound and logical manner. It will require that certain transfers be made after a thorough evaluation of changes in organization and procedures which, in most cases, have not yet crystallized. It is accordingly recommended that:

a. Transfers of funds take place from time to time, as necessitated by the transfer of personnel, organizations or functions, and as mutually recommended by the two Departments and approved by the Secretary of Defense.

b. Pending such transfers, the Budget Officer for the War Department (Department of the Army) continue to allocate funds for the support of the Air Force upon the recommendation of that Department.

SECTION IX

AGREEMENTS ON

ADJUTANT GENERAL FUNCTIONS

The following general areas of agreement have been reached; however, much detailed study is required before a decision can be made as to the date of transfer of such functions, the allocation of personnel authorizations and the transfer of individuals.

1. Current Records

The U. S. Air Force will assume custody of all <u>current</u> 201 files and records of active, retired, and reserve personnel who are transferred to the U. S. Air Force.

2. Associate Functions

Upon assuming custody of the above 201 files and records, the U. S. Air Force will also assume those functions, as they pertain to U. S. Air Force personnel, now being performed by the following sections of the Adjutant General's Office:

Personnel Actions Branch, Personnel Information Branch, Personnel Research and Procedures Branch, Decorations and Awards Branch, Assignment Branch and Reserve Branch.

3. Non-Current Records

The Adjutant General will continue to maintain and service all non-current records, and the U. S. Air Force initially will retire future non-current records to Army Records Centers.

4. Corrections Branch

The Adjutant General will continue to perform all functions now assigned to the Corrections Branch, AGO.

5. Military Personnel Procurement

The Adjutant General will continue, for the present, to perform the functions now assigned to the Military Personnel Procurement Division, AGO. These functions will be performed under joint policies established by the Director of Personnel and Administration for the Army and the Assistant Chief of Air Staff-1 for the Air Force.

6. Strength Accounting, etc.

    The U. S. Air Force will assume those functions, as they pertain to the Air Force, now performed by the following sections of the Adjutant General's Office: Strength Accounting Branch, Operations Branch and Security Classification Branch.

7. Office Service Branch

    The Adjutant General will continue to operate the Office Service Branch.

8. Other Functions

    Further study will be necessary in determining agreements on the functions now performed by the Army Publications Service, the Army Postal Service, and the Civilian Personnel Branch.

SECTION X

AGREEMENTS ON

INSPECTOR GENERAL FUNCTIONS

In view of the fact that the Army Air Forces has enjoyed almost complete autonomy insofar as inspector general functions are concerned for the past two years and the two agencies have worked in close harmony, there are no points of disagreement concerning the division of responsibilities incident to separation of the Air Forces from the U. S. Army. Formal agreement has been reached concerning the separation of the major functions of The Inspector General.

1. Annual General Inspections

All annual general inspection reports and action letters, Inspector General's Department, pertaining to Air Force activities, will be processed entirely by The Air Inspector. All inspection reports now in the hands of The Inspector General, concerning inspections of Air Force activities for the fiscal year 1948, will be transferred to the Air Inspector as the final repository. This also applies to any special inspections of Air Force activities excluding procurement inspections.

2. Procurement Inspections

Complete responsibility for procurement inspection will be transferred simultaneously with the transfer of complete responsibility for procurement.

3. Inspection of Air Force Disbursing Officers

Although since 1 July 1947 informal agreement has been in effect concerning inspection of fiscal matters, it is agreed that the Air Force will now accept all responsibility for inspection of accounts of Air Force disbursing officers, including the final filing of Forms No. 3, IGD. Any Forms No. 3, IGD, concerning Air Force disbursing officers, completed as a result of inspections since 1 July 1947 will be delivered by The Inspector General to The Air Inspector.

4. Complaints and/or Allegations

All complaints concerning Air Force personnel or installations made under army regulations will become the responsibility of The Air Inspector. All correspondence concerning complaints and/or allegations now in process will be completed by the agency now responsible.

5. Investigations

Any investigation pertaining to Air Force personnel or facilities, formerly conducted under the provisions of AR 20-30, will become the responsibility of The Air Inspector on and after 1 September 1947. All such investigations now in process will remain the responsibility of the responsible agency now conducting the investigation. Investigations concerning war frauds will continue to be the responsibility of The Inspector General until such time as the responsibility for the contracts involved is determined.

6. National Guard

It is agreed that until such time as Section 93, National Defense Act of 1920 is amended, The Air Inspector will be responsible for the inspection of Air National Guard units under the provisions of NGR No. 48.

7. Air ROTC Inspections

The inspection of Air ROTC units will be the responsibility of The Air Inspector.

8. General

a. It is mutually agreed that the agency conducting an inspection or investigation is authorized to cross such channels into the other agency as is necessary for completion of the inspection or investigation, following appropriate coordination with responsible commanders.

b. All of the matters stated in the agreements above are equally applicable to the Zone of Interior and Overseas commands.

c. With respect to those functions mutually agreed upon, The Inspector General interposes no objection to properly detailed air inspectors performing the functions heretofore reserved for inspectors general and the Air Inspector is authorized to continue to detail in the Inspector General's Department such officers as he may consider necessary, pending publication of Air Force regulations governing detail as Air Inspectors.

AGREEMENTS ON

CHAPLAIN FUNCTIONS

1. The Chaplain Corps, United States Army will continue to furnish Chaplains for duty with the United States Air Force.

2. Chaplains of the Army normally will be attached for duty with the U. S. Air Force for a three or four-year period. Such tours may be lengthened or shortened by agreement between the Department of the Army and Department of the Air Force. While attached for duty with the U. S. Air Force, Chaplains will be under the command and assignment jurisdiction of the Chief of Staff, U. S. Air Force.

3. Policy promulgated by the Chief of Chaplains as it affects the U. S. Air Force will be coordinated with the U. S. Air Force prior to publication.

4. The U. S. Air Force will compute their needs for Chaplains, Chaplains' equipment and religious supplies and defend the budget for these matters.

5. The U. S. Army will procure and furnish to the U. S. Air Force Chaplains, Chaplains' equipment and religious supplies in accordance with approved budget allowance.

AGREEMENTS ON

PROVOST MARSHAL GENERAL FUNCTIONS

1. GENERAL

a. There will be established a joint provost marshal staff (Army-Air Force level). Both parts of such staff would operate as a single unit and by mutual agreement on common functions. Each part of such staff would function independently insofar as the individual service is concerned. This would provide the necessary personnel to perform all functions and responsibilities assigned to the two services. Such joint staff section would be composed of the aggregate of troop spaces and civilian authorizations now available to The Provost Marshal General and the Air Provost Marshal Offices with subsequent (date to be decided) redistribution of those space and authorizations on a 60% - 40% Air Force ratio.

b. The joint staff established as above would conduct continuing studies during the two year transition period so that recommendations may be made from time to time to the Army and Air Force staffs for such transfers of personnel, equipment, etc., as are indicated by further divisions of responsibility in accordance with the principles laid down by higher authority.

c. Adjoining office space should be provided for efficient operation of the joint staff.

2. POLICE OF PUBLIC CARRIERS

Group movements are a command responsibility and the police of such movements is the responsibility of the commander of the station of origin. This responsibility begins at point of origin and continues through to destination. Where the density of individual travel or other circumstances warrant it, the local commander will take the necessary action with regard to police enforcements. No reallocation of personnel or spaces is involved.

3. SECURITY OF AIR FORCE BASES, POSTS, CAMPS AND STATIONS

Each department will be responsible for the security of its own installations. No reallocation of spaces or personnel is involved.

4. GUARD HOUSES

Each department will be responsible for the operation and control of its own guard houses. No reallocation of spaces or personnel is involved.

5. LOYALTY INVESTIGATIONS AND ALLIED SUBJECTS INCLUDING PLANT CLEARANCE

For the time being each department will remain responsible according to present division of responsibilities. A study is now under way to arrive at a satisfactory solution to this matter. It is not believed that any reallocation of spaces or personnel will be involved.

6. DOMESTIC DISTURBANCES

The Air Provost Marshall will have no direct responsibility in such matters.

7. OFF-POST AND OFF-BASE PATROLS

a. Where area frequented is contiguous to a post, camp, station or base of one service and only one service is involved, the using service will be responsible for the off-post, camp, station or base patrol of the frequented area.
b. Where personnel of both departments frequent a single area the responsibility for the police of that area is the responsibility of the service having the greater garrison strength. Personnel for patrols in such areas will be furnished by both departments as agreed between the local commanders concerned.

8. CRIMINAL INVESTIGATIONS

Each department will conduct both on and off station criminal investigation as it pertains to itself. No reallocation of spaces or personnel is involved.

9. APPREHENSIONS

Each department will be involved in the apprehension of deserters, escapes, etc. Each department will assist the other in this matter upon request.

10. MILITARY POLICE SCHOOL

The Army will operate the school and will supply the administrative staff required for its operation. The faculty, except for civilian members thereof, will be allocated between the two departments according to the participation of the two services in the school. Troop spaces will be transferred from the Army to the Air Force in accordance with this agreement. Civilian instructors will be furnished by the Army. Each department will participate in the establishment of the curriculum of the school.

11. MILITARY POLICE BOARD

Each department will have representation on the Board; the Air Force furnishing two members, the Army three.

AGREEMENTS ON

PUBLIC INFORMATION FUNCTIONS

1. The following functions are now performed by War Department
Public Information Division for the Public Information Division,
AAF and will be continued for the U.S. Air Force.
    a. Mimeographing of releases.
    b. Distribution of releases to media and individuals.
    c. Clearance of releases for security and policy except when
        covered by a certification from the Air Forces that sub-
        ject matter pertains only to the Air Forces. On matters
        of mutual interest and where there is doubt concerning
        the War Department policy, releases will be submitted to
        War Department Public Information Division.
    d. Press room will be used mutually with free access by the
        Air Forces to representatives of the press.
    e. Clearance and accreditation of correspondents to overseas
        theaters is the responsibility of the Liaison Section,
        WDPID. The Air Force makes use of these facilities.
2. Apart from the foregoing, the Air Forces has been given the
authority to operate autonomously in all Public Information matters.
3. This arrangement has functioned satisfactorily and it is recommended that it be continued as long as Headquarters of the Air
Forces remain in the Pentagon. The Air Forces will eventually
assume the mimeographing and distribution, outside of local
requirements, of their releases. The clearance of releases will
become the responsibility of the Air Forces.

AGREEMENTS ON

LEGISLATIVE AND LIAISON FUNCTIONS

1. CONGRESSIONAL LIAISON
    This covers in general the type of personalized service now being rendered the Congress by the Liaison Branch of Legislative and Liaison Division with respect to congressional inquiries directed to the War Department either in writing or verbal. It does not cover the field of legislative liaison nor the field of liaison with Congressional Investigation Committees.
    It is agreed that the Legislative and Liaison Division will turn over to the Legislative Services Division of the Air Force the functions of primary interest to the Air force together with personnel presently engaged in carrying out those functions. It is estimated that complete transfer of both functions and personnel can be affected within thirty (30) days following approval of this agreement.

2. LEGISLATIVE FORMULATION, PROCESSING AND LIAISON
    The transfer of functions in this field it is agreed should be an evolutionary process. Legislative and Liaison Division will continue to be responsible for monitoring the processing and presentation of the current War Department legislative program, both Army and Air Force, pending before the 90th Congress. Personnel of the Legislative Services Division of the Air Force will participate in carrying out these functions under the close coordination and supervision of the Chief of the Legislative and Liaison Division. It is anticipated that such personnel will gain sufficient experience by the end of the 80th Congress to permit the functions of formulation, processing and presentation of the Air Force legislative program to be presented to the 81st Congress to be placed under the direct control of the legislative Services Division.
    Legislative problems originating subsequent to the date of this agreement may be of such a nature as to indicate independent handling by the Legislative Services Division. In such event the Chief of Legislative and Liaison Division is agreeable to such action. It is felt that any transfer of personnel from the Legislative Branch of Legislative and Liaison Division should take place after final session of the 80th Congress.

3. CONGRESSIONAL INVESTIGATIONS
    In the field of congressional investigations, it is agreed that those matters now under investigation by congressional committees should continue to be handled under the supervision and

control of Legislative and Liaison Division. New matters of investigation by committees will be the responsibility of Legislative and Liaison Division or Legislative Services Division, depending upon whether the mater primarily pertains to the Army or Air Force. Matters of mutual interest will be closely coordinated between the two offices. No personnel is to be transferred to the Air Force until the close of the last session of the 80th Congress.

4. SENATE AND HOUSE LIAISON OFFICES

These offices are a part of the Liaison Branch of Legislative and Liaison Division and as such their functions and personnel are a part of the agreement included under paragraph 1 above. It is felt, however, that their organization and composition subsequent to the adjournment of the 80th Congress will be contingent upon the wishes of the 81st Congress and upon decision of the Secretary of Defense. For these reasons it is agreed that pending decision by higher authority these offices will continue under Legislative and Liaison Division during the remainder of the 80th Congress but will serve Legislative Services Division directly in all matters affecting the Air Force. In the event that the Secretary of Defense does not establish by the beginning of the 81st Congress, an office to serve the entire military establishment, Legislative Services Division will establish congressional liaison offices in both the House of Representatives and Senate, comparable to those now existing for Legislative and Liaison Division and the Navy.

5. WAR DEPARTMENT LIAISON OFFICERS ASSIGNED TO SENATE AND HOUSE ARMED SERVICES COMMITTEES.

The primary function of these officers is to assist the Armed Services Committees, and thereby serve the War Department, in receiving, analyzing, and processing the legislative proposals of the War Department. The Navy has liaison officers with these same committees who perform similar functions for the Navy. It is agreed that the officers of Legislative and Liaison Division now performing this duty continue serving both the War Department and the Air Force for the duration of the 80th Congress. As a matter of interest, one of the two committee liaison officers is an Air Force Officer. This arrangement is considered in harmony with the previously stated agreement that all current legislation will remain the responsibility of Legislative and Liaison Division during the 80th Congress. Closest liaison is to be maintained between Legislative and Liaison division and Legislative Services Division on this function.

AGREEMENTS OF

TROOP INFORMATION AND EDUCATION FUNCTIONS

The Troop Information and Education Division, EDSS, and its three field installations in the past established policies, planned operation, and furnished services for the TI&E program for the U.S. Army including the Army Air Force. In addition, the Navy has participated actively in this program by acting jointly with the Army in operating the U.S. Armed Force Institute and the Armed Forces Radio service, and by using informational materials produced for the Army. Consequently, the WD Troop Information and Education operation is already largely unified with the Air Force and the Navy. The following satisfactory mutual agreements have been reached:

1. The Army Air Force will continue to participate in the present Troop Information and Education program being conducted for the U.S. Army.

2. The U.S. Armed Forces Institute, the Armed Forces Radio Service, and the Armed Forces Press Service will continue to serve the Army Air Force in the same way they serve the Army.

3. The Army Air Force will continue to receive the weekly Armed Forces Talk and other materials furnished by this Special Staff Division in the same manner as it has in the past.

4. The Army Air Force will furnish its proportionate share of personnel to conduct the TI&E program. The replacement of present Army personnel with Air Force personnel is to be a gradual operation.

5. The Army Air Force will have a voice in establishing policies governing the TI&E activities and in the operation of the field agencies. This voice will be obtained initially through the Air Force in establishing policies governing TI&E activities. In the interim period, the Air Force will have an equal status with the Army in all matters common to both forces. This coordination will be direct through Chief, TI&E Division, WDSS, and AC/AS-1.

6. The Army Air Force will continue to utilize the facilities of the Army Information School for the training of Information and Education officers.

AGREEMENTS OF

CIVIL AFFAIRS FUNCTIONS

1. There are no Civil Affairs Division problems, projects or functions to be transferred to or from the Air Force.
2. All Air Force personnel now with Civil Affairs Division could be transferred to the Air Force -- if this transfer were accomplished gradually. However, it would be most desirable if at least two or three Air Force Officers would remain in Civil Affairs Division to facilitate resolution of Civil Affairs/Military Government problems with aviation implications.
3. It is emphasized that the above comments apply only to Civil Affairs Division and do not prejudge dispositions within the theaters of occupation by the theater commanders.

AGREEMENTS ON

HISTORICAL FUNCTIONS

1. The Historical Division, WDSS, and the Air Force Historical office were organized independently and are administratively auto- nomous. Since the ending of hostilities the major task of each organization has been to prepare its part of the official history of the "U.S. Army in World War II." Close liaison and coor- dination exists between the two historical organizations with the result that all matters such as scope, standards, access to records, distribution, etc., have been resolved. It is believed that the mutual clearance and concurrence that each organization receives from the other before the volumes are published should continue so that each organization can profit from the other's experience and that the public will know that the histories as produced have the official approval of both the U.S. Army and the U.S. Air Force.

2. In writing of the history of World War II it would be impossible to present a clear and factual account if the air and ground story were not integrated just as they were integrated during the war. It will be necessary for certain Air officers to remain on the staff of the Historical Division until the history is complete to make certain that tactical air phase is complete and receives adequate treatment within the ground volumes.

3. Recently a special fund was established with the Army Central Welfare Agency as custodian to insure the completion and publica- tion of the official history, "U.S. Army in World War II" (Ground Forces, Air Forces, Service Forces). It is known that some volu- mes will cost more to produce than others so it is recommended that any decision partitioning this account into separate funds for the Air Force and Army be postponed until more experience and more adequate cost analyses can be obtained. Pending final deci- sion on division of the fund it is recommended that the Chief Air Historical Office continue as a member of the Council admi- nistering the fund.

4. a. The Historical Division is planning to develop a unit histories section to execute those responsibilities assigned to the Division by War Department Circular No. 204, 2 August 1947. Part II of the Circular, Distinctive Insignia, lifts the prohibi- tion on manufacture of distinctive unit insignia and outlines the procedure and priority by which the insignia may be secured by units. Prior to World War II the Historical Section, Army War College determined and prepared for the Quartermaster General the histories of units, including Air, on which the designs of Coats

of Arms and Units insignia are based. During the past war the preparation and issuance of coats of arms and unit insignia was
suspended, but the Historical Section, Army War College maintained
unit files in anticipation of the reopening of the program. A
short time ago, the Historical Section, Army War College was combined with the Historical Division, WDSS, along with the above
mentioned files. These files will be the records upon which the
unit histories will be based.

      b. The files are now being maintained by one warrant officer
who files orders showing changes in status of units such as activation, inactivation, redesignation, change of station, etc., as
published by the Adjutant General, Army Areas, and Air Commands.
It is believed that the Air Force unit files should be transferred
to the AAG Record Administrator for maintenance when the Air
Adjutant General assumes the function of recording changes in status of air units now being performed for the Air Force by the
Adjutant General.

      c. In line with the above it is believed that the Air Force
should assume responsibility as soon as possible for the determination and compilation of data on Air Force units. This recommendation is made for the following reasons:

      (1) On assumption by the Air Adjutant General of those
functions performed for the Air Force by the Adjutant General, the
Historical Division will be unable to maintain the unit historical
files for Air Forces units unless complicated and expensive
liaison is maintained between the Air Adjutant General and the
Historical Division.

      (2) As the program for design and issuance of unit
insignia and coats of arms is just being implemented and has not
started actual operation as yet, it is believed that the Air Force
might be desirous of revising regulations and directives concerning the unit history, battle honors, unit insignia, etc.,
along lines more suitable to the Air Force.

5. The Historical Division is preparing an Order of Battle and a
day by day chronology of the war. It may be that the Air Force
will desire to do the work applicable to the Air Force under their
supervision but as the work has not advanced far enough for a
decision it is recommended that the Historical Division remain
responsible for its completion at this time.

AGREEMENTS ON

STATISTICAL OFFICE FUNCTIONS

1. The enactment of the National Security Act of 1947 raises three broad problems with respect to the functions of the Central Statistical Office, the Statistical Control Division of Army Air Forces and other statistical and reporting services as follows:

a. The coordination among the Army, the Navy, and the Air Force on common reporting and statistical services and particularly in submitting to the Joint Staff and the Secretary of Defense reports in comparable units, terminology, and periods so as to enable evaluation and comparison of data obtained from the three departments.

b. The transfer to the U. S. Air Force of responsibility for statistical and reporting services pertaining to the U. S. Air Force which have heretofore been processed through the War Department.

c. The servicing of the Office, Secretary of Defense with statistical analyses and studies required for planning, policy, and operating decisions.

2. In connection with the problems outlined above, until such time as the organization of the Office, Secretary of Defense and the Joint Staff are formulated, specific proposals with respect to paragraph 1 c must await further development.

3. As regards paragraphs 1 a and b above the following agreements have been reached.

a. That the Central Statistical Office and the Statistical Control Division be designated as the agencies for their respective departments to effect any necessary actions or coordination required by 1 a above .

b. That the Air Force will continue to furnish reports necessary for publication of documents such as the Civilian Personnel Statistics Bulletin, The War Department Troop Program, Strength Reports of the Army, and The War Department Troop List, as prescribed by the Central Statistical Office. The discontinuance of the joint Army-Air character of each of these publications and the institution of separate publications for each Department will be accomplished as rapidly as feasible but of necessity will be governed by the requirements for presenting joint Army-Air Statistics to budget and common supply and service agencies.

c. That field reports will be separated as rapidly as is consistent with the shift of functions from the War Department to the Departments of Army and Air so as to provide for reports on Air Force matters going direct to the Headquarters, U. S. Air Force.

BASIC DOCUMENTS

AGREEMENTS ON

MANAGEMENT OFFICE FUNCTIONS

1. Since the work of the Management Office is basically internal, concerned almost exclusively with administrative and management operations within the Staff area, rather than Army-wide matters, there will not be very many points at which there is potential overlap of functions between this office and its counterpart in the Air Force.

2. There are three principal areas in which this office will be affected in the separation of the Air Force.

    a. Withdrawal of USAF officers from agencies of the War Department Groups.

    b. Administration of USAF personnel remaining in the War Department Groups or subsequently assigned to the War Department Groups.

    c. Allocation of funds.

3. On the first of these points -- the withdrawal of Air Force officers from the War Department agencies -- it is understood that the Air Force will withdraw its officers individually over an extended period rather than establish percentage quotas for specific dates. It is also understood that the Career Management Branch, P & A Division will be primarily concerned with filling the resulting vacancies with Army officers. Apparently, there is no action necessary by the Management Office on this problem until the actual withdrawal of Air Force officers begins.

4. The problem indicated in paragraph 2 b above, regarding the authorization and administration of USAF personnel remaining in the War Department Groups or subsequently assigned to the War Department Groups, breaks into two parts: (a) the administration of Air personnel assigned to Army agencies and (b) the administration of Air and Army personnel assigned to Joint agencies. This is being worked out by O & T, P & A, the Manpower Board, and the Management Office. The proposed plan worked out by these agencies will be submitted to Headquarters, AAF for concurrence. The Allocations Branch of A-3 has already indicated its willingness to go along with whatever arrangement is worked out by the Army.

5. As far as the administration of the joint agencies is concerned, there are four subdivisions of this problem:

    a. Civilian and military personnel authorization.

    b. Military personnel administration.

    c. Civilian personnel administration.

    d. Civilian personnel budget.

The Joint Chiefs of Staff have not been able as yet to give any indication as to how the administration of their agencies will be

146

handled under the new setup. There are two alternatives: either to have the administration of the Joint Staff handled by a central agency at their level or in the Office of the Secretary of Defense, or to have the present system of Army-Navy contributions of personnel and money on a roughly 50-50 basis broadened so that there will be one third participation by Army, Navy, and Air in contributing to the support of the Joint Staff. This office and most of the Army and Air Agencies with whom the problem has been discussed favor the first alternative -- the creation of an operating management office in the Office of the Secretary of Defense to take care of administrative matters for his immediate office plus the Joint Staff, the Munitions Board, the Research and Development Board, and any other committees or agencies which may be established at that level. However, until this basic decision is reached, it will not be possible to arrive at any definite agreement with the Air Force on the administration of the joint agencies. Agreements have been reached to handle the administration of the Air Force share of the Joint Staff authorization, budget, and personnel, if it is decided that the Joint Staff will be supported on a three-way contribution basis.

6. The allocation of budgetary funds to the Air Force will be handled by the Management Office insofar as the payment of salaries for departmental civilian personnel in Staff is concerned. However, it will not be possible to determine precisely the amount of money involved in the transfer until each of the Staff agencies has come to an agreement with the Air Force regarding the number of people involved in the split-off of functions between Army and Air. For example, the amount of money that should be transferred from the Intelligence Division to A-2 cannot be determined until those two organizations come to an agreement as to the functions which will be carried by each organization. As soon as these determinations have been made and approved, arrangements will be made with the Budget Division and the Air Comptroller for the transfer of the necessary funds. At this point, it does not seem likely that there will be any large amount of money involved in the transfer since the Staff agencies will need to maintain the bulk of their present staff for strictly Army activities.

AGREEMENTS ON

STAFF COMMUNICATIONS OFFICE FUNCTIONS

1. Staff Communications Office will continue to perform present service to the Air Forces.

2. If, at a future date, the above agreement is found to be impractical, a survey will be made to determine whether or not these functions should be assumed by an Air Force Staff agency.

AGREEMENTS ON

JUDGE ADVOCATE GENERAL FUNCTIONS

1. The Department of Air will assume all functions, as they pertain to the Department of Air, now charged to The Judge Advocate General (except these pertaining to real estate and construction contracts). This transfer of functions will be accomplished gradually as the Air Force becomes prepared to assume them.
2. The Department of Air will not assume responsibility for appellate review as provided by Article of War 50½ pending passage, by the Congress, of necessary legislation.
3. Reallocation of space authorizations and personnel between the Office of The Judge Advocate General and The Air Judge Advocate is being studied and will be presented at a later date.

(NOTE: The above agreements, except for the portion shown in parentheses will hold after the separation of the Air Force. Further discussions are being held concerning the portion shown in parentheses).

(7) Key West Agreement, 21 April 1948

The incongruities between the National Security Act of 1947 and its companion Executive Order 9877 attracted Secretary of Defense James Forrestal's attention. These incongruities were due to President Harry S. Truman's urgent desire to issue both documents concurrently, while the drafters of the order had planned a meeting to iron out the inconsistencies between the two documents prior to issuing the executive order. On 20 January 1948, Forrestal sent for comment a proposed redraft of the Executive Order to the service secretaries and the Joint Chiefs of Staff (JCS). None of the service secretaries approved of the proposed redraft and, since it did not provide the clear-cut guidance Forrestal desired, he withdrew it from consideration. Moreover, the Secretary found no solid ground on which to base his roles and missions assignments since the JCS had not completed any strategic plans to underpin mission assignments. By February, Forrestal had decided to await further JCS progress in strategic planning, after which he would issue a directive on roles and missions simultaneously with a presidential recission of Executive Order 9877.

Prior to Forrestal's withdrawal of his redraft, the JCS had referred the document to an ad hoc committee for study. While the committee favored a new redraft of an executive order, the JCS preferred a guidance statement from the Secretary of Defense. But, by then Forrestal had become aligned with that approach, and the committee was instructed to begin work on a statement of service functions to replace Executive Order 9877.

The disagreements between the services engendered by the attempts to redraft Executive Order 9877 and draft a new statement of service functions prompted Secretary Forrestal to arrange a conference of the Joint Chiefs and himself at Key West, Florida, from 11 to 14 March 1948. The JCS efforts to agree on service functions had foundered over fundamental disagreements: whether the Navy's carrier aviation should have a role in strategic air operations, and whether the Army or the Air Force should assume primary responsibility for land-based air defense. The Army tended to side with the Air Force on the naval air issue and urged limitations on naval aviation and the Marine Corps, while the Navy stoutly resisted their efforts to limit naval freedom of action. These issues were resolved by Forrestal in his opening remarks at Key West, in which he assigned primary responsibility for strategic bombing and overall air warfare to the Air Force, though not restricting the Navy from acquiring and maintaining an air component, and by restricting the size of the Marine Corps. Under the guidance of these opening remarks, the JCS drafted a new statement of roles and missions, although final refinements were completed in Washington, D.C., following a 20 March meeting. The President approved the functions statement on 21 April 1948.

The Key West Agreement, labelled "Functions of the Armed Forces and the Joint Chiefs of Staff," contrasted with the broad missions statements in Executive Order 9877 by being far more detailed, spelling out clearly the primary and secondary missions of each service. In general terms, the division of service responsibilities remained the same, with the Navy assigned primacy in combat operations at sea; the Army assigned land combat and responsibility for providing antiaircraft artillery for air defense; the Marine Corps assigned amphibious warfare; and the Air Force assigned strategic air warfare, defense of the United States against air attack, and air and logistic support of ground units.

Aside from the statement on primary missions, each service was assigned a number of collateral missions, in conjunction with a general statement on how to handle missions which involved forces from more than one service. Certain collateral missions were delineated at the time, allowing the services to provide for mutual support in performance of primary missions. The generalized statement provided a mechanism through which future missions could be parcelled out with a minimum of acrimony. Specific collateral missions assigned to the Air Force involved assistance to the Navy in sea lane interdiction, antisubmarine warfare, and aerial minelaying operations.

****
Steven L. Rearden, History of the Office of the Secretary of Defense, The Formative Years 1947-1950, (Washington, D.C.; OSD Historical Office, 1984) pp 393-97.

THE SECRETARY OF DEFENSE

21 April 1948

MEMORANDUM FOR:
The Secretary of The Army
The Secretary of the Navy
The Secretary of The Air Force
Joint Chiefs of Staff

Attached is a signed copy of the paper defining the functions of the Armed Forces and the Joint Chiefs of Staff

Attached also is a photostatic copy of President Truman's letter, approving this paper.

The only change in the paper, as executed, occurs in the third line from the bottom of page 1 where the words "by direction of the President" have been added.

/s/ James Forrestal

THE WHITE HOUSE

April 21, 1948

Honorable James Forrestal
Secretary of Defense
Washington, D.C.
My dear Mr. Secretary:

In reply to your letter of March 27, 1948, I have today issued
an Executive Order revoking Executive Order 9877, of July 26,
1947. In its stead, I wish you to issue the statement of functions of the Armed Forces and the Joint Chiefs of Staff which has
been drawn up by you and the Joint Chiefs of Staff.

Very sincerely yours,
/s/ Harry S. Truman

21 April 1948

Functions of the Armed Forces
and the Joint Chiefs of Staff

Index

Introduction

Congress, in the National Security Act of 1947, has described
the basic policy embodied in the Act in the following terms:
"In enacting this, legislation, it is the intent of Congress
to provide a comprehensive program for the future security of the
United States; to provide for the establishment of integrated
policies and procedures for the departments, agencies, and functions of the government relating to the national security; to pro-

vide three military departments for the operation and administration of the Army, the Navy (including naval aviation and the United States Marine Corps), and the Air Force, with their assigned combat and service components; to provide for their authoritative coordination and unified direction under civilian control but not to merge them; to provide for the effective strategic direction of the armed forces and for their operation under unified control and for their integration into an efficient team of land, naval and air forces."

In accordance with the policy declared by Congress, and in accordance with the provisions of the National Security Act of 1947, and to provide guidance for the departments and the joint agencies of the National Military Establishment, the Secretary of Defense, by direction of the President, hereby promulgates the following statement of the functions of the Armed Forces and the Joint Chiefs of Staff.

Section I--Principles

1. There shall be the maximum practicable integration of the policies and procedures of the departments and agencies of the National Military Establishment. This does not imply a merging of Armed Forces, but does demand a consonance and correlation of policies and procedures throughout the National Military Establishment in order to produce an effective, economical, harmonious and businesslike organization which will insure the military security of the United States.

2. The functions stated herein shall be carried out in such a manner as to achieve the following:

a. Effective strategic direction of the Armed Forces.

b. Operation of Armed Forces under unified command, wherever such unified command is in the best interest of national security.

c. Integration of the Armed Forces into an efficient team of land, naval, and air forces.

d. Prevention of unnecessary duplication or overlapping among the Services, by utilization of the personnel, intelligence, facilities, equipment, supplies and services of any or all Services in all cases where military effectiveness and economy of resources will thereby be increased.

e. Coordination of Armed Forces operations to promote efficiency and economy and to prevent gaps in responsibility.

3. It is essential that there be full utilization and exploitation of the weapons, techniques, and intrinsic capabilities of each of the Services in any military situation where this will contribute effectively to the attainment of over-all military objectives. In effecting this, collateral as well as primary

functions will be assigned. It is recognized that assignment of collateral functions may establish further justification for stated force requirements, but such assignment shall not be used as the basis for establishing additional force requirements.

    4. Doctrines, procedures, and plans covering joint operations and joint exercises shall be jointly prepared. Primary responsibility for development of certain doctrines and procedures is hereinafter assigned.

    5. Technological developments, variations in the availability of manpower and natural resources, changing economic conditions, and changes in the world politico-military situation may dictate the desirability of changes in the present assignment of specific functions and responsibilities to the individual Services. This determination and the initiation of implementing action are the responsibility of the Secretary of Defense.

Section II--Common Functions of the Armed Forces

A. General

    As prescribed by higher authority and under the general direction of the Joint Chiefs of Staff, the armed forces shall conduct operations wherever and whenever necessary for the following purposes:

    1. To support and defend the Constitution of the United States against all enemies, foreign or domestic.

    2. To maintain, by timely and effective military action, the security of the United States, its possessions and areas vital to its interest.

    3. To uphold and advance the national policies and interests of the United States.

B. Specific

    1. In accordance with guidance from the Joint Chiefs of Staff, to prepare forces and to establish reserves of equipment and supplies for the effective prosecution of war and to plan for the expansion of peacetime components to meet the needs of war.

    2. To maintain in readiness mobile reserve forces, properly organized, trained, and equipped for employment in emergency.

    3. To provide adequate, timely, and reliable intelligence for use within the National Military Establishment.

    4. To organize, train, and equip forces for joint operations.

    5. To conduct research, to develop tactics, techniques and organization, and to develop and procure weapons, equipment, and supplies essential to the fulfillment of the functions hereinafter assigned, each Service coordinating with the others in all matters of joint concern.

    6. To develop, garrison, supply, equip, and maintain bases

and other installations, to include lines of communication, and to provide administrative and logistical support of all forces and bases.

    7. To provide, as directed by proper authority, such forces, military missions, and detachments for service in foreign countries as may be required to support the national interests of the United States.

    8. As directed by proper authority, to assist in training and equipping the military forces of foreign nations.

    9. Each Service to assist the others in the accomplishment of their functions, including the provision of personnel, intelligence, training, facilities, equipment supplies, and services as may be determined by proper authority.

    10. Each Service to support operations of the others.

    11. Each Service to coordinate operations (including administrative, logistical, training, and combat) with those of the other Services as necessary in the best interests of the United States.

    12. Each Service to determine and provide the means of communications by which command within the Service is to be exercised.

    13. To refer all matters of strategic significance to the Joint Chiefs of Staff.

Section III--Functions of the Joint Chiefs of Staff

A. General

    The Joint Chiefs of Staff, consisting of the Chief of Staff, U.S. Army; the Chief of Naval Operations; the Chief of Staff, U.S. Air Force; and the Chief of Staff to the Commander-in-Chief, if there be one, are the principal military advisers to the President and to the Secretary of Defense.

B. Specific

    Subject to the authority and direction of the President and the Secretary of Defense, it shall be the duty of the Joint Chiefs of Staff:

    1. To prepare strategic plans and to provide for the strategic direction of the Armed Forces, to include the general direction of all combat operations.

    2. To prepare joint logistic plans and to assign to the military Services logistic responsibilities in accordance with such plans.

    3. To prepare integrated joint plans for military mobilization, and to review major material requirements and personnel qualifications and requirements of the Armed Forces in the light of strategic and logistic plans.

4. To promulgate to the individual departments of the National Military Establishment general policies and doctrines in order to provide guidance in the preparation of their respective detailed plans.

5. As directed by proper authority, to participate in the preparation of combined plans for military action in conjunction with the armed forces of other nations.

6. To establish unified commands in strategic areas when such unified commands are in the interest of national security, and to authorize commanders thereof to establish such subordinate unified commands as may be necessary.

7. To designate, as necessary, one of their members as their executive agent for:

a. A unified command;

b. Certain operations, and specified commands;

c. The development of special tactics, technique, and equipment, except as otherwise provided herein; and

d. The conduct of joint training, except as otherwise provided herein.

8. To determine what means are required for the exercise of unified command, and to assign to individual members the responsibility of providing such means.

9. To approve policies and doctrines for:

a. Joint operations, including joint amphibious and airborne operations, and for joint training.

b. Coordinating the education of members of the Armed Forces.

10. To recommend to the Secretary of Defense the assignment of primary responsibility for any function of the Armed Forces requiring such determination.

11. To prepare and submit to the Secretary of Defense, for his information and consideration in furnishing guidance to the Departments for preparation of their annual budgetary estimates and in coordinating these budgets, a statement of military requirements which is based upon agreed strategic considerations, joint outline war plans, and current national security commitments. This statement of requirements shall include: tasks, priority of tasks, force requirements, and general strategic guidance concerning development of military installations and bases, equipping and maintaining the military forces, and research and development and industrial mobilization programs.

12. To provide United States representation on the Military Staff Committee of the United Nations, in accordance with the provisions of the Charter of the United Nations and representation on other properly authorized military staffs, boards, councils, and missions.

Section IV--Functions of the United States Army

The United States Army includes land combat and service forces and such aviation and water transport as may be organic therein. It is organized, trained, and equipped primarily for prompt and sustained combat operations on land. Of the three major Services, the Army has primary interest in all operations on land, except in those operations otherwise assigned herein.

A. Primary Functions

1. To organize, train, and equip Army forces for the conduct of prompt and sustained combat operations on land. Specifically:

    a. To defeat enemy land forces.

    b. To seize, occupy, and defend land areas.

2. To organize, train, and equip Army antiaircraft artillery units.

3. To organize and equip, in coordination with the other Services, and to provide Army forces for joint amphibious and airborne operations, and to provide for the training of such forces in accordance with policies and doctrines of the Joint Chiefs of Staff.

4. To develop, in coordination with the other Services, tactics, technique, and equipment of interest to the Army for amphibious operations and not provided for in Section V, paragraph A 4 and paragraph A 11 c.

5. To provide an organization capable of furnishing adequate, timely, and reliable intelligence for the Army.

6. To provide Army forces as required for the defense of the United States against air attack, in accordance with joint doctrines and procedures approved by the Joint Chiefs of Staff.

7. To provide forces, as directed by proper authority, for occupation of territories abroad, to include initial establishment of military government pending transfer of this responsibility to other authority.

8. To develop, in coordination with the Navy, the Air Force, and the Marine Corps, the doctrines, procedures, and equipment employed by Army and Marine forces in airborne operations. The Army shall have primary interest in the development of these airborne doctrines, procedures and equipment which are of common interest to the Army and the Marine Corps.

9. To formulate doctrines and procedures for the organization, equipping, training, and employment of forces operating on land, at division level and above, including division corps, army, and general reserve troops, except that the formulation of doctrines and procedures for the organization, equipping, training, and employment of Marine Corps units for amphibious operations shall be a function of the Department of the Navy, coordinating as

required by paragraph A 11 c, Section V.

    10.   To provide support, as directed by higher authority, for the following activities.

      a.   The administration and operation of the Panama Canal.

      b.   River and harbor projects in the United States, its territories, and possessions.

      c.   Certain other civil activities prescribed by law.

B. Collateral Functions. The forces developed and trained to perform the primary functions set forth above shall be employed to support and supplement the other Services in carrying out their primary functions, where and whenever such participation will result in increased effectiveness and will contribute to the accomplishment of the over-all military objectives. The Joint Chiefs of Staff member of the Service having primary responsibility for a function shall be the agent of the Joint Chiefs of Staff to present to that body the requirements for and plans for the employment of all forces to carry out the function. He shall also be responsible for presenting to the Joint Chiefs of Staff for final decision any disagreement within the field of his primary responsibility which has not been resolved. This shall not be construed to prevent any member of the Joint Chiefs of Staff from presenting unilaterally any issue of disagreement with another Service. Certain specific collateral functions of the Army are listed below:

    1.   To interdict enemy sea and air power and communications through operations on or from land.

    2.   To provide forces and equipment for and to conduct controlled mine field operations.[1]

Section V--Functions of the United States Navy and Marine Corps

    Within the Department of the Navy, assigned forces include the entire operating forces of the United States Navy, including naval aviation, and the United States Marine Corps. These forces are organized, trained, and equipped primarily for prompt and sustained combat operations at sea, and for air and land operations incident thereto. Of the three major Services, the Navy has primary interest in all operations at sea, except in those operations otherwise assigned herein.

A. Primary Functions

    1.   To organize, train, and equip Navy and Marine Forces for the conduct of prompt and sustained combat operations at sea, including operations of sea-based aircraft and their land-based

---

[1]This collateral function was transferred from the Army to the Navy by the direction of the Secretary of Defense on 24 May 1949.

naval air components. Specifically:

a. To seek out and destroy enemy naval forces and to suppress enemy sea commerce.

b. To gain and maintain general sea supremacy.

c. To control vital sea areas and to protect vital sea lines of communication.

d. To establish and maintain local superiority (including air) in an area of naval operations.

e. To seize and defend advanced naval bases and to conduct such land operations as may be essential to the prosecution of a naval campaign.

2. To conduct air operations as necessary for the accomplishment of objectives in a naval campaign.

3. To organize and equip, in coordination with the other Services, and to provide Naval forces, including Naval close air support forces, for the conduct of joint amphibious operations, and to be responsible for the amphibious training of all forces as assigned for joint amphibious operations in accordance with the policies and doctrines of the Joint Chiefs of Staff.

4. To develop, in coordination with the other Services, the doctrines, procedures, and equipment of naval forces for amphibious operations, and the doctrines and procedures for joint amphibious operations.

5. To furnish adequate, timely, and reliable intelligence for the Navy and Marine Corps.

6. To be responsible for naval reconnaissance, antisubmarine warfare, the protection of shipping, and for mine laying, including the air aspects thereof.[2]

7. To provide air transport essential for naval operations.

8. To provide sea-based air defense and the sea-based means for coordinating control for defense against air attack, coordinating with the other Services in matters of joint concern.

9. To provide naval (including naval air) forces as required for the defense of the United States against air attack, in accordance with joint doctrines and procedures approved by the Joint Chiefs of Staff.

10. To furnish aerial photography as necessary for naval and Marine Corps operations.

11. To maintain the United States Marine Corps, which shall include land combat and service forces and such aviation as may be organic therein. Its specific functions are:

a. To provide Fleet Marine Forces of combined arms, together

---

[2]The words "and controlled mine field operations" were added to this paragraph by direction of the Secretary of Defense on 24 May 1949.

with supporting air components, for service with the Fleet in the seizure or defense of advanced naval bases and for the conduct of such land operations as may be essential to the prosecution of a naval campaign. These functions do not contemplate the creation of a second land army.

b. To provide detachments and organizations for service on armed vessels of the Navy, and security detachments for the protection of naval property at naval stations and bases.

c. To develop, in coordination with the Army, the Navy, and the Air Force, the tactics, technique, and equipment employed by landing forces in amphibious operations. The Marine Corps shall have primary interest in the development of those landing force tactics, technique, and equipment which are of common interest to the Army and the Marine Corps.

d. To train and equip, as required, Marine Forces for air-borne operations, in coordination with the Army, the Navy, and the Air Force in accordance with policies and doctrines of the Joint Chiefs of Staff.

e. To develop, in coordination with the Army, the Navy, and the Air Force, doctrines, procedures, and equipment of interest to the Marine Corps for airborne operations and not provided for in Section IV, paragraph A 8.

12. To provide forces, as directed by proper authority for the establishment of military government, pending transfer of this responsibility to other authority.

B. Collateral Functions. The forces developed and trained to perform the primary functions set forth above shall be employed to support and supplement the other Services in carrying out their primary functions, where and whenever such participation will result in increased effectiveness and will contribute to the accomplishment of the over-all military objectives. The Joint Chiefs of Staff member of the service having primary responsibility for a function shall be the agent of the Joint Chiefs of Staff to present to that body the requirements for and plans for the employment of all forces to carry out the function. He shall also be responsible for presenting to the Joint Chiefs of Staff for final decision any disagreement within the field of his primary responsibility which has not been resolved. This shall not be construed to prevent any member of the Joint Chiefs of Staff from presenting unilaterally any issue of disagreement with another Service. Certain specific collateral functions of the Navy and Marine Corps are listed below:

1. To interdict enemy land and air power and communications through operation at sea.

2. To conduct close air support for land operations.

3. To furnish aerial photography for cartographic purposes.

4. To be prepared to participate in the over-all air effort as directed by the Joint Chiefs of staff.

Section VI--Functions of the United States Air Force

The United States Air Force includes air combat and service forces. It is organized, trained, and equipped primarily for prompt and sustained combat operations in the air. Of the three major Services, the Air Force has primary interest in all operations in the air, except in those operations otherwise assigned herein.

A. Primary Functions

1. To organize, train and equip Air Force forces for the conduct of prompt and sustained combat operations in the air. Specifically:

a. To be responsible for defense of the United States against air attack in accordance with the policies and procedures of the Joint Chiefs of Staff.

b. To gain and maintain general air supremacy.

c. To defeat enemy air forces.

d. To control vital air areas.

e. To establish local air superiority except as otherwise assigned herein.

2. To formulate joint doctrines and procedures, in coordination with the other Services, for the defense of the United States against air attack, and to provide the Air Force units, facilities, and equipment required therefor.

3. To be responsible for strategic air warfare.

4. To organize and equip Air Force forces for joint amphibious and airborne operations, in coordination with the other Services, and to provide for their training in accordance with policies and doctrines of the Joint Chiefs of Staff.

5. To furnish close combat and logistical air support to the Army, to include air lift, support, and resupply of airborne operations, aerial photography, tactical reconnaissance, and interdiction of enemy land power and communications.

6. To provide air transport for the Armed Forces except as otherwise assigned.

7. To provide Air Force forces for land-based air defense, coordinating with the other Services in matters of joint concern.

8. To develop, in coordination with the other Services, doctrines, procedures, and equipment for air defense from land areas, including the continental United States.

9. To provide an organization capable of furnishing adequate, timely, and reliable intelligence for the Air Force.

10. To furnish aerial photography for cartographic purposes.

11. To develop, in coordination with the other Services, tactics, technique, and equipment of interest to the Air Force for amphibious operations and not provided for in Section V, paragraph A 4 and paragraph A 11 c.

12. To develop, in coordination with the other Services, doctrines, procedures, and equipment employed by Air Force forces in airborne operations.

B. Collateral Functions. The forces developed and trained to perform the primary functions set forth above shall be employed to support and supplement the other Services in carrying out their primary functions, where and whenever such participation will result in increased effectiveness and will contribute to the accomplishment of the over-all military objectives. The Joint Chiefs of Staff member of the Service having primary responsibility for a function shall be the agent of the Joint Chiefs of Staff to present to that body the requirements for and plans for the employment of all forces to carry out the function. He shall also be responsible for presenting to the Joint Chiefs of Staff for final decision any disagreement within the field of his primary responsibility which has not been resolved. This shall not be construed to prevent any member of the Joint Chiefs of Staff from presenting unilaterally any issue of disagreement with another Service. Certain specific collateral functions of the Air Force are listed below:

1. To interdict enemy sea power through air operations.
2. To conduct antisubmarine warfare and to protect shipping.
3. To conduct aerial minelaying operations.

Section VII--Glossary of Terms and Definitions

The usual and accepted definitions and interpretations of the English language, as contained in Webster's New International Dictionary (Unabridged), are applicable to this document, except that for purposes of clarity and to ensure a common understanding of its intent, certain words and phrases are defined specifically as follows:

Air Defense--All measures designed to nullify or reduce the effectiveness of the attack of hostile aircraft or guided missiles after they are airborne.

Air Superiority--That degree of capability (preponderance in morale and material) of one air force over another which permits the conduct of air operations by the former at a given time and place without prohibitive interference by the opposing air force.

Air Supremacy--That degree of air superiority wherein the opposing air force is incapable of effective interference.

Amphibious Operation--An attack launched from the sea by

naval and landing forces embarked in ships or craft involving a landing on a hostile shore. An amphibious operation includes final preparation of the objective area for the landing and operations of naval, air and ground elements in over water movements, assault, and mutual support. An amphibious operation may precede a large-scale land operation in which case it becomes the amphibious phase of a joint amphibious operation. After the troops are landed and firmly established ashore the operation becomes a land operation.

Antisubmarine Operations-Operations contributing to the conduct of antisubmarine warfare.

Antisubmarine Warfare--Operations conducted against submarines, their supporting forces, and operating bases.

Base--A locality from which operations are projected or supported. May be preceded by a descriptive word such as "air" or "submarine," which indicates primary purpose.

Close Air Support--The attack by aircraft of hostile ground or naval targets which are so close to friendly forces as to require detailed integration of each air mission with the fire and movement of those forces.

Functions--Responsibilities, missions and tasks.

In coordination with--In consultation with. This expression means that agencies "coordinated with" shall participate actively; their concurrence shall be sought; and that if concurrence is not obtained, the disputed matter shall be referred to the next higher authority in which all participants have a voice.

Joint--As used in this paper, and generally among the Armed Forces, connotes activities, operations organizations, etc., in which elements of more than one Service of the National Military Establishment participate.

Military--A term used in its broadest sense meaning of or pertaining to war or the affairs of war, whether Army, Navy or Air Force.

Naval Campaign--An operation or a connected series of operations conducted essentially by naval forces including all surface, sub-surface, air, amphibious, and Marines, for the purpose of gaining, extending, or maintaining control of the sea.

Operation--A military action, or the carrying out of a military mission, strategic, tactical, service, training, or administrative; the process of carrying on combat on land, on sea, or in the air, including movement, supply, attack, defense, and maneuvers needed to gain the objectives of any battle or campaign.

Strategic Air Operations--Air operations contributing to the conduct of strategic air warfare.

Strategic Air Warfare--Air combat and supporting operations designed to effect, through the systematic application of force to

BASIC DOCUMENTS

a selected series of vital targets, the progressive destruction
and disintegration of the enemy's war-making capacity to a point
where he no longer retains the ability or the will to wage war.
Vital targets may include key manufacturing systems, sources of
raw material, critical material, stock piles, power systems,
transportation systems, communications facilities, concentrations
of uncommitted elements of enemy armed forces, key agricultural
areas, and other such target systems.

/s/ James Forrestal

(8) **Executive Order 9950, 21 April 1948**

    With this order, issued immediately prior to
Secretary Forrestal's publication of the "Functions of
the Armed Forces and the Joint Chiefs of Staff,"
President Truman revoked Executive Order 9877.   This
allowed Forrestal's "functions" paper to provide the
operative guidance on mission assignments (see Key West
Agreement, Document 7).

EXECUTIVE ORDER 9950

Revoking Executive Order No. 9877 of July 26, 1947,
Prescribing the Functions of the Armed Forces

By virtue of the authority vested in me by the Constitution
and laws of the United States, and as President of the United
States and Commander in Chief of the Armed Forces of the United
States, it is ordered that Executive Order No. 9877 of July 26,
1947, prescribing the assignment of primary functions and responsibilities to the three armed services, be, and it is hereby,
revoked.

Harry S Truman

THE WHITE HOUSE
April 21, 1948

(9) **Secretary of Defense James V. Forrestal's Memorandum Creating the Military Air Transport Service (MATS) 3 May 1948**

Air transport grew in importance during World War II, as it provided the sole means of supply in many cases of crucial need. Both the Army Air Forces (AAF) and the Navy operated world-wide air transport systems that greatly aided the Allied war effort. During the war, air transport subsumed several different facets within it, including aircraft ferrying and delivery, airborne troop operations, and long- and short-range transport of men and materiel. In the postwar period, the air transport mission came to mean primarily movement of personnel, materiel, mail, and strategic materials, while airborne assault troop carriers remained assigned to tactical forces.

In an attempt to garner the fruits of unification's efficiency, Secretary Forrestal created the Military Air Transport Service (MATS) on 3 May 1948. Composed of the Air Transport Service (of the U.S. Air Force's (USAF) Air Transport Command, which also contained communications and weather services) and the Naval Air Transport Service, the consolidated service came under the command and direction of the USAF Chief of Staff. Organizationally, MATS operated as both a USAF major command and a National Military Establishment (later Department of Defense) agency. MATS received responsibility for air transportation of personnel, materiel, mail, strategic materials and other cargoes for the National Military Establishment. This did not include tactical transportation of airborne troops, initial supply of troops in forward combat areas, or transport required by the Navy for internal administration or over routes of sole interest to the Navy.

Secretary Forrestal assigned to MATS all of the personnel, property, and facilities assigned to the Air Transport Service, and the property and facilities of the Naval Air Transport Service (except those needed to maintain their own internal air transport).

Forrestal intended "to establish a single air transport service for the Military Establishment in the interest of economy and efficiency and with no interruption of service." Emphasizing the central control over this air transport operation, Forrestal prohibited delay or diversion of aircraft or crews by theater, area, fleet, air force, or other commander unless such actions were necessary for the safety of the crew or aircraft.

171

BASIC DOCUMENTS

****

Robert F. Futrell, <u>Ideas, Concepts, and Doctrine: A History of Basic Thinking in the United States Air Force 1907-1964</u>, (Maxwell AFB, Ala:Air University, 2nd. edition, 1974) pp 93-94, 100, and 102-105.

Alfred Goldberg, ed., <u>A History of the United States Air Force 1907-1957</u>, (New York: D. Van Nostrand Company, Inc, 1957) pp 147-48.

Herman S. Wolk, <u>Planning and Organizing the Postwar Air Force, 1943-1947</u>, (Washington, D.C.:Office of Air Force History, 1984) pp 220-21.

3 May 1948

MEMORANDUM FOR THE SECRETARY OF THE ARMY
                SECRETARY OF THE NAVY
                SECRETARIES OF THE AIR FORCE
                JOINT CHIEFS OF STAFF

SUBJECT: Organization and Mission of Military Air Transport
           Service (MATS)

1.   The Air Transport Service (ATS) of the Air Force Air
Transport Command (ATC) and the Naval Air Transport Service (NATS)
will be consolidated effective 1 June 1948. The consolidated service will be known as the Military Air Transport Service
(hereinafter referred to as "MATS") and will be under the command
and direction of the Chief of Staff, United States Air Force.

2.   The Military Air Transport Service (MATS) will be commanded by a Commander appointed by the Chief of Staff, United
States Air Force, with the consent of the Secretary of Defense.
Naval as well as Air Force officers will be eligible for the
office.

3.   MATS will be responsible for:

a.   The transportation by air of personnel (including the
evacuation of sick and wounded), materiel, mail, strategic
materials and other cargoes for all agencies of the National
Military Establishment and as authorized for other government
agencies of the United States, subject to established priorities.
The responsibility for air transportation for the National
Military Establishment does not include responsibility for the
tactical air transportation of airborne troops and their equipment, the initial supply and resupply of units in forward combat
areas, or that required for the fulfillment of the mission by the
Navy, or air transport over routes of sole interest to the Naval
forces where the requirements cannot be met by the facilities of
MATS. Nothing in this paragraph shall preclude the Navy or the
Air Force from using their equipment as a secondary function for
the evacuation of sick and wounded when circumstances require.

b.   The establishment, control, operation and maintenance
of facilities assigned to MATS within the United States and on air
routes outside the United States which facilities are or maybe
made, the responsibility of the Chief of Staff, United States Air
Force. In such areas outside the continental limits of the United
States, where there is no other United States military authority
charged with that responsibility, the Commander of MATS will have

and will exercise all normal responsibilities and prerogatives of Commands of theaters of operation, area commands or base commands.

c. In order to assure safety of flight over established routes outside the United States which are, or may be, assigned as the specific responsibility of MATS, to the extent permitted by law, and to insure the orderly utilization of facilities assigned to MATS flight control of all aircraft utilizing said specific routes is vested in MATS. This authority extends to the control of clearance of aircraft into all Mats [sic] facilities.

d. The control, operation and maintenance of such facilities and personnel required for ports of aerial embarkation as may be necessary to the performance of the MATS mission.

e. The additional training of personnel assigned or attached to MATS to meet approved qualifications and standards of operation of MATS.

f. Administration of priorities for air transportation in accordance with policies and procedures established by proper authority.

g. In coordination with other departments and agencies of the National Military Establishment the preparation of plans and requirements for transport flight operations and equipment. In collaboration with other agencies of the National Military Establishment specifically responsible for the design and specifications for transport type aircraft; participation in the redesign, modification and flight testing of new types of transport aircraft which may eventually be assigned to MATS; the making of studies, analyses and recommendations for the improvement and standardization of transport flight control practices, procedures and systems; and the service test and final operational development of prospective MATS air transport equipment, techniques and procedures.

In pursuance of the foregoing, MATS will maintain liaison with all agencies which design, develop, utilize or supervise the use of transport type aircraft, and effect interchange of information with such agencies with respect thereto that is not restricted by considerations of military security.

MATS responsibilities will include participation in the development of "all weather" transport flight technique, but will not include responsibility for the operation or development of either transport type aircraft or procedures employed in the Air transportation of airborne troops in tactical operations.

h. Preventive and progressive maintenance on all transport aircraft assigned to MATS. (The Navy will provide all maintenance to aircraft it assigns to MATS until such time as MATS is able to assume the successive phases of maintenance responsibility. The Navy will retain a maintenance unit to provide pre-

ventive and progressive maintenance and overhaul to its own
transport aircraft.)

i. In coordination with other Departments and agencies
of the Military Establishment and in order to assure the most
efficient utilization of the capacities of the civil air carriers,
all requests by agencies of the National Military Establishment
for services to be performed by or for the use of facilities or
personnel of such carriers, or negotiations therefor, shall first
be coordinated with the Commander of MATS. This is not intended
to include commercial air transportation furnished on regular
schedules.

j. The direction, supervision and control of contrac-
tors, either in operations or maintenance, furnishing services in
support of MATS, except contracting, auditing or purchasing
responsibility.

k. Acting in an advisory capacity to the Secretary of
Defense and the Secretaries of the Army, the Navy and the Air
Force in matters pertaining to air transportation and related ser-
vices under the jurisdiction of MATS.

l. Preparation for submission to the Secretary of
Defense after consultation with appropriate agencies in the
National Military Establishment and the civil departments and
agencies of the Government, and maintenance in current status of
plans for the employment and expansion of MATS in time of national
emergency. These plans will allow for the expansion of air
transport retained under Naval control as required by the
Department of the Navy for internal administration or required for
the fulfillment of the mission of the Navy, and further shall
allow for air transport over routes of sole interest to the Naval
forces where the requirements cannot be met by the facilities of
MATS. Such plans will include the utilization to the maximum
extent possible of the services, facilities and personnel of the
civil air carriers and other appropriate civil enterprises related
to air transportation, and in the development of such plans,
direct contact with such carriers and other civil enterprises is
authorized. Plans to utilize the services, facilities or personnel of the civil air carriers, or negotiations therefor, are the
responsibility of the Commander of MATS, who will consult with the
appropriate agencies of the National Military Establishment.

m. The development and maintenance of such cost
accounting records and operational statistics as will reflect the
degree of efficiency and economy of the operations conducted by
MATS, and show the utilization of funds, manpower and equipment.
These figures will be made available at quarterly intervals to the
Military Air Transport Board and the Secretary of Defense.

n. The determination of and advice to the Chief of

Staff, USAF and the Chief of Naval Operations of the requirements of MATS with respect to personnel, equipment, facilities, and services. These requirements will be expressed according to rules to be determined later which will permit proportionate participation.

o. The preparation of budgetary and other fiscal requirements of MATS coordinated with participating agencies and proportionate to their participation.

4. The Navy will continue to be responsible for the development and operation of large seaplane transports.

5. MATS is hereby authorized and will be responsible for the control, administration and disposition of all personnel, property and facilities presently assigned to the Air Transport Service (ATS) and the property and facilities presently assigned to the Naval Air Transport Service (NATS), except such property and facilities as are required by the Department of Navy (including the establishment, maintenance and operation of the air transport service required by the Navy for internal administration and the fulfillment of its mission, as provided in paragraph 3a hereof). Prior to the disposition by MATS of property and facilities obtained from NATS, the Navy will have the opportunity of reclamation thereof. In accordance with existing law, the administration of Naval personnel assigned to MATS will be a responsibility of the Department of the Navy exercised through the Senior Naval officer in MATS headquarters who will report to the Chief of Naval Operations for additional duty for this purpose. In addition to his other duties, he will be responsible for normal and routine administrative inspection of the Naval component MATS in accordance with current directives and policies promulgated by the Chief of Naval Operations. In addition, inspection or investigation of the Naval component may be made by competent Naval authority when so directed by the Secretary of the Navy or the Chief of Naval Operations, with the Commander, MATS, being notified in each instance.

6. Property and facilities on order for ATS and NATS (except those which may be required in connection with the Air transport function reserved to the Navy), when acquired, will be placed under the jurisdiction of MATS with full authority to control, administer and dispose of the same.

7. To the extent practicable, during the Fiscal Years 1948 and 1949, it is anticipated that the personnel and property acquired by MATS from NATS will be maintained by the Navy at approximately their present level. No Naval air facilities will be turned over to the MATS organization. However, at those Naval stations which MATS transits and serves, full Naval support will be provided in the same manner in which such support is now

accorded NATS. The intent of this directive is to establish a single air transport service for the Military Establishment in the interest of economy and efficiency and with no interruption of service. It is realized that due to difference in methods of personnel management and allocation utilized by the two participating services, the consolidation can be accomplished only as a phased operation over a period of time. Commander, MATS will inform the Secretary of Defense, the Secretary of the Navy, and other interested agencies when this phased operation is completed. Initially, it is expected that the Chief of Naval Operations and the Chief of Staff, USAF, will determine the amount of airlift to be performed by the respective components of MATS, and in accordance with their established formulae will respectively provide units and personnel in adequate numbers to perform the assigned tasks. In the interest of final equitable relative contribution of personnel to MATS by the participating services, parallel policies on manpower utilization, aircraft utilization, priorities and other related matters will be established by the Commander, MATS, with the concurrence of the Chief of Naval Operations, as early as practicable, and when so established, personnel of both participation g [sic] services will be adjusted on an equitable proportionate basis in accordance with such policies. Final determination of ratios of personnel to airlift will be based upon the above outlined policies. The personnel, property and facilities furnished by the Navy will be used to provide air transport of primary interest to the Navy insofar as practicable. As a matter of policy, officer personnel will be assigned to duty for a period of not less than thirty (30) months, reserving however, to the Navy Department, after appropriate notification of the Department of the Air Force, the right to withdraw, add to or substitute.

8. The Department of the Army and the arms and services thereof; the Department of the Navy and the bureaus thereof; and the Department of the Air Force and the executive agencies and the commands thereof; Area, Theater and Fleet Commands, and similar commands concerned, and their subordinate activities will take all necessary action to facilitate the efficient and economic operation of MATS (including the assignment of personnel and the furnishing of facilities, services and equipment). The Department of the Army will within its capabilities and in consonance with its other missions provide and assign to MATS such specialized or technical personnel, units and equipment as may from time to time be requested by the Chief of Staff, USAF, for the accomplishment of the mission of MATS.

9. Aircraft and crews of MATS engaged in the operation of air transport and ferrying services together with their enroute

cargoes will not be delayed or diverted by Theater, Area, Fleet, Air Force, or similar Commanders unless conditions make such action necessary for the security of MATS aircraft and crews.

10. The Department of the Air Force and the Department of the Army will make available, within existing funding procedures, to MATS, as necessary, unexpended balances of existing appropriations and the appropriations for the Fiscal Year 1949 which otherwise would have been made available for ATS, and the Navy Department will make available to MATS such similar balances as otherwise would have been utilized by NATS, excepting funds required for the conduct of air transport and maintenance reserved to the Navy.

11. The Department of the Navy and the Department of the Air Force will, at all times, keep the Commander of MATS fully informed concerning the personnel, equipment and facilities being used in the operation of air transport services, reserved to them; except as specifically required for such services, transport and cargo type aircraft will be assigned only to MATS.

12. A Military Air Transport Board consisting of three members, one each to be appointed by the Secretary of the Army, Secretary of The Navy, and the Secretary of the Air Force is hereby established. The Board shall recommend to the Secretary of Defense the policies to be adhered to by MATS with respect to categories of passengers and cargo to be transported by air. The board will also act in an advisory capacity to the Commander, MATS, for the purpose of making recommendations for the settling of disputes arising in connection with the following matters:

a. Establishment, maintenance and operation of military air transport services.

b. The question of what constitutes trunk routes and scheduled air transport service.

c. Complaints of any department that it is not receiving adequate service or fair treatment from MATS.

d. Questions with respect to the utilization of property, personnel or facilities.

e. Questions with respect to the provision of personnel, facilities, services and equipment required to be furnished MATS by the agencies of the National Military Establishment.

f. The question of execution or non-execution of the directives of the Joint Chiefs of Staff and theater or fleet commanders on the allocations or lift capacities and routes subject to the capabilities of MATS.

JAMES FORRESTAL

(10) Newport Agreement, 21 August 1948

The atmosphere of agreement that grew out of the Key West conference proved short-lived, as arguments between the Navy and the Air Force surfaced within days of the "functions" paper's publication. The ostensible cause of acrimony, an Air Force request to be named executive agent for the Armed Forces Special Weapons Project which handled and assembled nuclear weapons, merely reflected the struggle between the services over control of nuclear weapons. All of the services had recognized that nuclear weapons carried with them a large portion of the armed forces budget, and in an era of declining defense budgets struggles over spending priorities were bound to exacerbate internal divisions. The fundamental debate centered on strategic bombing, with the Air Force the traditional exponent and operator resisting incursion by the Navy, which wanted to ensure that it was not relegated to second place and had nuclear weapons available to perform its primary mission.

Alarmed by the apparent inability of the services to resolve roles and missions conflicts peacefully in the national interest, Secretary of Defense James V. Forrestal called on two retired officers, Gen. Carl A. Spaatz and Adm. John H. Towers. He asked for their views regarding strategic warfare requirements and the Key West division of functions, including the role of aircraft carriers, control of nuclear weapons, and the role of naval aircraft in air-atomic operations. The two officers agreed that the Key West Agreement was "a satisfactory document," provided each service recognized that primary responsibility for a mission area did not preclude supporting efforts from another service. However, they conceded that varying interpretations were possible and proceeded to apply that judgement to their views on management of nuclear weapons, with each arguing that his own service should possess operational control of these weapons. Both were in favor of compromise, provided the services recognized that exclusive responsibility in a given field did not confer "preclusive participation."

In hopes of converting this favorable attitude into a working doctrine, Forrestal convened a conference at the Naval War College in Newport, Rhode Island, from 20 to 22 August 1948, with the Joint Chiefs of Staff. The broad-ranging conference provided agreement on two roles and missions subjects. The first involved compromise on the strategic bombing question, and the

179

mechanism for compromise was a clarifying supplement to the Key West Agreement, which defined primary missions such that the Air Force could not deny the Navy access to atomic weapons or exclude the Navy from strategic air operations planning. In return, the Navy dropped its opposition to the Air Force receiving control of the Armed Forces Special Weapons Project on an interim basis (see paragraphs 1 and 2 of Document 11).

The second agreement attempted to preclude later disagreement over roles and missions which would arise over the introduction of new weapons. This agreement helped establish a Weapons Systems Evaluation Group (WSEG), reporting to the JCS and providing impartial technical evaluations of modern weapons. Forrestal had endorsed the formation of this group when it had been proposed by the Chairman of the Research and Development Board, Dr. Vannevar Bush. Though the Joint Chiefs of Staff were lukewarm about WSEG, they were persuaded by Forrestal to endorse its formation.

****

Steven L. Rearden, History of the Office of the Secretary of Defense, The Formative Years 1947-1950, (Washington, D.C.:OSD History Office, 1984, pp 397-402.

OFFICE OF THE SECRETARY OF DEFENSE
Washington

23 August 1948

MEMORANDUM FOR THE RECORD

SUBJECT: Newport Conference--Summary of Conclusions Reached and
    Decisions Made (Decisions with respect to command arrangements
    are included in a separate Memorandum for the Record, dated 23
    August 1948, and entitled "Newport Conference--Decisions with
    Respect to Command").

At the conferences in Newport from 20 August to 22 August, the
following actions were taken:

    1. CONTROL AND DIRECTION OF ATOMIC OPERATIONS. (Herein of the
Armed Forces Special Weapons Project)

    a. Planning for the Atomic Aspects of "Halfmoon": It was
agreed that, as an interim measure, the Chief of Staff, U.S. Army,
the Chief of Naval Operations and the Chief of Staff, U.S. Air
Force should, as heretofore proposed by General Bradley, direct
the Chief, Armed Forces Special Weapons Project to report to the
Chief of Staff, U.S. Air Force for instructions of the atomic
aspects of "Halfmoon". This directive should be identical with
the proposed directive attached to the memorandum from General
Bradley to the Secretary of Defense of 3 August 1948, except that
its title would be modified by inserting the word "interim" at the
front of the title.
    b. Permanent Organization: It was agreed to postpone any
decision concerning the permanent future organization for the
control and direction of atomic operations until the current study
of the Military Liaison Committee could be completed.

    2. CLARIFICATION OF THE TERM "PRIMARY MISSION" IN THE
FUNCTIONS PAPER

    a. The Joint Chiefs of Staff recommended, and the Secretary of
Defense approved the issuance of the following supplement to his
paper on "Functions of the Armed forces and the Joint Chiefs of
Staff" which was attached to his memorandum to the Joint Chiefs of
Staff of 21 April 1948:

"Subject to control by higher authority, each service, in the
fields of its primary missions, must have exclusive responsibility
for planning and programming and the necessary authority. In the
execution of any mission of the armed services, all available

resources must be used to the maximum overall effectiveness. For this reason, the exclusive responsibility and authority in a given field do not imply preclusive participation. In providing for our armed forces, including the preparation of the annual budget and the preparation of mobilization plans, it is essential to avoid duplication and the wastage of resources therefrom. For this reason the service having the primary function must determine the requirements, but in determining those requirements must take into account the contributions which may be made by forces from other services."

b. It was agreed that the effectiveness of the foregoing decision would depend upon (1) the spirit in which it was carried out; (2) general acceptance of the view that the decision was not in any wise a victory or defeat for any service, and (3) mutual acceptance on the part of all concerned of the obligation to work amicably to settle any differences arising under the decision, and to anticipate, and resolve in advance, any prospective differences. To this end, it was agreed that the Secretary of Defense, together with the three service Chiefs of Staff, should assemble the top members of their staffs at a meeting on Tuesday, 24 August for the purpose of describing and explaining the foregoing decision. It was also suggested that an effort should be made to secure newspaper cooperation in making clear the precise consequences of the decision, putting it up to the various journalist protagonists that this program could only work with their cooperation.

3. ESTABLISHMENT OF A WEAPONS EVALUATION GROUP

a. It was agreed that the establishment of a weapons evaluation group is desirable and necessary.
b. Although no final decision was reached as to the precise form of organization for a weapons evaluation group, it appeared to be the consensus of opinion that the group should be organized directly under the Joint Chiefs of Staff but that the Joint Chiefs of Staff should call upon Dr. Bush to organize the group and get it operating. It was also suggested that the civilian chief or civilian deputy chief of the group (depending on which of these two jobs was made a civilian job) might well be nominated by the Research and Development Board.
c. It was agreed that Mr. Forrestal and Mr. Carpenter would discuss this organizational problem further with Dr. Bush, as soon as Dr. Bush returned to Washington, specifically suggesting the solution referred to in b. above. Thereafter, and depending upon the outcome of the meeting with Bush, there should be another meeting with the Joint Chiefs of Staff.

4. PARTICIPATION OF DR. BUSH IN THE WORK OF THE JOINT CHIEFS OF STAFF

It was the consensus of opinion that Dr. Bush should be invited to participate more directly in the work of the Joint Chiefs of Staff, and that he should be asked to sit with the Joint Chiefs of Staff on all appropriate occasions.

5. CREATION OF A MILITARY GROUP IN THE OFFICE OF THE SECRETARY OF DEFENSE

It was the consensus of opinion that there was a definite requirement for the creation of a small military group in the Office of the Secretary of Defense. There was no specific decision concerning the totality of functions of this group, but suggestions were made that it should perform some or all of the following duties:
(a) Keep the Secretary generally advised of matters of military significance in the several services and the Joint Chiefs of Staff;
(b) follow-up in the several services and in the Joint Chiefs of Staff on matters of military significance which emanated from the Office of the Secretary of Defense, or in which the Secretary was interested;
(c) bring to the attention of the Secretary of Defense matters of military significance which required some action, or were not being properly taken care of, in this respect acting as sort of a "dust pan";
(d) coordinate joint matters of a policy or operating nature in the military or politico-military field which could not be handled by the Joint Chiefs of Staff or by any single service, and as to those matters which could be so handled, see that they were properly channeled and monitored;
(e) serve as a convenient means of liaison between each of the services and the Office of the Secretary of Defense on military and perhaps on other matters, and
(f) assist in bringing about a more orderly relationship between the National Military Establishment and the State Department.

There was discussion of, but no definite agreements concerning the following additional matters relating to the establishment of this group:
(a) The size of the group (requirements of from three to 20 were suggested by various people);
(b) the extent to which persons assigned by the several services to this group would act as representatives of their respec-

tive services, or would serve exclusively as representatives of the Secretary of Defense, and

(c) whether the individual selected to head this group should also have the Joint Staff under his direction.

Similarly, there was no decision as to the identity of the man who should direct this group, but there was wide sentiment among the conferees to the effect that Lt. General Hull would be an excellent selection. In connection with discussions concerning the precise functions of the group, Mr. Forrestal suggested that the director should be selected, and allowed to develop his own charter. It was agreed that Mr. Forrestal, before proceeding further, should discuss these questions with Secretaries Symington and Sullivan (who were not present during the discussion of this item), and that this discussion would take place at the earliest possible moment.

6. FAMILIARIZING THE SERVICES WITH THE ORGANIZATION OF THE OFFICE OF THE SECRETARY OF DEFENSE AND WITH THE FUNCTIONS AND RESPONSIBILITIES OF THE VARIOUS SECTIONS AND INDIVIDUALS IN THAT OFFICE

It was the feeling of many of the conferees that the Office of the Secretary of Defense should make much clearer to the services than had heretofore been done, the organization of the Office of the Secretary of Defense and the functions of the various individuals and divisions thereof. Secretary Forrestal requested the action be taken in this direction.

7. ESTABLISHMENT OF A COMMAND HEADQUARTERS BEHIND THE RHINE

It was agreed that it was imperative immediately to establish a stationary Western European Headquarters behind the Rhine which could plan and coordinate the evacuation of dependents from Germany; the withdrawal of troops from Germany, and the defense of the Rhine; and which could, in the event war should come, control those operations. (As to related matters, see separate memorandum for the record on decisions with respect to command.)

8. MISCELLANEOUS MATTERS

During the course of the meeting, the following points were made, although no decision with respect to them was taken:
a. There was a necessity for the early clarification of a situation which had arisen concerning base rights in Labrador.
b. There was an immediate need to take stock of the status of our base rights generally.

c. The base rights situation in Iceland should be improved.

d. As a matter of urgency, some method should be found to provide the money to create, rehabilitate and ship surpluses to France, etc.

9. PRESS RELEASE CONCERNING CONFERENCE

The conferees agreed on the release to the press of the statement attached hereto.

JOHN H. OHLY
Special Assistant to the Secretary

Attachment [not printed]

(11) National Security Act Amendments of 1949, 10 August 1949

Shortly after Secretary of Defense James V. Forrestal took office he began to question the efficacy of the National Security Act, which placed limits on his power to invoke procedural and substantive changes in National Military Establishment (NME) matters. One difficulty stemmed from the organization's nebulous existence as an "establishment" rather than an executive department. Each of the services was an executive department, and the lack of precedent or parallel for the establishment (while conferring a certain freedom of action) thwarted Forrestal's ability to unseat deep-rooted service traditions of autonomy. Also, the act did not provide for a staff for the Secretary of Defense. Thus without statutory authority, the staff operated as merely an extension of the Secretary himself. The act limited Forrestal to exercise "general direction, authority and control," which in Forrestal's mind made him a policymaker rather than an administrator. The Secretary leaned on his three statutory agencies -- the Joint Chiefs of Staff (JCS), the Munitions Board, and the Research and Development Board -- to provide the technical expertise lacking in his staff and to analyze issues for his consideration. The status of the services as executive departments, though each was an integral part of the NME, left all of the powers and duties not specifically conferred on the Secretary of Defense with the service secretaries. The result of this arrangement was a largely horizontal organization, rather than the more normal pyramidal structure, and left the military departments largely self-administered. Though unified in name, the NME could be more accurately called a tripartite alliance.

Despite several successes in his term, Forrestal found himself unable to quell deep-seated and traditional interservice rivalries, which had been exacerbated by reduced funding in the postwar era. The tensions aroused by contending for funding priorities caused difficulties among the JCS, who were unable to agree on strategic plans or the allocation of funds. Without a consensus on strategic matters, other portions of the NME were hamstrung in their efforts to deal with issues. Both the Research and Development Board and the Munitions Board were unable to deal with their more pressing issues because the JCS could not provide the basic premises with which to underpin

187

deliberations. Other problems contributed to the boards' paralysis, not least of which was the divisive nature of the issues confronted. Forrestal also faced a mounting administrative burden and the skepticism of the services on the extent of his powers as delineated in the act. Reluctantly, Forrestal concluded that the act contained serious flaws, some of which he had helped to engineer.

The first indications of Forrestal's concern over the act appeared in a February 1948 report to President Harry S. Truman, though it stopped short of seeking legislative adjustment. During the latter half of 1948, Forrestal sought input on possible modifications from a variety of sources, including the services. The Navy opposed any major changes, while the Army and the Air Force favored more centralized authority. In his first annual report, published in December 1948, Forrestal came out in favor of amendments to the act. His report outlined six changes he felt were needed to improve his office and the NME:

1) appoint an undersecretary to act as an alter-ego,
2) designate a head of the JCS,
3) remove the limit on the size of the joint staff,
4) create a Personnel Board to institute uniform personnel practices,
5) remove the service secretaries from the National Security Council,
6) clarify the powers of the Secretary of Defense.

In early March 1949, President Truman sent to Congress his recommendations for amending the National Security Act.

Though the amendments to the National Security Act that were signed into law on 10 August 1949 were not identical to those submitted by Truman, they were sufficiently similar to receive his approval. Congress had accepted the recommendations of two groups, one led by Herbert Hoover and the other by Ferdinand Eberstadt, on government organization, and added Title IV to the act, which set up uniform budgetary and fiscal procedures for the Department of Defense (DOD), as the NME was renamed. The amendments converted the NME to DOD, made it an executive department, and reduced the services to military departments, removing their free access to the President and the Bureau of the Budget in addition to removing the service secretaries from the National Security Council. The free access permissions were replaced by the right to make reports to Congress. The Secretary of Defense received unqualified "direction, authority, and control" over the new executive department and was named the President's principal assistant in all matters relating to DOD. He was also granted a Deputy Secretary of Defense who would function in the Secretary's absence or disability and who ranked second directly after the Secretary himself.

These amendments marked a turn away from the concept of decentralized authority in favor of a strong executive, primarily in order to realize the economic savings judged inherent in unified armed forces. The Air Force absorbed no change in its own structure, since the amendments were operative at a higher level than within the service. The Air Force had backed these changes, feeling that a stronger executive would provide clearer definition of authority and responsibility. The strong leadership that could be provided under these amendments would be seen in later actions regarding the Air Force.

****

Steven L. Rearden, History of the Office of the Secretary of Defense, The Formative Years 1947-1950, (Washington, D.C.: OSD Historical Office, 1984), pp 35-43, and 50-55.

PUBLIC LAW 216--August 10, 1949

Public Law 216   Chapter 412

An Act

To reorganize fiscal management in the National Military
Establishment to promote economy and efficiency, and for other
purposes.

Be it enacted by the Senate and House of Representatives of the
United States of America in Congress assembled.

SHORT TITLE

Section 1. This Act may be cited as the "National Security Act
Amendments of 1949".
Sec. 2. Section 2 of the National Security Act of 1947 is
amended to read as follows:
"Sec. 2. In enacting this legislation, it is the intent of
Congress to provide a comprehensive program for the future
security of the United States; to provide for the establishment of
integrated policies and procedures for the departments, agencies,
and functions of the Government relating to the national security;
to provide three military departments, separately administered,
for the operation and administration of the Army, the Navy
(including naval aviation and the United States Marine Corps), and
the Air Force, with their assigned combat and service components;
to provide for their authoritative coordination and unified direction under civilian control of the Secretary of Defense but not to
merge them; to provide for the effective strategic direction of
the armed forces and for their operation under unified control and
for their integration into an efficient team of land, naval, and
air forces but not to establish a single Chief of Staff over the
armed forces nor an armed forces general staff (but this is not to
be interpreted as applying to the Joint Chiefs of Staff or Joint
Staff)."

CHANGE IN COMPOSITION OF THE NATIONAL SECURITY COUNCIL

Sec. 3. The fourth paragraph of section 101 (a) of the National
Security Act of 1947 is amended to read as follows:
"The Council shall be composed of-
    "(1) the President;
    "(2) the Vice President;
    "(3) the Secretary of State;

"(4) the Secretary of Defense;

"(5) the Chairman of the National Security Resources Board; and

"(6) The Secretaries and Under Secretaries of other executive departments and of the military departments, the Chairman of the Munitions Board, and the Chairman of the Research and Development Board, when appointed by the President by and with the advice and consent of the Senate, to serve at his pleasure."

CONVERSION OF THE NATIONAL MILITARY ESTABLISHMENT INTO AN EXECUTIVE DEPARTMENT

Sec. 4. Section 201 of the National Security Act of 1947 is amended to read as follows:

"Sec. 201. (a) There is hereby established, as an Executive Department of the Government, the Department of Defense, and the Secretary of Defense shall be the head thereof.

(b) There shall be within the Department of Defense (1) the Department of the Army, the Department of the Navy, and the Department of the Air Force, and each such department shall on and after the date of enactment of the National Security Act Amendments of 1949 be military departments in lieu of their prior status as Executive Departments, and (2) all other agencies created under title II of this Act.

"(c) Section 158 of the Revised Statutes, as amended, is amended to read as follows:

"'Sec. 158. The provisions of this title shall apply to the following Executive Departments:

"'First. The Department of State.

"'Second. The Department of Defense.

"'Third. The Department of the Treasury.

"'Fourth. The Department of Justice.

"'Fifth. The Post Office Department.

"'Sixth. The Department of the Interior.

"'Seventh. The Department of Agriculture.

"'Eighth. The Department of Commerce.

"'Ninth. The Department of Labor.'

"(d) Except to the extent inconsistent with the provisions of this Act, provisions of title IV of the Revised Statutes as now or hereafter amended should be applicable to the Department of Defense."

THE SECRETARY OF DEFENSE

Sec. 5. Section 202 of the National Security Act of 1947, as amended, is further amended to read as follows:

"Sec. 202. (a) There shall be a Secretary of Defense, who shall be appointed from civilian life by the President, by and with the advice and consent of the Senate: Provided, That a person who has within ten years been on active duty as a commissioned officer in a Regular component of the armed services shall not be eligible for appointment as Secretary of Defense.

"(b) The Secretary of Defense shall be the principal assistant to the President in all matters relating to the Department of Defense. Under the direction of the President, and subject to the provisions if this Act, he shall have direct authority, and control over the Department of Defense.

"(c) (1) Notwithstanding any other provision of this Act, the combatant functions assigned to the military services by sections 205 (e), 206 (b), 206 (c), and 208 (f) hereof shall not be transferred, reassigned, abolished, or consolidated.

"(2) Military personnel shall not be so detailed or assigned as to impair such combatant functions.

"(3) The Secretary of Defense shall not direct the use and expenditure of funds of the Department of Defense in such manner as to effect the results prohibited by paragraphs (1) and (2) of this subsection.

"(4) The Departments of the Army, Navy, and Air Force shall be separately administered by their respective Secretaries under the direction, authority, and control of the Secretary of Defense.

"(5) Subject to the provisions of paragraph (1) of this subsection no function which has been or is hereafter authorized by law to be performed by the Department of Defense shall be substantially transferred, reassigned, abolished or consolidated until after a report in regard to all pertinent details shall have been made by the Secretary of Defense to the Committees on Armed Services of the Congress.

"(6) No provision of this Act shall be so construed as to prevent a Secretary of a military department or a member of the Joint Chiefs of Staff from presenting to the Congress on his own initiative, after first so informing the Secretary of Defense, any recommendation relating to the Department of Defense that he may deem proper.

"(d) The Secretary of Defense shall not less often than semiannually submit written reports to the President and the Congress covering expenditures, work and accomplishments of the Department of Defense, accompanied by (1) such recommendations as he shall deem appropriate, (2) separate reports from the military departments covering their expenditures, work and accomplishments, and (3) itemized statements showing the savings of public funds and the eliminations for unnecessary duplications and overlappings that have been accomplished pursuant to the provisions of this

Act.

"(e) The Secretary of Defense shall cause a seal of office to be made for the Department of Defense, of such design as the President shall approve, and judicial notice shall be taken thereof.

"(f) The Secretary of Defense may, without being relieved of his responsibility therefor, and unless prohibited by some specific provision of this Act or other specific provision of law, perform any function vested in him through or with the aid of such officials or organizational entities of the Department of Defense as he may designate."

DEPUTY SECRETARY OF DEFENSE; ASSISTANT SECRETARIES OF DEFENSE; MILITARY ASSISTANTS; AND CIVILIAN PERSONNEL

Sec. 6 (a) Section 203 of the National Security Act of 1947 is amended to read as follows:

"Sec. 203. (a) There shall be a Deputy Secretary of Defense, who shall be appointed from civilian life by the President, by and with the advice and consent of the Senate: Provided, That a person who has within ten years been on active duty as a commissioned officer in a Regular component of the armed services shall not be eligible for appointment as Deputy Secretary of Defense. The Deputy Secretary shall perform such duties and exercise such powers as the Secretary of Defense may prescribe and shall take precedence in the Department of Defense next after the Secretary of Defense. The Deputy Secretary shall act for, and exercise the powers of the Secretary of Defense during his absence or disability.

"(b) There shall be three Assistant Secretaries of Defense, who shall be appointed from civilian life by the President, by and with the advice and consent of the Senate. The Assistant Secretaries shall perform such duties and exercise such powers as the Secretary of Defense may prescribe and shall take precedence in the Department of Defense after the Secretary of Defense, the Deputy Secretary of Defense, the Secretary of the Army, the Secretary of the Navy, and the Secretary of the Air Force.

"(c) Officers of the armed services may be detailed to duty as assistants and personal aides to the Secretary of Defense, but he shall not establish a military Staff other than that provided for by section 211 (a) of this Act."

"(b) Section 204 of the National Security Act of 1947 is amended to read as follows:

"Sec 204. The Secretary of Defense is authorized, subject to the civil service laws and the Classification Act of 1923, as amended, to appoint and fix the compensation of such civilian personnel as

194

may be necessary for the performance of the functions of the Department of Defense other than those of the Departments of the Army, Navy, and Air Force."

CREATING THE POSITION OF CHAIRMAN OF THE JOINT CHIEFS OF STAFF AND PRESCRIBING HIS POWERS AND DUTIES

Sec. 7. (a) Section 210 of the National Security Act of 1947 is amended to read as follows:

"Sec. 210. There shall be within the Department of Defense an Armed Forces Policy Council composed of the Secretary of Defense, as Chairman, who shall have power of decision; the Deputy Secretary of Defense; the Secretary of the Army; The Secretary of the Navy; the Secretary of the Air Force; the Chairman of the Joint Chiefs of Staff; the Chief of Staff, United States Army; the Chief of Naval Operations; and the Chief of Staff, United States Air Force. The Armed Forces Policy Council shall advise the Secretary of Defense on matters of broad policy relating to the armed forces and shall consider and report on such other matters as the Secretary of Defense may direct."

"(b) Section 211 of the National Security Act of 1947 is amended to read as follows:

"Sec 211. (a) There is hereby established within the Department of Defense the Joint Chiefs of Staff, which shall consist of the Chairman, who shall be the presiding officer thereof but who shall. have no vote; the Chief of Staff, United States Army, the Chief of Naval Operations: and the Chief of Staff, United States Air Force. The Joint Chiefs of Staff shall be the principal military advisers to the President, the National Security Council, and the Secretary of Defense.

"(b) Subject to the authority and direction of the President and the Secretary of Defense, the Joint Chiefs of Staff shall perform the following duties, in addition to such other duties as the President or the Secretary of Defense may direct:

"(1) preparation of strategic plans and provision for the strategic direction of the military forces;

"(2) preparation of joint logistic plans and assignment to the military services of logistic responsibilities in accordance with such plans;

"(3) establishment of unified commands in strategic areas;

"(4) review of major material and personnel requirements of the military forces in accordance with strategic and logistic plans;

"(5) formulation of policies for joint training of the military forces;

"(6) formulation of policies for coordinating the military

education of members of the military forces; and

"(7) providing United States representation on the Military Staff Committee of the United Nations in accordance with the provisions of the Charter of the United Nations.

"(c) The Chairman of the Joint Chiefs of Staff (hereinafter referred to as the 'Chairman') shall be appointed by the President, by and with the advice and consent of the Senate from among the Regular officers of the armed services to serve at the pleasure of the President for a term of two years and shall be eligible for one reappointment, by and with the advice and consent of the Senate, except in time of war hereafter declared by the Congress when there shall be no limitation on the number of such reappointments. The Chairman shall receive the basic pay and basic and personal money allowances prescribed by law for the Chief of Staff, United States Army, and such special pays and hazardous duty pays to which he may be entitled under other provisions of law.

"(d) The Chairman, if in the grade of general, shall be additional to the number of officers in the grade of general provided in the third proviso of section 504 (b) of the Office Personnel Act of 1947 (Public Law 381, Eightieth Congress) or, of [sic] in the rank of admiral, shall be additional to the number of officers having the rank of admiral provided in section 413 (a) of such Act. While holding such office he shall take precedence over all other officers of the armed services: Provided, That the Chairman shall not exercise military command over the Joint Chiefs of Staff or over any of the military services.

"(e) In addition to participating as a member of the Joint Chiefs of Staff in the performance of the duties assigned in subsection (b) of this section, the Chairman shall, subject to the authority and direction of the President and the Secretary of Defense, perform the following duties:

"(1) serve as the presiding officer of the Joint Chiefs of Staff;

"(2) provide agenda for meetings of the Joint Chiefs of Staff and assist the Joint Chiefs of Staff to prosecute their business as promptly as practicable; and

"(3) inform the Secretary of Defense and, when appropriate as determined by the President or the Secretary of Defense, the President, of those issues upon which agreement among the Joint Chiefs of Staff has not been reached."

"(c) Section 212 of the National Security Act of 1947 is amended to read as follows:

"Sec. 212. There shall be, under the Joint Chief of Staff, a Joint Staff to consist of not to exceed two hundred and ten officers and to be composed of approximately equal numbers of officers appointed by the Joint Chiefs of Staff from each of the three armed services. The Joint Staff, operating under a Director thereof appointed by the Joint Chiefs of Staff, shall perform such duties as may be directed by the Joint Chiefs of Staff. The Director shall be an officer junior in grade to all members of the Joint Chiefs of Staff."

CHANGING THE RELATIONSHIP OF THE SECRETARY OF DEFENSE TO THE MUNITIONS BOARD

Sec. 8. Section 213 of the National Security Act of 1947 is amended to read as follows:

"Sec. 213. (a) There is hereby established in the Department of Defense a Munitions Board (hereinafter in this section referred to as the 'Board').

"(b) The Board shall be composed of a Chairman, who shall be the head thereof and who shall, subject to the authority of the Secretary of Defense and in respect to such matters authorized by him, have the power of decision upon matters falling within the jurisdiction of the Board, and an Under Secretary or Assistant Secretary from each of the three military departments, to be designated in each case by the Secretaries of their respective departments. The Chairman shall be appointed from civilian life by the President, by and with advice and consent of the Senate, and shall receive compensation at the rate of $14,000 a year.

"(c) Subject to the authority and direction of the Secretary of Defense, the Board shall perform the following duties in support of strategic and logistic plans and in consonance with guidance in those fields provided by the Joint Chiefs of Staff, and such other duties as the Secretary of Defense may prescribe:

"(1) coordination of the appropriate activities with regard to industrial matters, including the procurement, production, and distribution plans of the Department of Defense;

"(2) planning for the military aspects of industrial mobilization;

"(3) assignment of procurement responsibilities among the several military departments and planning for standardization of specifications and for the greatest practicable allocation of purchase authority of technical equipment and common use items on the basis of single procurement;

"(4) preparation of estimates of potential production, procurement, and personnel for use in evaluation of the logistic feasibility of strategic operations;

"(5) determination of relative priorities of the various segments of the military procurement programs;

"(6) supervision of such subordinate agencies as are or

may be created to consider the subjects falling within the scope of the Board's responsibilities;

"(7) regrouping, combining, or dissolving of existing interservice agencies operating in the fields of procurement, production, and distribution in such manner as to promote efficiency and economy;

"(8) maintenance of liaison with other departments and agencies for the proper correlation of military requirements with the civilian economy, particularly in regard to the procurement or disposition of strategic and critical material and the maintenance of adequate reserves of such material, and making of recommendations as to policies in connection therewith; and

"(9) assembly and review of material and personnel requirements presented by the Joint Chiefs of Staff and by the production, procurement, and distribution agencies assigned to meet military needs, and making of recommendations thereon to the Secretary of Defense.

"(d) When the Chairman of the Board first appointed has taken office, the Joint Army and Navy Munitions Board shall cease to exist and all its records and personnel shall be transferred to the Munitions Board.

"(e) The Secretary of Defense shall provide the Board with such personnel and facilities as the Secretary may determine to be required by the Board for the performance of its functions."

CHANGING THE RELATIONSHIP OF THE SECRETARY OF DEFENSE TO THE RESEARCH AND DEVELOPMENT BOARD

Sec. 9. Section 214 of the National Security Act of 1947 is amended to read as follows:

"Sec 214. (a) There is hereby established in the Department of Defense a Research and Development Board (hereinafter in this section referred to as the 'Board'). The Board shall be composed of a Chairman, who shall be the head thereof and who shall, subject to the authority of the Secretary of Defense and in respect to such matters authorized by him, have the power of decision on matters falling within the jurisdiction of the Board, and two representatives from each of the Departments of the Army, Navy, and Air Force, to be designated by the Secretaries of their respective Departments. The Chairman shall be appointed from civilian life by the president, by and with the advice and consent of the Senate, and shall receive compensation at the rate of $14,000 a year. The purpose of the Board shall be to advise the Secretary of Defense as to the status of scientific research relative to the national security, and to assist him in assuring adequate provision for research and development on scientific problems relating to the national security.

"(b)   Subject to the authority and direction of the Secretary of Defense, the Board shall perform the following duties and such other duties as the Secretary of Defense may prescribe:

"(1)   preparation of a complete and integrated program of research and development for military purposes;

"(2)   advising with regard to trends in scientific research relating to national security and the measures necessary to assure continued and increasing progress;

"(3)   coordination of research and development among the military departments and allocations among them of responsibilities for specific programs;

"(4)   formulation of policy for the Department of Defense in connection with research and development matters involving agencies outside the Department of Defense; and

"(5)   consideration of the interaction of research and development and strategy, and advising the Joint Chiefs of Staff in connection therewith.

"(c)   When the Chairman of the Board first appointed has taken office, the Joint Research and Development Board shall cease to exist and all its records and personnel shall be transferred to the Research and Development Board.

"(d)   The Secretary of Defense shall provide the Board with such personnel and facilities as the Secretary may determine to be required by the Board for the performance of its functions."

COMPENSATION OF SECRETARY OF DEFENSE, DEPUTY SECRETARY OF DEFENSE,
    SECRETARIES OF MILITARY DEPARTMENTS, AND CONSULTANTS

Sec. 10. (a) Section 301 of the National Security Act of 1947 is amended to read as follows:

"Sec. 301. (a) The Secretary of Defense shall receive the compensation prescribed by law for heads of executive departments.

"(b)   the Deputy Secretary of Defense shall receive compensation at the rate of $14,000 a year, or such other compensation plus $500 a year as may hereafter be provided by law for under secretaries of executive departments. The Secretary of the Army, the Secretary of the Navy, and the Secretary of the Air Force shall each receive compensation at the rate of $14,000 a year, or such other compensation as may hereafter be provided by law for under secretaries of executive departments."

(b)   Section 302 of the National Security Act of 1947 is amended to read as follows:

"Sec. 302. The Assistant Secretaries of Defense and the Under Secretaries and Assistant Secretaries of the Army, the Navy and the Air Force shall each receive compensation at the rate of

$10,330 a year or at the rate hereafter prescribed by law for assistant secretaries of executive departments and shall perform such duties as the respective Secretaries may prescribe."

(c) Section 303 (a) of the National Security Act of 1947 is amended to read as follows:

"(a) The Secretary of Defense, the Chairman of the National Security Resources Board, the Director of Central Intelligence, and the National Security Council, acting through its Executive Secretary, are authorized to appoint such advisory committees and to employ, consistent with other provisions of this Act, such part-time advisory personnel as they may deem necessary in carrying out their respective functions and the functions of agencies under their control. Persons holding other offices or positions under the United States for which they receive compensation, while serving as members of such committees, shall receive no additional compensation for such service. Other members of such committees and other part-time advisory personnel so employed may serve without compensation or may receive compensation at a rate not to exceed $50 for each day of service, as determined by the appointing authority."

REORGANIZATION OF FISCAL MANAGEMENT TO PROMOTE
ECONOMY AND EFFICIENCY

Sec. 11. The National Security Act of 1947 is amended by inserting at the end thereof the following new title:

. . . .

[Ed. Note] Material omitted (Title IV) can be found in: Alice C. Cole, et al, eds., The Department of Defense: Documents on Establishment and Organization, 1944-1978, (Washington, D.C.: OSD Historical Office, 1978), pp. 100-106, or in: Joint Army and Air Force Bulletin Number 22, 22 August 1949.

(12) Army and Air Force Authorization Act of 1949, 10 July 1950

The general terms used in the National Security Act which permitted the Air Force much latitude in generating its own internal organization proved a double-edged sword. The latitude proved a boon to an essentially new service, but certain disadvantages accrued since there was no specific authorization for its strength and it was bound by old laws which limited appropriations to a two-year life. Therefore, the Air Force supported Army and Air Force authorization legislation when its leaders were asked to testify before Congress in 1949.

The Army and Air Force Authorization Act, signed into law on 10 July 1950, provided for an Air Force composed of the Regular Air Force, the Air National Guard of the United States, the Air National Guard while in U.S. service, and the Air Force Reserve. The act authorized an Air Force strength not to exceed seventy groups and whatever separate squadrons were required. To carry out its missions, the Air Force received 502,000 officers and airmen, with the officer corps limited to 27,500 and warrant officers limited to 4,800. The Air National Guard was authorized 150,000 persons overall, while the Air Force Reserve was apportioned 100,000. The Air Force was limited to either 24,000 aircraft or 25,000 airframe tons, exclusive of guided missiles, whichever the Secretary of the Air Force deemed appropriate. In addition, the Air Force received authority to develop and procure new aircraft and guided missiles as needed. One of the most important aspects of the act was the provision that appropriations remained available until expended.

****

Robert F. Futrell, Ideas, Concepts and Doctrine: A History of Basic Thinking in the United States Air Force 1907-1964, (Maxwell AFB, Ala: Air University, 2nd. edition, 1974) pp 158-59.

PUBLIC LAW 604--July 10, 1950

Public Law 604   Chapter 454

An Act

To announce the composition of the Army of the United States and
the Air Force of the United States, and for other purposes.

Be it enacted by the Senate and House of Representatives of the
United States of America in Congress assembled,

SHORT TITLE

Section 1. That this Act may be cited as the "Army and Air Force
Authorization Act of 1949".

DECLARATION OF POLICY

Sec. 2. In enacting this legislation, it is the intent of
Congress to provide an Army of the United States and an Air Force
of the United States capable, in conjunction with the other armed
services, of preserving the peace, security, and providing for the
defense of the United States, its Territories, possessions, and
occupied areas wherever located, of supporting the national policies, of implementing the national objectives, and of overcoming
any nations responsible for aggressive actions imperiling the
peace and security of the United States.

. . . .
[Ed. Note] (The material omitted [Title I-ARMY] can be found in
Public Law 604, 64 Stat., 81st Cong. 2nd Sess., Chapter 454, July
10, 1950.)

TITLE II--AIR FORCE

The Air Force of the United States

Sec. 201. (a) The Air Force of the United States shall consist
of the United States Air Force (the Regular Air Force), the Air
National Guard of the United States, the Air National Guard while
in the service of the United States, and the United States Air
Force Reserve: and shall include persons inducted, enlisted, or
appointed without specification of component into the Air Force of
the United States: and shall further include all of those Air
Force units and other Air Force organizations, with their
installations and supporting and auxiliary combat, training, admi-

nistrative, and logistic elements and all personnel, including those not assigned to units, necessary to form the basis for a complete and immediate mobilization for the national defense in the event of an national emergency.

(b) Effective on the date of enactment of this Act, and subject to the limitations imposed by sections 202 and 203 of this Act, the Air Force of the United States shall have an authorized strength of not to exceed seventy United States Air Force groups and such separate United States Air Force squadrons, reserve groups, and supporting and auxiliary United States Air Force and reserve units as may be required.

Authorized Personnel Strength

Sec. 202. (a) There is hereby authorized for the Air Force of the United States an active-duty personnel strength of five hundred and two thousand officers, warrant officers, and enlisted persons exclusive of such one-year enlistees as are or may be authorized by law, officer candidates, aviation cadets, and personnel of the Reserve components on active duty for training purposes only, persons paid under the appropriations for the Air National Guard and United States Air Force Reserve, and personnel of the Reserve components ordered to active duty in an emergency hereafter declared.

(b) Of the active duty personnel strength authorized in subsection (a) of this section, not to exceed twenty-seven thousand five hundred, exclusive of any numbers authorized by special provision of law providing for officers in designated categories as additional numbers may be active list commissioned officers of the United States Air Force and four thousand eight hundred may be active list warrant officers of the United States Air Force.

(c) There is hereby authorized for the Air National Guard and the Army National Guard of the United States a personnel strength, to be distributed among the several States, Territories, Puerto Rico, and the District of Columbia of one hundred and fifty thousand officers, warrant officers and enlisted persons, excluding those serving on active duty in the Air Force of the United States who are counted within the personnel strength of five hundred and two thousand authorized in subsection (a) of this section.

(d) There is hereby authorized for the United States Air Force Reserve personnel strength of five hundred thousand officers, warrant officers, and enlisted persons, including those members of the United States Air Force Reserve on active duty in the Air Force of the United States who are not counted within the personnel strength of the five hundred and two thousand authorized in subsection (a) of this section. Persons may be appointed as warrant officers in the United States Air Force Reserve under such regulations and in such numbers as the Secretary of the Air Force may prescribe.

Aircraft Authorization

Sec. 203. The Air Force of the United States is hereby authorized twenty-four thousand serviceable aircraft or two hundred and twenty-five thousand airframe tons aggregate of serviceable aircraft, whichever amount the Secretary of the Air Force may determine is more appropriate to fulfill the requirements of the Air Force of the United states for aircraft necessary to carry out the purposes of this Act: PROVIDED, That guided missiles shall not be included within the number of aircraft or airframe tons herein authorized.

Procurement Authorization

Sec. 204. The Secretary of the Air Force is authorized to procure (1) the number of aircraft or airframe tons authorized by section 203 and to replace such aircraft as he may determine to be unserviceable or obsolete, (2) guided missiles, and (3) spares, spare parts, equipment, and facilities necessary for the maintenance and operation of the Air Force of the United States.

Research and Development Authorization

Sec. 205. The Secretary of the Air Force is hereby authorized to conduct, engage, and participate in research and development programs related to activities of the Air Force of the United States and to procure, or contract for the use of such facilities, equipment, services, and supplies as may be required to effectuate such programs.

Saving Provision

Sec. 206. No provision of this title shall be construed as modifying the existing status of the Air National Guard of the United States as a reserve component of the Air Force of the United States, or as amending or modifying in any way section 60 of the National Defense Act of 1916, as amended.

Repeal of Existing Law

Sec. 207. Section 8 of the Act of July 2, 1926 (44 Stat. 780), as amended by section 1 of the Act of April 3, 1939 (53 Stat. 555), is hereby repealed.

TITLE III--GENERAL PROVISIONS

Saving Provision

Sec. 301. The provisions of this Act shall be subject to the duties and authority of the Secretary of Defense and the military departments and agencies of the Department of Defense as provided in the National Security Act of 1947, as amended.

Separability Provision

Sec. 302. If any provision of this Act or the application thereof to any person or circumstances is held invalid, the validity of the remainder of the Act and of the application of such provision to other persons and circumstances shall not be affected thereby.

Appropriation

Sec. 303. (a) There are hereby authorized to be appropriated out of any moneys in the Treasury of the United States not otherwise appropriated such sums as may be necessary to carry out the purposes of this Act.

(b) Moneys appropriated to the Departments of the Army, Navy, or Air Force for procurement of technical military equipment and supplies, the construction of public works, and for research and development, including moneys appropriated to the Department of the Navy for the procurement, construction, and research and development of guided missiles, which are hereby authorized for the Department of the Navy, shall remain available until expended unless otherwise provided in the appropriation Act concerned.

Limitation of Authority

Sec. 304. Nothing contained in this Act shall be construed to authorize the Department of Defense to expend any money appropriated pursuant to authority conferred by this Act for the design or development of any prototype aircraft intended primarily for commercial use.

Approved July 10, 1950.

(13) Secretary of Defense Louis A. Johnson's Guided Missile Memorandum, 21 March 1950

Responsibility for guided missile development and operational employment proved a contentious issue in the post-World War II era. Initially, competition grew between the Army Ordnance Department, the Army Air Forces, and the Navy over development of guided missiles. Twice prior to 1950, the Army Air Forces had been assigned developmental responsibility for guided missiles, first on 2 October 1944, and again on 7 October 1946. Effective 19 July 1948, the recently formed Air Force was relieved of responsibility for development of guided missiles intended to fulfill Army roles and missions.

Increasing developmental programs in all three services for guided missiles prompted the Joint Chiefs of Staff (JCS) to forward to Secretary of Defense Louis A. Johnson a meaningful division of responsibility for missile development which would provide the least overlap in capabilities. The basic factor in the lack of clear delineation of responsibility was the ambiguity regarding future weapons growing out of developmental programs. On 15 March 1950, the JCS forwarded to Secretary Johnson a set of guidelines on missile responsibility which he approved on 21 March 1950.

The JCS felt it impractical to assign responsibility for the entire guided missile field, and stated that guided missiles would be employed by the services according to their assigned functions. Undesirable duplication would be avoided by having the Research and Development Board assign research responsibility where appropriate. In general, the Air Force was assigned responsibility for missiles which replaced or supplemented fighter interceptors (in conjunction with the Navy); missiles which replaced or supplemented ground support aircraft (in conjunction with the Army); and missiles which supplemented, extended the capabilities of, or replaced aircraft other than ground support aircraft. In addition, the Air Force (with the Navy) received responsibility for air-to-air missiles and air-to-surface missiles. Specific projects authorized for continued development under Air Force auspices were: Falcon (air-to-air); Rascal (air-to-surface); Wizard (surface-to-air, continued as system study project); Navaho (surface-to-surface); and Snark (surface-to-surface, only as a guidance system test project). The end

207

result of this set of agreements left the Air Force in possession of responsibility for missiles designed for strategic bombardment, to the exclusion of the other services.

This staff paper was signed on 17 November 1949 by JCS Chairman Gen. Omar N. Bradley for the JCS. His signature block appeared in the final version which in this volume corresponds to pages 212 and 218.

****

Robert F. Futrell, <u>Ideas, Concepts and Doctrine: A History of Basic Thinking in the United States Air Force 1907-1964</u>, (Maxwell AFB, Ala: Air University, 2nd. edition, 1974) pp 237-42.

NOTE BY THE SECRETARIES

to the

JOINT CHIEFS OF STAFF

on

ASSIGNMENT OF RESPONSIBILITY FOR GUIDED MISSILES
Reference: J.C.S. 1620 Series

On 17 November 1949 the Joint Chiefs of Staff agreed to forward the memorandum in the Enclosure hereto to the Secretary of Defense.

W. G. Lalor,

J. H. Ives,

Joint Secretariat

ENCLOSURE

MEMORANDUM FOR THE SECRETARY OF DEFENSE

Subject: Assignment of Responsibility for
Guided Missiles.

Reference: Your memorandum of 25 May 1949,
same subject

1. The Joint Chiefs of Staff, after having studied for the past several months the problem outlined in the reference memorandum, have reached the conclusion that it is impracticable at this time to assign to the several Services, in accordance with their assigned functions, responsibilities for the entire guided missile field.

2. As a general rule, guided missiles will be employed by the Services in the manner and to the extent required to accomplish their assigned functions. Undesirable duplications in research and development should be avoided by careful screening of projects and assignment of research responsibility by the Research and Development Board where appropriate.

3. Development of guided missiles of certain categories has progressed to a point where the fields of their normal employment may be recognized. Subject to a periodic review, responsibilities are assigned as follows:

a. Surface-to-air.

(1) Guided missiles which supplement, extend the capabilities of, or replace antiaircraft artillery will be a responsibility of the U.S. Army and the U.S. Navy as required by their assigned functions.

(2) Guided missiles which supplement or replace fighter interceptors will be a responsibility of the U.S. Air Force and the U.S. Navy as required by their assigned functions.

b. Surface-to-Surface.

(1) Surface launched guided missiles which supplement or extend the capabilities of, or replace the fire of artillery or naval guns will be the responsibility of the U.S. Army and U.S. Navy as required by their functions.

(2) Surface-launched guided missiles which supplement or
extend the capabilities of, or replace, support aircraft
will be the responsibility of the U.S. Air Force and U.S.
Army, as required by their functions.

(3) Ship-launched guided missiles which supplement,
extend the capabilities of, or replace naval aircraft will
be a responsibility of the U.S. Navy, as required by its
functions.

(4) Surface-launched guided missiles which supplement,
extend the capabilities of, or replace Air Force aircraft
(other than support aircraft) will be a responsibility of
the U.S. Air Force, as required by its functions.

(5) Unnecessary duplication will be avoided by the
periodic review to be accomplished by the Joint Chiefs of
Staff.

c. Air-to-Air.

Guided missiles which are used for air-to-air combat will
be a responsibility of the U.S. Air Force and the U.S. Navy as
required by their functions.

d. Air-to-surface.

Guided missiles which are used by aircraft against surface objectives will be a responsibility of the U.S. Air Force and
the U.S. Navy as required by their functions.

e. In connection with the requirements of the various
Services for guided missiles, the needs of the Marine Corps will
be met from the Service having appropriate responsibility.

4. In order to establish a firm basis for the development and
employment of new weapons or improved existing weapons, the Joint
Chiefs of Staff recommend that you approve and issue the
following statement of policy to the Department of Defense:

"Employment of new or improved weapons, and related equipment, resulting from research and development will not be
restricted by reason of the interest or responsibility of a
particular Service in the development of a weapon. On the
contrary, new weapons developed by the programs of the several
Services will be considered available for employment by any

211

Service which requires them in the discharge of its assigned functions as determined by the Joint Chiefs of Staff within the structure of the approved 'Functions of the Armed Forces and the JCS'. The initial determination of such requirement shall be made by individual Services, subject to final approval by the Joint Chiefs of Staff on the basis of its contribution to the over-all war effort in any case where conflicts of functions or economy may arise. A Service charged with primary responsibility for development of a weapon shall invite the participation of any other Service having an operational interest in the weapon. This policy in no way alters the existing responsibilities of the Research and Development Board for the allocation of research and development responsibility to the various Services."

THE SECRETARY OF DEFENSE

Washington

21 March 1950

MEMORANDUM FOR THE JOINT CHIEFS OF STAFF

SUBJECT: Department of Defense Guided Missiles Program

I approve the recommendations of the Joint Chiefs of Staff as presented to me orally on 20 March 1950, with one proviso: namely, that the Interdepartmental Operational Requirements Group, which is to be established pursuant to the recommendations, will advise the Joint Chiefs of Staff every ninety days as to requirements for the guided missiles program.

I understand that the recommendations referred to above are identical with those set forth in a memorandum to me from the Chairman, Joint Chiefs of Staff, subject, "Department of Defense Guided Missiles Program", dated 15 March 1950. [Enclosure to JCS 1620/17](added)

signed

Louis A. Johnson

E N C L O S U R E

MEMORANDUM FOR THE SECRETARY OF DEFENSE

15 March 1950

1. The Joint Chiefs of Staff have reviewed the report of the Special Interdepartmental Guided Missiles Board, dated 3 February 1950[*] and have also reviewed the Joint Chiefs of Staff recommendations made to you in a memorandum dated 17 November 1949[**] on the assignment of responsibility for guided missiles. With respect to the projects or guided missiles which are at present being pursued by the three Departments, the recommendations of the Joint Chiefs of Staff are listed below:

Project	Responsibility	Recommendation
Air-to-Air Missiles		
(1) FALCON	Air Force	Continue
(2) SPARROW	Navy	Continue
(3) METEOR	Navy	Continue
Air-to-Surface Missiles		
(4) DOVE	Navy	Continue
(5) PETREL	Navy	Continue
(6) RASCAL	Air Force	Continue Systems Study
Land-to-Air Missiles		
(7) NIKE	Army	Continue
(8) WIZARD	Air Force	Continue
Ship-to-Air Missiles		
(9) TERRIER-TALOS	Navy	Continue
(10) ZEUS	Navy	Discontinue

[*] Appendix "D" to JCS 1620/13

[**] Enclosure to JCS 1620/12

Project	Responsibility	Recommendation
	Land-to-Surface Missiles	
(11) HERMES (A-1)	Army	Discontinue as a weapon
(12) HERMES (A-3, C-1)	Army	Continue
(13) HERMES (B-1)	Army	Discontinue as a weapon
(14) HERMES (B-2)	Army	Discontinue
(15) HERMES (A-2)	Army	Continue
(16) HERMES II	Army	Discontinue as a weapon. Continue as a cellular ram jet development.
(17) CORPORAL E	Army	Discontinue
(18) SNARK	Air Force	Discontinue as a weapon. Continue the project as development of missile guidance system only and test vehicle therefor.
(19) *NAVAHO (A-2)	Air Force	Continue
(20) LACROSSE	Navy	Transfer responsibility to Army and continue. Marine Corps continue close liaison in connection with amphibious applications.
	Ship-to-Surface Missiles	
(21) REGULUS	Navy	Continue
(22) RIGEL	Navy	Continue

*Design study and development of components of NAVAHO (A-6) to
 continue. NAVAHO may be land- or air-launched

(23) GREBE	Navy	Limit development to 3-mile range version for the present, but continue design studies for longer range adaptation.
(24) TRITON	Navy	Continue as a research and design project, insuring integration of results from NAVAHO

2. With reference to the recommendations by the Special Interdepartmental Guided Missiles Board with respect to operation and utilization of flight test facilities, General Bradley informed you by memorandum dated 24 February 1950[*] that the Joint Chiefs of Staff agree that there is a requirement for three ranges, and further agree that the assignment of responsibility for these ranges should be

White Sands/Holloman	-	Department of the Army
Point Mugu	-	Department of the Navy
Banana River	-	Department of the Air Force.

The Joint Chiefs of Staff further recommend that, with the one amendment to recommendation a of the Special Interdepartmental Guided Missiles Board as indicated herein, you approve the recommendations of that board as outlined in Enclosure 3 of its report. These recommendations, with the one amendment referred to above, are that:

"a. The present White Sands Proving Ground and Holloman Air Force Base be consolidated into a single facility under the command and management of the Department of the Army~,. provided the Wherry Housing Bill commitments can be worked out to the satisfaction of all concerned. (This amendment recommended since the Air Force has cancelled the Wherry Bill housing at Holloman Air Force Base.

"b. Subject to approval of the foregoing, the three guided missile proving grounds be assigned to Departments as indicated below, the indicated Department to have

---

[*] Enclosure to JCS 1620/14

command, management, operational and budgetary responsibility.

White Sands/Holloman	-	Department of the Army
Point Mugu	-	Department of the Navy
Banana River	-	Department of the Air Force.

"c. The Joint Chiefs of Staff revoke its recommendation
for a 'Joint Long-Range Proving Ground Command.' (This
refers to the Banana River Range which the Joint Chiefs
of Staff previously recommended be a joint command.)

"d. Each of these proving grounds be available to
all three Services for appropriate flight testing; the
cost of any special instrumentation required to be borne
by the Department cognizant of the missile project under
test.

"e. An Interdepartmental Operational Requirements Group
for Guided Missiles . . . be charged with formulation and
initiation of such common policies as may be necessary,
for issuance by the respective Departments, to insure
the integrated and efficient operation of all guided missile proving grounds and ranges in such a manner as to
serve all three Departments. Such policies shall not
conflict with the policies of the Research and Development
Board."

3. The Joint Chiefs of Staff agree with the proposal of the
Special Interdepartmental Guided Missiles Board contained in
Enclosure 4 of its report to the effect that an Interdepartmental
Operational Requirements Group be established for the purpose of
advising on the coordinating and integrating of the operational
features of the three Services guided missiles program, with the
proviso that the Group will be responsible for advising the Joint
Chiefs of Staff as well as the Military Departments. As one of
its first tasks the Group would formulate and recommend to the
Joint Chiefs of Staff a requirements program for guided missiles
research and development, and for production of operational guided
missiles, for their first annual review of the program in
September. The Joint Chiefs of Staff will provide the necessary
guidance as to priorities.

4. With reference to the Joint Chiefs of Staff memorandum of
17 November 1949 on the subject of assignment of responsibility
for guided missiles, the Joint Chiefs of Staff recommend that
paragraph 3 b of that memorandum be deleted and that the following be substituted therefor:

"<u>b</u>. Surface-to-Surface

"(1) Surface-launched guided missiles which supplement or extend the capabilities of, or replace the fire of artillery or naval guns will be the responsibility of the U. S. Army and U. S. Navy as required by their functions.
"(2) Surface-launched guided missiles which supplement or extend the capabilities of, or replace, support aircraft will be the responsibility of the U. S. Air Force and U. S. Army, as required by their functions.
"(3) Ship-launched guided missiles which supplement, extend the capabilities of, or replace naval aircraft will be a responsibility of the U. S. Navy, as required by its functions.
"(4) Surface-launched guided missiles which supplement, extend the capabilities of, or replace Air Force aircraft (other than support aircraft) will be a responsibility of the U. S. Air Force, as required by its functions.
"(5) Unnecessary duplication will be avoided by the periodic review to be accomplished by the Joint Chiefs of Staff."

5. Subject to your approval of the recommendations contained in paragraphs 1, 2, 3, and 4 above, it is the intention of the Joint Chiefs of Staff to review annually from the military point of view the entire guided missiles program. The first annual review will be initiated about 1 September 1950

(14) **Vandenberg-Collins Agreement, 1 August 1950**

One of the missions assigned the Air Force was to provide air defense of the continental United States. Providing this air defense required integration of Army antiaircraft artillery battalions with Air Force interceptor squadrons into one operational entity. During the late 1940s, the Air Force Air Defense Command (ADC) theoretically provided the interceptor squadrons, while the Army provided, on paper, antiaircraft artillery battalions. Prior to 1950, discussions over doctrinal issues remained theoretical, since both the Army and the Air Force intended to mobilize the necessary forces from their respective National Guard forces. Following the explosion of a Soviet nuclear weapon in August 1949, the Air Force issued requirements for an operational air defense system by 1952, while the Army established an Army Antiaircraft Command to assume responsibility for field air defense matters. One outcome of this new emphasis on air defense was the separation of ADC from the Continental Air Command, and its reestablishment as an Air Force major command, effective 1 January 1951. One other outcome was an agreement between Air Force Chief of Staff, Gen. Hoyt S. Vandenberg, and Army Chief of Staff, Gen. J. Lawton Collins.

The Vandenberg-Collins agreement, signed on 1 August 1950, stated that the targets to be defended would be settled upon jointly by the Army and Air Force (in the absence of a Joint Chiefs of Staff (JCS)-approved plan); that the Air Force would accept an Army officer accompanied by an "appropriately sized" Army staff at each echelon of the Air Force air defense organization; that the Air Force commander responsible for air defense would set the principles of engagement (as mutually agreed upon); and that the "location of each antiaircraft defense will be prescribed geographically by mutual agreement."

This agreement cleared the way for integrating the two air defense systems but provided less than an overall air defense organization. ADC acquired the Eastern and Western Air Defense Forces and set up the Central Air Defense Force. The Army set up the Army Antiaircraft Command in close proximity to HQ ADC in Colorado Springs and likewise formed three defense forces adjacent to their air counterparts.

****

Robert F. Futrell, <u>Ideas, Concepts and Doctrine: A</u>

BASIC DOCUMENTS

History of Basic Thinking in the United States Air Force 1907-1964, (Maxwell AFB, Ala: Air University, 2nd edition, 1974) p 158.

MEMORANDUM OF AGREEMENT

The undersigned agree to the following statement which covers certain aspects of control of antiaircraft units of the U. S. Army by various command echelons of the U. S. Air Force charged with air defense responsibilities.

1. The Air Force accepts at each echelon of the Air Force command structure charged with air defense, including the Continental Air Command, an Army officer with an appropriately sized Army staff section to serve as the AAA element on the staff of the respective air defense command. The Army officer will, in addition, serve as the principal antiaircraft adviser to the respective air defense commander.

2. The Air Force commander charged with the air defense of the United States will announce the basic principles of engagement for antiaircraft fire units and fighter units as mutually agreed herein for use throughout the continental United States as part of the instructions included in the Standing Operating Procedures promulgated for air defense. Such procedures will be designed and prescribed with the object of assuring the maximum combined effectiveness of fighter defense units and antiaircraft artillery under the varying local conditions of geography and deployment. Decision regarding engagement in any particular situation will be the responsibility of the appropriate air defense commander in accordance with the following basic principles of engagement which will govern the employment of antiaircraft artillery in air defense of the United States:

a. Air Defense commanders will establish conditions of fire for antiaircraft artillery units which will provide the greatest flexibility to firing units and which will prescribe hold fire conditions only when such a condition is necessary and then for periods of time as short as possible.

b. Regardless of hold fire orders, antiaircraft commanders may fire at aircraft committing hostile acts. Hostile acts will be defined by Commanding General, Continental Air Command, in collaboration with appropriate AA commanders.

      c. Local antiaircraft commanders may fire at aircraft recognized or identified as hostile except in exceptional cases when it may be imperative to hold fire in areas of secondary importance in order to permit fighters to reach areas of primary importance.

      d. Antiaircraft artillery commanders may fire at any aircraft over a prohibited area except when temporary restrictions are ordered to permit necessary passage of friendly aircraft.

      3. The normal condition of readiness, after establishment of a state of emergency by the appropriate authority, for each antiaircraft artillery local defense will be determined by the appropriate air defense commander after examination of all factors and in conformance with JCS approved plan for air defense.

      4. Vital geographical areas in the United States to be afforded AA defense against air attack will be determined by mutual agreement of the Department of the Air Force and the Department of the Army in the absence of a JCS approved plan.

      5. The location of each local antiaircraft defense will be prescribed geographically by mutual agreement. Each local antiaircraft defense will be commanded by an antiaircraft artillery officer. Tactical disposition of antiaircraft artillery units at each area being defended is a function of the antiaircraft commander.

      6. Within each Air Defense Division, operational control insofar as engagement and disengagement of fire is concerned, will be exercised directly by the Commander of the Air Defense Division over appropriate Air Force and AA units subject to the principles outlined above.

/s/ <u>Hoyt S. Vandenberg</u>   /s/ <u>J. Lawton Collins</u>
/t/ <u>HOYT S. VANDENBERG</u>   /t/ <u>J. LAWTON COLLINS</u>
    General, USAF   General, USA

(15) Air Force Organization Act, 19 September 1951

Following the passage of the Army and Air Force Authorization Act, Air Force leaders had to contend with House Military Affairs Committee Chairman Carl Vinson, who wanted to codify Headquarters USAF organization as much as possible. Air Force leaders felt that it would be better to let the organization evolve before codifying its structure. When the Air Force proved reluctant to draft a legislative measure for consideration, Congress seized the initiative and produced a document known as the Air Force Organization Act of 1951. The House version of the bill provided for the Chief of Staff to supervise the members and organizations of the Air Force, and that the major commands would be Continental Air Command, Strategic Air Command (SAC), Tactical Air Command (TAC), Air Materiel Command, and the European Support Command. The measure provided for the statutory positions of Air Adjutant General, Inspector General, and Provost Marshal General, while the Army's Surgeon General and the Navy's Medical Department would service the Air Force, along with the Army's Quartermaster General, Chief of Engineers, Judge Advocate General, and Chief of Chaplains.

Air Force leaders were reluctant to codify the organizational structure, but in deference to Chairman Vinson, declined to oppose the draft legislation, provided certain objectionable clauses could be altered. The major sticking point grew out of the clause stating that the Chief of Staff of the Air Force would supervise -- rather than command -- the Air Force. Air Force Chief of Staff General Hoyt S. Vandenberg proved willing to supervise Air Force support activities, but reluctant to relinquish command of strategic and air defense forces, since the prerogative of command was firmly stated in the National Security Act. Vandenberg and Air Force Secretary Thomas K. Finletter also opposed formation of the statutory positions of special staff agencies like the Inspector General and the Adjutant General. During committee meetings, the Air Force won over the members, such that the special agencies were dropped, although the Air Force agreed to establish an Air Staff comprised of the Chief of Staff and not more than five Deputy Chiefs of Staff. These deliberations also produced agreement that only three commands (SAC, TAC, and ADC) would be established by law, leaving the Secretary of the Air Force free to establish other commands as necessary.

The Air Force Organization Act passed the House of Representatives on 24 January 1951 and proved acceptable to the Air Force, except for the distinction between supervision versus command for the Chief of Staff. Finletter argued before the Senate that the Chief of Staff should command the fighting commands of the Air Force, which the Senate agreed to when it passed its version of the bill on 21 June 1951. A conference committee revised the bill, signed into law by President Harry S. Truman on 19 September 1951, which provided for a Chief of Staff who commanded SAC, TAC, and ADC, or any similar superseding commands, while supervising all other Air Force activities. The sole special agency provided for in the act was the Judge Advocate General, appointed by the President for a four-year term.

****

Robert F. Futrell, <u>Ideas, Concepts and Doctrine: A History of Basic Thinking in the United States Air Force 1907-1964</u>, (Maxwell AFB, Ala: Air University, 2nd edition, 1974) pp 159-60.

Public Law 150   Chapter 407

AN ACT

To provide for the organization of the Air Force and the
Department of the Air Force, and for other purposes.

Be it enacted by the Senate and House of Representatives of the
United States of America in Congress assembled,

Short Title

Section 1. This Act may be cited as the "Air Force Organization
Act of 1951".

Table of Contents

Definitions

Sec. 2. As used in this Act--
(a) The terms "United States Air Force" and "Air Force" are
synonymous and mean the United States Air Force established by the
National Security Act of 1947; and said terms include the components and persons prescribed in section 301 of this Act.
(b) The term "members of the Air Force" means all persons
appointed, enlisted, or inducted in, or transferred to, any of the
components of the Air Force; all persons appointed, enlisted or
inducted in, or transferred to the Air Force without specification
of component; and all persons serving as members of the Air Force
under call or conscription under any provision of law. The term
"officers of the Air Force" means all members of the Air Force
appointed to and holding a commissioned or warrant officer grade.
The term "airman" is synonymous with "enlisted members" and means
all members of the Air Force in any enlisted grade.
(c) The term "Air Force Establishment" means all commands,
organizations, forces, agencies, installations, and activities,
including the Department of the Air Force, all members of the Air
Force, all property of every kind and character -- real, personal,

and mixed -- and all civilian personnel, under the control or supervision of the Secretary of the Air Force.

(d) The term "Department of the Air Force" means the executive part of the Air Force Establishment at the seat of government.

TITLE I--SECRETARY, UNDER SECRETARY, AND ASSISTANT SECRETARIES OF THE AIR FORCE

Sec. 101. (a) The Secretary of the Air Force shall be responsible for and shall have the authority necessary to conduct all affairs of the Air Force Establishment, including, but not limited to, those necessary or appropriate for the training, operations, administration, logistical support and maintenance, welfare, preparedness, and effectiveness of the Air Force, including research, and development, and such other activities as may be prescribed by the President or the Secretary of Defense as authorized by law. There are authorized to be appropriated such sums as may be necessary to conduct the affairs of the Air Force Establishment.

(b) The Secretary of the Air Force may assign to the Under Secretary of the Air Force and to the Assistant Secretaries of the Air Force such of his functions, powers, and duties as he may consider proper. Officers of the Air Force shall report regarding any matters to the Secretary, Under Secretary, or either Assistant Secretary of the Air Force, as the Secretary of the Air Force may prescribe.

(c) The Secretary of the Air Force or, as he may prescribe, the Under Secretary of the Air Force or either Assistant Secretary of the Air Force, shall, in addition to other duties, be charged (1) with supervision of the procurement activities of the Air Force Establishment, of plans for the mobilization of materials and industrial organizations essential to wartime needs of the Air Force, and of other business pertaining thereto, and (2) with supervision of all activities of the reserve components of the Air Force.

(d) The Secretary of the Air Force may make such assignments and details of members of the Air Force and civilian personnel as he thinks proper, and may prescribe the duties of the members and civilian personnel so assigned; and such members and civilian personnel shall be responsible for, and shall have the authority necessary to perform, such duties as may be so prescribed for them.

(e) The Secretary of the Air Force may cause to be manufactured or produced at Government arsenals, depots, or Government-owned factories of the United States all those supplies needed by the Air Force which can be manufactured or produced upon an economical basis at such arsenals, depots, or factories.

Sec. 102. (a) There shall be in the Department of the Air Force an Under Secretary of the Air Force and two Assistant Secretaries of the Air Force, who shall be appointed by the President, by and with the advice and consent of the Senate, and who shall receive the compensation prescribed by law.

(b) In case of the death, resignation, removal from office, absence, or disability of the Secretary of the Air Force, the officer of the United States who is highest on the following list, and who is not absent, or disabled, shall, until the President directs some other person to perform such duties in accordance with section 179, Revised Statutes (5 U.S.C.6), perform his duties until a successor is appointed, or until such absence or disability shall cease-

(1) the Under Secretary of the Air Force;

(2) the Assistant Secretaries of the Air Force in the order fixed by their length of service as such; and

(3) the Chief of Staff.

(c) If the Chief of Staff by reason of succession assumes, or if he or any other officer of the Air Force is designated in accordance with option 179, Revised Statutes (5 U.S.C.6), to perform the duties of the Secretary of the Air Force, section 1222, Revised Statutes (10 U.S.C. 576), shall not apply to him by reason of his temporarily performing such duties.

TITLE II--CHIEF OF STAFF AND THE AIR STAFF

Sec. 201. (a) There shall be in the Department of the Air Force a staff which shall be known as the Air Staff, and which shall consist of-

(1) the Chief of Staff;

(2) a Vice Chief of Staff;

(3) not to exceed five Deputy Chiefs of Staff; and

(4) such other members of the Air Force and such civilian officers and employees in or under the jurisdiction of the Department of the Air Force as may be assigned or detailed under regulations prescribed by the Secretary of the Air Force.

(b) The Air Staff shall be organized in such manner, and its members shall perform such duties and bear such titles, as the Secretary of the Air Force may prescribe: PROVIDED, That there shall be in the Air Staff a general officer who shall assist and advise the Secretary of the Air Force and the Chief of Staff on all matters relating to the reserve components of the Air Force and who shall perform such other duties in connection therewith as may be assigned by the Secretary or the Chief of Staff.

(c) Except in time of war or national emergency hereafter declared by the Congress, not more than two thousand eight hundred officers of the Air Force shall be detailed or assigned to permanent duty in the Department of the Air Force: PROVIDED, That the numerical limit prescribed in this subsection shall not apply upon a finding by the President that an increase in the number of officers in the Department of the Air Force is in the national interest: PROVIDED FURTHER, That the Secretary of the Air Force shall report quarterly to the Congress the number of officers in the Department of the Air Force and the justification therefor.

(d) A commissioned officer of the Air Force now or hereafter detailed or assigned to duty in the Department of the Air Force shall serve for a tour of duty not to exceed four years, except that such tour of duty may be extended beyond four years upon a special finding by the Secretary of the Air Force that the extension is necessary in the public interest. Upon relief from such duty no such officer shall again be detailed or assigned within two years to duty in the Department of the Air Force except upon a like finding by the Secretary of the Air Force. This subsection shall not take effect until one year after the enactment of this Act, and shall be inapplicable in time of war or national emergency hereafter declared by the Congress.

Sec. 202. The Chief of Staff shall be appointed by the President by and with the advice and consent of the Senate, from the general officers of the Air Force, to serve during the pleasure of the President, but no person shall serve as Chief of Staff for a term of more than four years unless reappointed by the President, by and with the advice and consent of the Senate. The Chief of Staff, while holding office as such, shall have the grade of general without vacation of his permanent grade in the Air Force, and shall take rank as prescribed by law. He shall receive the compensation prescribed by law and shall be counted as one of the officers authorized to be serving in grade above lieutenant general under the provisions of the Officer Personnel Act of 1947 (61 Stat. 886), as amended.

Sec. 203. (a) The Vice Chief of Staff and the Deputy Chiefs of Staff shall be general officers of the Air Force detailed to those positions. In case of a vacancy in the office or the absence or disability of the Chief of Staff, the Vice Chief of Staff or the senior Deputy Chief of Staff, who is not absent or disabled, shall unless otherwise directed by the President, perform the duties of Chief of Staff until his successor is appointed or such absence or disability shall cease.

(b) In case of a vacancy in the position, or the absence or disability, of the Vice Chief of Staff, the senior Deputy Chief of Staff who is not absent or disabled shall, unless otherwise directed by the Secretary of the Air Force, perform the duties of the Vice Chief of Staff until his successor is designated or such absence or disability shall cease.

Sec. 204. (a) Under the direction of the Secretary of the Air Force, the Chief of Staff shall exercise command over the air defense command, the strategic air command, the tactical air command, and such other major commands as may be established by the Secretary under section 308 (b), and shall have supervision over all other members and organizations of the Air Force, shall perform the duties prescribed for him by the National Security Act of 1947, as amended, and by other laws, and shall perform such other military duties not otherwise assigned by law as may be assigned to him by the President.

(b) The Chief of Staff shall preside over the Air Staff. Subject to the provisions of section 101 of this Act, and of subsection (c) of this section, he shall be directly responsible to the Secretary of the Air Force for the efficiency of the Air Force, its state of preparation for military operations, and plans therefor. He shall transmit to the Secretary of the Air Force the plans and recommendations of the Air Staff, shall advise him in regard thereto, and, upon the approval of such plans or recommendations by the Secretary of the Air Force, he shall act as the agent of the Secretary of the Air Force in carrying the same into effect.

(c) Except as otherwise prescribed by law, the Chief of Staff shall perform his duties under the direction of the Secretary of the Air Force.

Sec. 205. (a) The Air Staff shall render professional aid and assistance to the Secretary of the Air Force, the Under Secretary of the Air Force, the Assistant Secretaries of the Air Force, and the Chief of Staff.

(b) It shall be the duty of the Air Staff-

(1) to prepare such plans for the national security, and the use of the Air Force for that purpose both separately and in conjunction with land and naval forces, and for recruiting, organizing, supplying, equipping, training, serving, mobilizing, and demobilizing the Air Force, as will assist the execution of any power vested in duty imposed upon, or function assigned to the Secretary of the Air Force or the Chief of Staff;

(2) to investigate and report upon all questions affecting the efficiency of the Air Force and its state of preparation for military operations,

(3) to prepare detailed instructions for the execution of approved plans and to supervise the execution of such plans and instructions;

(4) to act as the agents of the Secretary of the Air Force and the Chief of Staff in coordinating the action of all orga-

nizations of the Air Force Establishment; and
(5) to perform such other duties not otherwise assigned by law as may be prescribed by the Secretary of the Air Force.

TITLE III--COMPOSITION AND ORGANIZATION OF THE AIR FORCE

Sec. 301. The United States Air Force shall consist of the Regular Air Force, the Air Force Reserve, the Air National Guard of the United States and the Air National Guard while in the service of the United States; and shall include persons inducted, enlisted, or appointed without specification of component in the Air Force, and all persons serving in the Air Force under call or conscription under any provision of law, including members of the Air National Guard of the several States, Territories, and the District of Columbia when in the service of the United States pursuant to call as provided by law.

Sec. 302. (a) The Regular Air Force is that component of the Air Force which consists of persons whose continuous service on active duty in both peace and war is contemplated by law, and of persons who are retired members of the Regular Air Force.

(b) The Regular Air Force shall include the commissioned officers, warrant officers, and airmen holding appointments or enlisted in the Regular Air Force as now or hereafter provided by law, the retired commissioned officers, warrant officers, and airmen of the Regular Air Force, and such other persons as are now or may hereafter be specified by law. No person who is now a member of the Regular Air Force, active or retired, shall, by reason of the enactment of this Act, be deprived of his membership in the Regular Air Force.

Sec. 303. The Air Force Reserve referred to in the Army and Air Force Authorization Act of 1949 shall be a reserve component of the Air Force to provide a reserve for military service, and shall consist of all persons appointed or enlisted therein, or transferred therein, as now or hereafter provided by law.

Sec. 304. The Air National Guard of the United States referred to in the Army and Air Force Authorization Act of 1949 shall be a Reserve component of the Air Force to provide a reserve for military service, and shall consist of all federally recognized units and organizations of the Air National Guard of the several States, Territories, and District of Columbia, and of all personnel of the Air National Guard of the several States, Territories, and District of Columbia who shall have been appointed or enlisted in the Air National Guard of the United States, or who shall have been temporarily extended Federal recognition by the Secretary of the Air Force pursuant to section 530 of the Career Compensation Act of 1949 (63 Stat. 802).

Sec. 305. The Air National Guard referred to in the Army and Air Force Authorization Act of 1949, which consists of those units, organizations, and personnel of the National Guard (as that term is defined in section 71 of the National Defense Act, as amended) for which Federal responsibility has been vested in the Secretary of the Air Force or the Department of the Air Force pursuant to law, shall be while in the service of the United States, a component of the Air Force.

Sec. 306. All persons inducted in or holding appointments or enlistments in the Air Force or transferred therein pursuant to the National Security Act of 1947, as amended, on the effective date of this Act, shall be deemed, without further action, to hold their military status in the corresponding components set forth in section 301 of this Act or in the Air Force without specification of component and without specification of any arm, branch, service, or corps.

Sec. 307. (a) Qualified members of the Air Force shall be designated to perform medical, dental, medical service, veterinary, nursing, women's medical specialist, judge advocate, chaplain, or other duties requiring special training or experience, under regulations prescribed by the Secretary of the Air Force. Qualifications for designations under this subsection shall be prescribed by the Secretary of the Air Force in conformity with qualifications specified in any of the following statutory provisions for the respective types of duties:

(1) Act of August 5, 1947 (ch. 494, title II, sec. 201; 61 Stat. 777 (10 U.S.C.91a, 121a)).

(2) Act of April 23, 1907 (ch. 150, sec. 4, 35 Stat. 67 (10 U.S.C. 93)).

(3) Act of April 16, 1947 (ch. 38, title I, sec. 101 (c); 61 Stat. 41, 10 U.S.C. 166(c)).

(4) Act of April 16, 1947 (ch. 38, title I, sec. 102 (c); 61 Stat. 42, 10 U.S.C.166a(c)).

(5) Act of March 2, 1899 (ch. 352, sec. 7, 30 Stat. 979; 10 U.S.C. 232).

(6) Act of April 16, 1947 (ch. 38, title I, sec. 116; 61 Stat. 46, 10 U.S.C. 376).

(7) Act of August 7, 1947 (ch. 512, title V, sec. 506; 61 Stat. 890, 10 U.S.C.506c).

(8) Act of May 16, 1950 (ch. 186, sec. 1; 64 Stat. 160, 10 U.S.C. 166b-1,2).

(b) Original appointments made with a view to designation for the performance of duties under subsection (a) of this section shall be in the grades prescribed in any of the following statutory provisions for the respective types of duties:

(1) Act of August 5, 1947 (ch. 494, title II, sec. 201; 61

Stat. 777, 10 U.S.C. 91a, 121a).

(2) Act of April 16, 1947 (ch. 38 title I, sec. 101 (c); 61 Stat. 41, 10 U.S.C. 166(c)).

(3) Act of April 16, 1947 (ch. 38, title I, sec. 102 (c); 61 Stat. 42, 10 U.S.C. 166a (c)).

(4) Act of April 16, 1947 (ch. 38, title I, sec. 104; 61 Stat. 43, as amended May 16, 1950; ch. 186, sec. 3 (b); 64 Stat. 160, 10 U.S.C. 166c).

(5) Act of April 16, 1947 (ch. 38, title I, sec. 105; 61 Stat. 43, 10 U.S.C. 166d).

(6) Act of April 16, 1947 (ch. 38, title I, sec. 116; 61 Stat. 46, 10 U.S.C. 376).

(7) Act of August 7, 1947 (ch. 512, title V, sec. 506; 61 Stat. 890, 10 U.S.C. 506c).

(8) Act of May 16, 1950 (ch. 186, secs. 1, 2; 64 Stat. 160, 10 U.S.C. 166b-1,2,d-1).

(c) Members of the Air Force designated to perform duties under subsection (a) of this section shall, while performing such duties, have the benefits and be subject to the conditions provided by the following statutory provisions, insofar as the same are presently in effect, relating to their respective types of duties and components:

(1) Act of August 5, 1947 (ch. 494, title II, sec. 201: 61 Stat. 777, 10 U.S.C. 91a, 121a).

(2) Act of April 23, 1908 (ch. 150, sec. 5; 35 Stat. 67, 10 U.S.C. 101, 102).

(3) Act of March 3, 1909 (ch. 252, 35 Stat. 737, 10 U.S.C. 103).

(4) Act of June 3, 1916 (ch. 134, sec. 24c, as added June 4, 1920; ch. 227, sec. 24; 41 Stat. 774, and amended August 7, 1947; ch. 512, title V, sec. 507 (d) (1); 61 Stat. 894, 10 U.S.C. 125, 143a).

(5) Act of April 16, 1947 (ch. 38, title I, sec. 105; 61 Stat. 43, as amended May 16, 1950; ch. 186, secs. 1,2, 64 Stat. 160, 10 U.S.C. 166d).

(6) Act of April 16, 1947 (ch. 38, title I, sec. 106 Stat. 44, 10 U.S.C. 166e).

(7) Act of April 16, 1947 (ch. 38, title I, sec. 107; 61 Stat. 44, as amended May 16, 1950; ch. 186, sec. 3 (c), 64 Stat. 160, 10 U.S.C. 166f).

(8) Act of April 16, 1947 (ch. 38, title I, sec. 108 (a): 61 Stat. 44, as amended May 16, 1950; ch. 186, sec. 3 (d); 64 Stat. 160, 10 U.S.C. 166g (a)).

(9) Act of April 16, 1947 (ch. 38, title I, sec. 109; 61 Stat. 45, 10 U.S.C. 166h).

(10) Act of April 16, 1947 (ch. 38, title I, sec. 110; 61

Stat. 46, as amended May 16, 1950; ch. 186, sec. 3 (f); 64 Stat. 160, 10 U.S.C. 166i).

    (11) Revised Statutes, section 1122 (10 U.S.C. 235).

    (12) Act of June 24, 1948 (ch. 632, sec. 1; 62 Stat. 650, 10 U.S.C. 291 c-1).

    (13) Act of August 7, 1947 (ch. 512, title V, sec. 506 (c); 61 Stat. 890, 10 U.S.C. 506c (c)).

    (14) Act of August 7, 1947 (ch. 512, title V, sec. 505; 61 Stat. 888, 10 U.S.C. 559).

    (15) Act of August 7, 1947 (ch. 512, title V, sec. 517; 61 Stat. 909, 10 U.S.C. 559h).

    (16) Act of August 7, 1947 (ch. 512, title V, sec. 514 (d); 61 Stat. 902, 10 U.S.C. 941a (d)).

    (17) Act of May 29, 1928 (ch. 902, 45 Stat. 996, as amended January 29, 1938; ch. 12, sec. 2; 52 Stat. 8, 10 U.S.C. 953a).

    (18) Act of June 29, 1948 (ch. 708, title II, sec. 203 (d); 62 Stat. 1085, 10 U.S.C. 1003).

    (19) Act of October 12, 1949 (ch. 681; title II, sec. 203; 63 Stat. 809, 37 U.S.C. 234).

  (d) Separate promotion lists are authorized, within the discretion of the Secretary, for each of the categories of duties to which members of the Air Force are designated under section 307 (a) of this Act. Seniority and numbers in the several grades on the promotion lists so established under this section shall be as prescribed by the Secretary of the Air Force in accordance with the provisions of sections 505 (b) and 505 (d) of the Officer Personnel Act of 1947 (61 Stat. 888; 10 U.S.C. 559 (b), 559 (d)): PROVIDED, That such provisions of said section 505 (b) as relate to medical, dental, and chaplain officers shall, for the purposes of this section, also be applicable to officers designated to perform judge advocate duties in the Air Force.

  Sec. 308. (a) There shall be within the Air Force-

        (1) the following major air commands:

            (i) an air defense command:

            (ii) a strategic air command; and

            (iii) a tactical air command;

        (2) such other commands and organizations as may from time to time be established by the Secretary of the Air Force in the interest of efficiency and economy of operation.

  (b) For the duration of any war or national emergency declared by the President or the Congress, the Secretary of the Air Force may establish new major commands in lieu of, or discontinue or consolidate the major commands enumerated in, subsection (a) (1) of this section.

  Sec. 309. For Air Force purposes, the United States of America, its Territories and possessions, and other territory in which elements of the Air Force may be stationed or operate, may be divided into such areas as directed by the Secretary of the Air Force; and officers of the Air Force may be assigned to command of the Air Force activities, installations and personnel in such areas. In the discharge of the Air Force's functions or such other functions as may be authorized by other provisions of law, officers of the Air Force so assigned shall perform such duties and exercise such powers as the Secretary of the Air Force may prescribe.

Sec. 310. (a) There shall be in the Air Force a Judge Advocate General who shall be appointed, subject to the provisions of the Act of May 5, 1950 (64 Stat. 147; 50 U.S.C. 741), by the President, by and with the advice and consent of the Senate, for a term of four years, which term may be extended by the President at his discretion. An officer heretofore or hereafter appointed as Judge Advocate General of the Air Force shall not be a chief of a branch, arm, or service within the meaning of section 513 of the Officer Personnel Act of 1947 (61 Stat. 901; 10 U.S.C.559g) but he shall nevertheless, if he does not already hold a permanent appointment in the Regular Air Force in the grade of major general, be appointed by the President, by and with the advice and consent of the Senate, as a permanent major general in the Regular Air Force. The officer serving as Judge Advocate General on the effective date, of this Act shall, subject to the provisions of this section, continue to hold his appointment as Judge Advocate General and no reappointment of such officer as Judge Advocate General shall be required after the enactment of this Act.

(b) The Secretary of the Air Force, the Judge Advocate General of the Air Force, and officers heretofore or hereafter designated as judge advocates shall be vested with and shall exercise the same powers and duties with respect to the administration of military justice within the Air Force as are vested in the Secretary of the Army, the Judge Advocate General of the Army and judge advocates of the Army, respectively, with respect to the administration of military justice within the Army. The Judge Advocate General of the Air Force shall perform such other legal duties as may be directed by the Secretary of the Air Force.

TITLE IV--REPEALS, AMENDMENTS, AND SAVING PROVISIONS

Sec. 401. (a) The following laws and parts of laws are hereby repealed:
(1) The provision of section 401 of the Army Organization Act of 1950 and all laws and parts of laws set forth in said section to the extent applicable to the Department of the Air Force or the Air Force Establishment and not heretofore repealed;
(2) Sections 1, 2, and 3 of the Act of June 25, 1948 (62 Stat.

1014; 5 U.S.C. 627 j-1): PROVIDED, That such repeal shall not affect the existing applicability of the Articles of War to the Air Force and actions under such articles shall be enforced in the same manner and with the same effect as if this Act had not been passed.

(b) All other laws and parts of laws to the extent that they are inconsistent with the provisions of this Act are hereby repealed.

Sec. 402. The National Security Act of 1947, as amended, is hereby amended by striking out the words "command over the United States Air Force" in section 208 (b) thereof and substituting in lieu thereof the words "command over the air defense command, the strategic air command, the tactical air command, and such other major commands as may be established by the Secretary under section 308 (b) of the Air Force Organization Act of 1951, and shall have supervision over all other members and organizations of the Air Force."

Sec. 403. All laws and parts of laws not inconsistent with the provisions of this Act applicable to the Air Force Establishment, or to organizations, components or personnel thereof, whether so applicable by their terms or by operation of the National Security Act of 1947, as amended, shall continue in effect and shall be construed to apply to the Air Force Establishment and to the corresponding successive organizations, components, and personnel as set forth in this Act.

Sec. 404. (a) Nothing in this Act shall require the reappointment or redesignation of any person in the Air Force Establishment occupying a position or performing a duty as now prescribed by law.

(b) Except as otherwise expressly provided in this Act every power vested in and every duty imposed upon any office or officer, civilian or military, of the Air Force Establishment by any law, regulation, or order in force immediately prior to the effective date of this Act, shall continue to be applicable to such office and exercised and performed by such officer until the Secretary of the Air Force shall otherwise direct in accordance with the authority conferred upon him by this Act.

Sec. 405. Except as provided in section 305, nothing contained in this Act shall be construed to amend or repeal the provisions of law pertaining to the National Guard, the Air National Guard or the Chief of the National Guard Bureau.

Sec. 406. Under such regulations as may be prescribed by the Secretary of the Air Force, officers of the Air Force accountable for public moneys may intrust moneys to other officers of the Air Force for the purpose of having them make disbursements as their agents, and the officer to whom the moneys are intrusted, as well as the officer who intrusts the moneys to him, shall be held pecuniarily responsible therefore to the United States.

Sec. 407. Except as provided in section 402 of this Act, nothing in this Act shall be construed as amending, repealing, limiting, enlarging, or in any way modifying any provision of the National Security Act of 1947, as amended.

Sec. 408. If any provision of this Act or the application thereof to any person or circumstances be held invalid, the validity of the remainder of the Act and of the application of such provisions to other persons and circumstances shall not be affected thereby.

Approved September 19, 1951.

(16) Pace-Finletter Agreement, 2 October 1951

When it was formed out of the Army Air Forces in 1947, the Air Force received virtually all the aircraft formerly assigned to the Army. In the years following, the Army retained only those aircraft deemed "organic," such as small liaison aircraft and helicopters. An Army-Air Force agreement of 20 May 1949, known as the Bradley-Vandenberg Agreement, set the parameters of Army organic aviation at fixed-wing aircraft not exceeding 2,500 pounds in weight, and rotary-wing aircraft not exceeding 4,000 pounds. These aircraft were provided to expedite and improve ground combat procedures in forward battle areas, with specific tasks such as fire adjustment, route reconnaissance, and courier, although the Air Force would also maintain liaison squadrons to provide the same services.

On 2 October 1951, after extensive discussions between the staffs of the two services, Secretary of the Army Frank Pace and Secretary of the Air Force Thomas K. Finletter signed an agreement which removed the weight limitation on Army aviation and substituted a functional formula for eliminating duplication between the services. They chose to state the agreement by attempting to define the phrase contained in the National Security Act which provided the Army with, "such aviation...as may be organic therein." This took shape as aircraft used in the combat zone (itself limited to between 50 and 75 miles in depth), as an integral part of the combat organization, which expedited and improved ground combat and logistical procedures. The major limitation imposed stated that the Army could not duplicate Air Force capabilities in "close combat support, assault transport and other troop carrier airlift," reconnaissance, and interdiction.

****
Alfred Goldberg, and Lt. Col. Donald Smith, Army-Air Force Relations: The Close Air Support Issue (R-906-PR, SantaMonica, Oct. 1971), pp 6-11.

MEMORANDUM OF UNDERSTANDING BETWEEN THE SECRETARY OF THE ARMY
AND THE SECRETARY OF THE AIR FORCE

1. The National Security Act of 1947 as amended in 1949 provides, "in general the Army shall include land combat and service forces and such aviation and water transport as may be organic therein." It is the purpose of this memorandum to delineate in the foregoing quotation the phrase, "such aviation as may be organic therein," in order to insure that the U.S. Army may employ aircraft necessary for its internal requirements in the conduct of operations on land, without infringement upon the missions assigned to the U.S. Air Force.

2. Army organic aviation will consist of aircraft utilized by the Army within the Army combat zone as an integral part of its components for the purpose of expediting and improving ground combat and logistical procedures within the combat zone; subject, however, to the limitation that such aircraft will not duplicate the functions of the U.S. Air Force in providing the Army, by fixed wing and rotary type aircraft, close combat support, assault transport and other troop carrier airlift, aerial photography, tactical reconnaissance and interdiction of enemy land power and communications. Army organic aircraft are defined as fixed wing utility aircraft (light) and rotary type aircraft designed and utilized for the performance of the following functions:

   a. Aerial observation to amplify and supplement other Army methods of observation for the purpose of locating, verifying and evaluating targets, adjusting fire, terrain study, or obtaining information on enemy forces not otherwise obtained by air reconnaissance agencies of the other services; this includes limited aerial photography incident to these purposes.

   b. Control of Army forces.

   c. Command, liaison and courier missions pertinent to the combat zone and training therefor.

   d. Aerial wire laying within the combat zone.

   e. Transportation of Army supplies, equipment, and small units within the combat zone (by aircraft of the types referred to above), though it is recognized that the Air Force is assigned the primary function of supplying the necessary airlift to the Army.

3. Army organic aircraft will be used by the responsible Army commander as he considers necessary for the discharge of his military mission.

4. Policies and procedures to be followed by the Army and Air Force in matters related to the development, procurement, supply and maintenance of Army aircraft and allied equipment will be as prescribed in AR No. 700-30 and AFR No. 65-7, except for paragraph 2 (b) thereof.

5. The term "combat zone" as used herein shall be defined as follows:

The combat zone comprises that part of the theater of operations required for the conduct of war by the field forces. Its depth may be dependent upon the size of the forces assigned, the nature of the operations contemplated, the character of the lines of communications, the important terrain features, and the enemy capabilities. It may be divided for tactical control into army group, field army, corps, and division areas; each is controlled by the commander of the corresponding unit. The rear boundary of the combat zone is designated by the theater commander and is changed to conform to the movement of the armed forces.

It is understood that the combat zone will normally not exceed 50 to 70 miles in depth.

6. The provisions of this agreement, the impact thereon on future developments, and any major problems incident to the interpretation thereof which may arise shall be made the subject of consultation between the Chiefs of Staff and the Secretaries of the two Services upon request.

7. All regulations and agreements in conflict with the foregoing will be revised in accordance with the provisions of this memorandum.

/s/ Frank Pace Jr.
Secretary of the Army

/s/ Thomas K. Finletter
Secretary of the Air Force

(17) Pace-Finletter Agreement, 4 November 1952

Despite the apparent settlement reached in the Pace-Finletter Agreement of 2 October 1951, differences persisted between the two services. The Army continued to acquire more and larger helicopters, precipitating another round of conferences with the Air Force and JCS discussions. The result was a second Pace-Finletter Agreement on 4 November 1952.

This agreement returned to the weight restriction formula for fixed-wing aircraft, with the limit raised to 5,000 pounds. The renewed weight limit was subject to review by the Secretary of Defense when requested by the secretary of either service, as a hedge against technological developments or assignment of new missions. The agreement also expanded the definition of the combat zone, which was now described as "normally understood to be 50 to 100 miles in depth." In addition, the Army received expanded functions for its organic aircraft, including aeromedical evacuation within the battle zone, and artillery and topographic survey. This addition of functions was not to be construed as altering in any fashion the Key West Agreement on functions, as was explicitly stated in this second Pace-Finletter Agreement. However, the prevailing attitude in the Air Force was to acquiesce to the Army expanding into support roles for its organic aviation, as the Air Force pursued nuclear capabilities for its tactical forces as well as its strategic ones.

****

Alfred Goldberg, and Lt. Col. Donald Smith, Army-Air Force Relations: The Close Air Support Issue (R-906-PR, Santa Monica, Oct. 1971), pp 9-12.

241

November 4, 1952

MEMORANDUM OF UNDERSTANDING RELATING TO ARMY ORGANIC AVIATION

1.   The National Security Act of 1947 as amended in 1949 provides, "in general the Army shall include land combat and service forces and such aviation and water transport as may be organic therein." It is the purpose of this memorandum to delineate in the foregoing quotation the phrase, "such aviation as may be organic therein," in order to insure that the U. S. Army may employ aircraft necessary for its internal requirements in the conduct of operations on land, without infringement upon the missions assigned to the U. S. Air Force.

2.   Army organic aviation will consist of aircraft primarily utilized by the Army within the Army combat zone as an integral part of its components for the purpose of expediting and improving ground combat and logistical procedures, subject, however, to the limitation that such aircraft will not duplicate the functions of the U. S. Air Force in providing the Army, by fixed-wing and rotary-wing type aircraft, close combat support, assault transport and other troop carrier airlift, aerial photography, tactical reconnaissance and interdiction of enemy land power and communications. Army organic aircraft are defined as fixed-wing utility or observation type aircraft with an empty weight of not to exceed 5000 pounds and rotary-wing type aircraft, the total lift and propulsion of which are achieved solely from rotors, designed and utilized for the performance of the following functions; and these functions shall be used by the Army exclusively as a basis for developing Army requirements for the procurement of Army aircraft:

a. Aerial observation to amplify and supplement other Army methods of observation for the purpose of locating, verifying and evaluating targets, adjusting fire, terrain study, or obtaining information on enemy forces not otherwise obtained by air reconnaissance agencies of the other services; this includes limited aerial photography incident to these purposes.

b. Control of Army forces.

c. Command, liaison and courier missions pertinent to the combat zone and training therefor.

d. Aerial wire laying within the combat zone.

e. Transportation of Army supplies, equipment, and small units within the combat zone.

f. Aeromedical evacuation within the combat zone, to include battlefield pickup of casualties, their air transport to initial point of treatment and any subsequent move to hospital

facilities within the combat zone.
       g. Artillery and topographic survey.

    3. Army organic aircraft will be used by the responsible Army commander as he considers necessary for the discharge of his military mission.

    4. Army aircraft as defined in paragraph 2 above may be utilized in peacetime operations and in training for the functions outlined in paragraph 2 above, as required by Army units and activities.

    5. The weight limitations on Army fixed-wing aircraft will be subject to review by the Secretary of Defense upon request by the Secretary of the Army or the Secretary of the Air Force as required to keep this limitation realistic in the light of technical developments and assigned missions.

    6. Consistent with one of its primary functions, furnishing logistical air support to the Army, the Air Force will provide by fixed-wing or rotary wing aircraft the following airlift; and these functions shall be used by the Air Force exclusively as a basis for developing Air Force requirements for the procurement of Air Force aircraft:

       a. Airlift of Army supplies, equipment, personnel and units from exterior points to points within the combat zone.

       b. Airlift for the evacuation of personnel and materiel from the combat zone.

       c. Airlift for the air movement of troops, supplies and equipment in the assault and subsequent phases of airborne operations.

       d. Aeromedical evacuation for casualties from the initial point of treatment or point of subsequent hospitalization within the combat zone to points outside of the combat zone; and in airborne operations, the evacuation of all casualties from the objective area until such time as ground link-up is attained.

    7. For the purpose of this memorandum, the term "combat zone" shall be defined as follows:

    The combat zone comprises that part of the theater of operations required for the conduct of war by the field forces. Its rear boundary is designated by the theater commander and is dependent upon the size of the forces assigned, the nature of the operations contemplated, the character of the lines of communications, the important terrain features, and the enemy capabilities. It may be divided for tactical control into Army group, field Army, Corps, and Division areas; each is controlled by the

commander thereof. For the purposes of computing aircraft requirements, it is understood that the combat zone will normally be from
50 to 100 miles in depth.

    8.   The provisions of this agreement, the impact thereon on
future developments, and any major problems incident to the
interpretation thereof which may arise shall be made the subject
of consultation between the Chiefs of Staff and the Secretaries of
the two Services upon request.

    9.   The provisions of this memorandum are not intended to
apply to convertiplane-type aircraft, nor will this agreement be
interpreted to prohibit the continuing research, development and
testing of such aircraft for the Army.

    10.   This agreement supersedes the Memorandum of Understanding
Between the Secretary of the Army and the Secretary of the Air
Force, dated 2 October 1951. All regulations and agreements in
conflict with the foregoing will be revised in accordance with
the provisions of this memorandum. Nothing contained herein is
intended to or shall be construed as modifying, altering or
rescinding any of the assigned functions of the Armed Forces (The
Key West Agreement, dated 21 April 1948).

/s/ Frank Pace Jr.   /s/ Thomas K. Finletter
Secretary of the Army   Secretary of the Air Force

/s/ J. Lawton Collins   /s/ N. F. Twining
Chief of Staff, U. S. Army   Vice Chief of Staff, U. S. Air Force

(18) Reorganization Plan Number 6 of 1953, 30 April 1953

When Gen. Dwight D. Eisenhower became President in 1953, he brought to that office more than thirty years of military experience, which he focused on the organization of the Department of Defense (DOD). At this time a number of proposals had appeared for reorganizing DOD, including that prepared by outgoing Secretary of Defense Robert A. Lovett. Newly installed Defense Secretary Charles E. Wilson sought a comprehensive review of the department's organization and appointed a Committee on Department of Defense Organization headed by Nelson A. Rockefeller which issued a report on 11 April 1953. President Eisenhower accepted most of the committee's recommendations embodying them in his Reorganization Plan Number 6, transmitted to Congress on 30 April 1953. Congress failed to disapprove or amend the measure, despite extensive discussion, and the plan took effect 30 June 1953.

The reorganization fostered under this plan resulted in further centralization of authority, direction, and control in the Office of the Secretary of Defense. The plan abolished the Munitions Board, the Research and Development Board, and several other staff agencies (which were replaced by six new Assistant Secretaries of Defense), and granted the Chairman of the Joint Chiefs of Staff the authority to direct the Joint Staff. Moreover, President Eisenhower, in his letter of transmittal to Congress, proposed a change in the command channels for the unified commands, funneling responsibility through the service secretary (and the respective service), rather than the service Chief of Staff. This change came later and was not part of this 1953 reorganization.

President Eisenhower concurrently altered the National Security Council, adding the Secretary of the Treasury and the Director of the Bureau of the Budget to the Council, as well as establishing an NSC Planning Board and an Operations Coordinating Board later in the year.

****

Robert F. Futrell, Ideas, Concepts and Doctrine: A History of Basic Thinking in the United States Air Force 1907-1964, (Maxwell AFB, Ala: Air University, 2nd edition, 1974) pp 210-11.

BASIC DOCUMENTS

Alice C. Cole, ed., et al, <u>The Department of Defense,</u>
<u>Documents on Establishment and Organization 1944-1978,</u>
(Washington, D.C.: OSD Historical Office, 1978), pp
149-59.

Prepared by the President and transmitted to the Senate and the
   House of Representatives in Congress assembled, April 30, 1953,
   pursuant to the provisions of the Reorganization Act of 1949,
   approved June 20, 1949, as amended.

Department of Defense

Section 1. Transfers of functions--(a) All functions of the
Munitions Board, the Research and Development Board, the Defense
Supply Management Agency and the Director of Installations are
hereby transferred to the Secretary of Defense.

(b) The selection of the Director of the Joint Staff by the
Joint Chiefs of Staff, and his tenure, shall be subject to the
approval of the Secretary of Defense.

(c) The selection of the members of the Joint Staff by the Joint
Chiefs of Staff, and their tenure, shall be subject to the approval of the Chairman of the Joint Chiefs of Staff.

(d) The functions of the Joint Chiefs of Staff with respect to
managing the Joint Staff and the Director thereof are hereby
transferred to the Chairman of the Joint Chiefs of Staff.

Sec. 2. Abolition of agencies and functions.--(a) There are
hereby abolished the Munitions Board, the Research and Development
Board, and the Defense Supply Management Agency.

(b) The offices of Chairman of the Munitions Board, Chairman of
the Research and Development Board, Director of the Defense Supply
Management Agency, Deputy Director of the Defense Supply
Management Agency and Director of Installations are hereby
abolished.

(c) The Secretary of Defense shall provide for winding up any
outstanding affairs of the said abolished agency, boards, and
offices, not otherwise provided for in this reorganization plan.

(d) The function of guidance to the Munitions Board in connection with strategic and logistical plans as required by Section
213(c) of the National Security Act of 1947, as amended, is hereby
abolished.

Sec. 3. Assistant Secretaries of Defense.--Six additional
Assistant Secretaries of Defense may be appointed from civilian
life by the President, by and with the advice and consent of the
Senate. Each such Assistant Secretary shall perform such functions as the Secretary of Defense may from time to time prescribe
and each shall receive compensation at the rate prescribed by law
for assistant secretaries of executive departments.

Sec. 4. General Counsel.-- The President may appoint from civilian life, by and with the advice and consent of the Senate, a
General Counsel of the Department of Defense who shall be the
chief legal officer of the Department, and who shall perform such

functions as the Secretary of Defense may from time to time prescribe. He shall receive compensation at the rate prescribed by law for assistant secretaries of executive departments.

Sec. 5. Performance of functions.-- The Secretary of Defense may from time to time make such provisions as he shall deem appropriate authorizing the performance by any other officer, or by any agency or employee, of the Department of Defense of any function of the Secretary, including any function transferred to the Secretary by the provisions of this reorganization plan.

Sec. 6. Miscellaneous provisions.--(a) The Secretary of Defense may from time to time effect such transfers within the Department of Defense of any of the records, property, and personnel affected by this reorganization plan, and such transfers of unexpended balances (available or to be made available for use in connection with any affected function or agency) of appropriations, alloca- tions, and any other funds of such Department, as he deems necessary to carry out the provisions of this reorganization plan.

(b) Nothing herein shall affect the compensation of the Chairman of the Military Liaison Committee (63 Stat. 762).

(19) **Department of Defense Directive 5100.1,**
16 March 1954

Revisions of the Key West Agreement were
incorporated in the first edition of Department of
Defense (DOD) Directive 5100.1, "Functions of the Armed
Forces and the Joint Chiefs of Staff," dated 16 March
1954. The first change stated that no DOD function
could be performed "independent of the direction,
authority, and control of the Secretary of Defense."
This placed the Secretary firmly in command of the
department. The second change concerned the unified
commands and their control. Previously, the Joint
Chiefs of Staff (JCS) had designated one of their
members as executive agent for each of the unified
commands. The chain of command went from the
President, through the Secretary of Defense, through
the JCS to the service chief of staff to the unified
commander. Under this revision, one service would be
named as executive agent for a unified command, such
that the chain of command ran from the President, to
the Secretary of Defense, to the service secretary, and
to the unified commander. During combat operations and
emergency situations, the service chief of staff would
be authorized to act for the service department in his
capacity as executive agent in the name of the
Secretary of Defense and under his direction.

These measures were designed to provide civilian
control over the military, with the Secretary of
Defense clearly in command of the Defense Department.
Coupled with the 1953 reorganization, DOD became far
more centralized and able to implement Eisenhower's
"New Look" policy which emphasized air atomic power and
a less expensive defense.

****

Robert F. Futrell, Ideas, Concepts and Doctrine: A
History of Basic Thinking in the United States Air
Force 1907-1964, (Maxwell AFB, Ala: Air University,
2nd edition, 1974) pp 210-11.

DEPARTMENT OF DEFENSE DIRECTIVE

SUBJECT Functions of the Armed Forces and the Joint Chiefs of
Staff

Reference: Secretary of Defense memorandum, 21 April 1948 to the
Secretaries of Army, Navy and Air Force and the Joint
Chiefs of Staff, attaching the "Functions of the Armed
Forces and the Joint Chiefs of Staff", same date

Attached for information and guidance is a copy of the 1 October
1953 revision of "Functions of the Armed Forces and the Joint
Chiefs of Staff", commonly known as the "Key West Agreement."
There is also attached a copy of a document pointing up the
changes made in the original Key West Agreement, 21 April 1948.

(signed)
MAURICE W. ROCHE
Administrative Secretary

Attachments - 2

FUNCTIONS OF THE ARMED FORCES
AND THE JOINT CHIEFS OF STAFF

1 October 1953

Introduction

* Congress, in the National Security Act of 1947, as amended, * has described the basic policy embodied in the Act in the following terms:

"In enacting this legislation, it is the intent of Congress to provide a comprehensive program for the future security of the United States to provide for the establishment of integrated policies and procedures for the departments, agencies, and functions of the Government relating to the national security; to provide three military departments,
* separately administered, for the operation and administra- * tion of the Army, the Navy (including naval aviation and the United States Marine Corps), and the Air Force, with their assigned combat and service components; to provide for their authoritative coordination and unified direction under civi-
* lian control of the Secretary of Defense but not to merge * them; to provide for the effective strategic direction of the armed forces and for their operation under unified control and for their integration into an efficient team of land, naval,
* and air forces but not to establish a single Chief of Staff *
* over the armed forces nor an armed forces general Staff *
* (but this is not to be interpreted as applying to the Joint *
* Chiefs of Staff or Joint Staff)."
                                    *

In accordance with the policy declared by Congress, and in accordance with the provisions of the National Security Act of 1947, as amended, (including Reorganization Plan No. 6 of 1953)

---

* Corrected to reflect amendment of 1949

and to provide guidance for the departments and the joint agencies of the Department of Defense, the Secretary of Defense, by direction of the President, hereby promulgates the following statement of the functions of the armed forces and the Joint Chiefs of Staff.

SECTION I.--PRINCIPLES

1.   No function in any part of the Department of Defense, or in any of its component agencies, shall be performed independent of the direction, authority, and control of the Secretary of Defense.

2.   There shall be the maximum practicable integration of the policies and procedures of the departments and agencies of the Department of Defense. This does not imply a merging of armed forces, but does demand a consonance and correlation of policies and procedures throughout the Department of Defense, in order to produce an effective, economical, harmonious, and business-like organization which will insure the military security of the United States.

3.   The functions stated herein shall be carried out in such a manner as to achieve the following:

    (a) Effective strategic direction of the armed forces.

    (b) Operation of armed forces under unified command, wherever such unified command is in the best interest of national security.

    (c) Integration of the armed forces into an efficient team of land, naval, and air forces.

    (d) Prevention of unnecessary duplication or overlapping among the services, by utilization of the personnel, intelligence, facilities, equipment, supplies, and services of any or all services in all cases where military effectiveness and economy of resources will thereby be increased.

    (e) Coordination of armed forces operations to promote efficiency and economy and to prevent gaps in responsibility.

4.   It is essential that there be full utilization and exploitation of the weapons, techniques, and intrinsic capabilities of each of the services in any military situation where this

will contribute effectively to the attainment of over-all military objectives. In effecting this, collateral as well as primary functions will be assigned. It is recognized that assignment of collateral functions may establish further justification for stated force requirements, but such assignment shall not be used as the basis for establishing additional force requirements.

5. Doctrines, procedures, and plans covering joint operations and joint exercises shall be jointly prepared. Primary responsibility for development of certain doctrines and procedures is hereinafter assigned.

6. Technological developments, variations in the availability of manpower and natural resources, changing economic conditions, and changes in the world politico-military situation may dictate the desirability of changes in the present assignment of specific functions and responsibilities to the individual services. This determination and the initiation of implementing action are the responsibility of the Secretary of Defense.

SECTION II.--COMMON FUNCTIONS OF THE ARMED FORCES

A. General.--As prescribed by higher authority and under the direction of the Secretary of Defense with the advice of the Joint Chiefs of Staff, the armed forces shall conduct operations wherever and whenever necessary for the following purposes:

1. To support and defend the Constitution of the United States against all enemies, foreign or domestic.

2. To maintain, by timely and effective military action the security of the United States, its possessions, and areas vital to its interest.

3. To uphold and advance the national policies and interests of the United States.

4. To safeguard the internal security of the United States.

B. Specific

1. In accordance with continuous guidance from the Joint Chiefs of Staff, to prepare forces and to establish reserves of equipment and supplies, for the effective prosecution of war and to plan for the expansion of peacetime components to meet the needs of war.

2.   To maintain in readiness mobile reserve forces, properly organized, trained, and equipped for employment in emergency.

3.   To provide adequate, timely, and reliable intelligence for use within the Department of Defense.

4.   To organize, train, and equip forces for joint operations.

5.   To conduct research, to develop tactics, techniques, and organization, and to develop and procure weapons, equipment, and supplies essential to the fulfillment of the functions hereinafter assigned, each Service coordinating with the others in all matters of joint concern.

6.   To develop, garrison, supply, equip, and maintain bases and other installations, to include lines of communication, and to provide administrative and logistical support of all forces and bases.

7.   To provide, as directed by proper authority, such forces, military missions, and detachments for service in foreign countries as may be required to support the national interests of the United States.

8.   As directed by proper authority, to assist in training and equipping the military forces of foreign nations.

9.   Each service to assist the others in the accomplishment of their functions including the provision of personnel, intelligence, training, facilities, equipment, supplies, and services as may be determined by proper authority.

10.   Each service to support operations of the others.

11.   Each service to coordinate operations (including administrative, logistical, training, and combat) with those of the other services as necessary in the best interests of the United States.

12.   Each service to determine and provide the means of communications by which command within the service is to be exercised.

13.   To refer all matters of strategic significance to the Joint Chiefs of Staff.

14. Unified Commands

(a) The Secretary of Defense after consultation with the Joint Chiefs of Staff shall designate in each case one of the military departments to serve as the executive agency for unified commands and other matters requiring such designation.

(b) Under the arrangements herein established, the channel of responsibility will be from the Secretary of Defense to the designated civilian Secretary of a military department.

(c) For strategic direction and for the conduct of combat operations in emergency and wartime situations, the Secretary of the military department designated as executive agent shall forthwith authorize the military chief of such department in such situations to receive and transmit reports and orders and to act for such department in its executive agency capacity. The military chief will keep his Secretary, the Secretary of Defense, and the Joint Chiefs of Staff fully informed of decisions made and actions taken under such authority. The military chief will in such circumstances be acting in the name and under the direction of the Secretary of Defense. Promulgated orders will directly state that fact.

SECTION III.--FUNCTIONS OF THE JOINT CHIEFS OF STAFF

A. General.--The Joint Chiefs of Staff, consisting of the Chairman; the Chief of Staff, U. S. Army; the Chief of Naval Operations; and the Chief of Staff, U. S. Air Force are the principal military advisers to the President, the National Security Council and the Secretary of Defense. The Commandant of the U. S. Marine Corps has co-equal status with the members of the Joint Chiefs of Staff on matters which directly concern the Marine Corps.

B. Specific.--Subject to the authority and direction of the President and the Secretary of Defense, it shall be the duty of the Joint Chiefs of Staff:

1. To prepare strategic plans and to provide for the strategic direction of the Armed Forces, including guidance for the operational control of forces and for the conduct of combat operations.

2. To prepare joint logistic plans and to assign to the military services logistic responsibilities in accordance with

such plans.

    3.   To prepare integrated joint plans for military mobilization, and to review major material requirements and personnel qualifications and requirements of the Armed Forces in the light of strategic and logistic plans.

    4.   To promulgate to the individual departments of the Department of Defense general policies and doctrines in order to provide guidance in the preparation of their respective detailed plans.

    5.   As directed by proper authority, to participate in the preparation of combined plans for military action in conjunction with the armed forces of other nations.

    6.   To establish unified commands in strategic areas when such unified commands are in the interest of national security.

    7.   To determine what means are required for the exercise of unified command, and to recommend to the Secretary of Defense the assignment to individual military departments the responsibility of providing such means.

    8.   To approve policies and doctrines for:

    (a) Joint operations, including joint amphibious and airborne operations, and for joint training.

    (b) Coordinating the educations of members of the Armed Forces.

    9.   To recommend to the Secretary of Defense the assignment of primary responsibility for any function of the Armed Forces requiring such determination.

    10.   To prepare and submit to the Secretary of Defense, for his information and consideration in furnishing guidance to the Departments for preparation of their annual budgetary estimates and in coordinating these budgets, a statement of military requirements which is based upon agreed strategic considerations, joint outline war plans, and current national security commitments. This statement of requirements shall include: tasks, priority of tasks, force requirements, and general strategic guidance concerning development of military installations and bases, equipping and maintaining the military forces, and research and development and industrial mobilization program.

11. To provide United States representation on the Military Staff Committee of the United Nations, in accordance with the provisions of the Charter of the United Nations and representation on other properly authorized military staffs, boards, councils, and missions.

SECTION IV.--FUNCTIONS OF THE UNITED STATES ARMY

The United States Army includes land combat and service forces and such aviation and water transport as may be organic therein. It is organized, trained, and equipped primarily for prompt and sustained combat operations on land. Of the three major services, the Army has primary interest in all operations on land, except in those operations otherwise assigned herein.

A. Primary functions

1. To organize, train, and equip Army forces for the conduct of prompt and sustained combat operations on land. Specifically:

(a) To defeat enemy land forces.

(b) To seize, occupy, and defend land areas.

2. To organize, train, and equip Army antiaircraft artillery units.

3. To organize and equip, in coordination with the other services, and to provide Army forces for joint amphibious and airborne operations, and to provide for the training of such forces in accordance with policies and doctrines of the Joint Chiefs of Staff.

4. To develop, in coordination with the other services, tactics, technique, and equipment of interest to the Army for amphibious operations and not provided for in Section V, paragraph A 4 and paragraph A 11 (c).

5. To provide an organization capable of furnishing adequate, timely, and reliable intelligence for the Army.

6. To provide Army forces as required for the defense of the United States against air attack, in accordance with joint doctrines and procedures approved by the Joint Chiefs of Staff.

7. To provide forces, as directed by proper authority, for occupation of territories abroad, to include initial establishment

of military government pending transfer of this responsibility to other authority.

8.   To develop, in coordination with the Navy, the Air Force, and the Marine Corps, the doctrines, procedures, and equipment employed by Army and Marine forces in airborne operations. The Army shall have primary interest in the development of those airborne doctrines, procedures and equipment which are of common interest to the Army and the Marine Corps.

9.   To formulate doctrines and procedures for the organization, equipping, training, and employment of forces operating on land, at division level and above, including division corps, army and general reserve troops, except that the formulation of doctrines and procedures for the organization, equipping, training, and employment of Marine Corps units for amphibious operations shall be a function of the Department of the Navy, coordinating as required by paragraph A 11 (c), Section V.

10.   To provide support, as directed by higher authority, for the following activities:

   (a)   The administration and operation of the Panama Canal.

   (b)   River and harbor projects in the United States, its territories, and possessions.

   (c)   Certain other civil activities prescribed by law.

B.   Collateral Functions.--The forces developed and trained to perform the primary functions set forth above shall be employed to support and supplement the other services in carrying out their primary functions, where and whenever such participation will result in increased effectiveness and will contribute to the accomplishment of the over-all military objectives. The Joint Chiefs of Staff member of the service having primary responsibility for a function shall be the agent of the Joint Chiefs of Staff to present to that body the requirements and plans for the employment of all forces to carry out the function. He shall also be responsible for presenting to the Joint Chiefs of Staff for final decision any disagreement within the field of his primary responsibility which has not been resolved. This shall not be construed to prevent any member of the Joint Chiefs of Staff from presenting unilaterally any issue of disagreement with another service. Certain specific collateral functions of the Army are listed below:

1. To interdict enemy sea and air power and communications through operations on or from land.

SECTION V.--FUNCTIONS OF THE UNITED STATES NAVY AND MARINE CORPS

Within the Department of the Navy, assigned forces include the entire operating forces of the United States Navy, including naval aviation, and the United States Marine Corps. These forces are organized, trained, and equipped primarily for prompt and sustained combat operations at sea, and for air and land operations incident thereto. Of the three major services, the Navy has primary interest in all operations at sea, except in those operations otherwise assigned herein.

A. Primary Functions

1. To organize, train, and equip Navy and Marine Forces for the conduct of prompt and sustained combat operations at sea, including operations of sea-based aircraft and their land-based naval air components. Specifically:

(a) To seek out and destroy enemy naval forces and to suppress enemy sea commerce.

(b) To gain and maintain general sea supremacy.

(c) To control vital sea areas and to protect vital sea lines of communication.

(d) To establish and maintain local superiority (including air) in an area of naval operations.

(e) To seize and defend advanced naval bases and to conduct such land operations as may be essential to the prosecution of a naval campaign.

2. To conduct air operations as necessary for the accomplishment of objectives in a naval campaign.

3. To organize and equip, in coordination with the other services, and to provide naval forces, including naval close air-support forces, for the conduct of joint amphibious operations, and to be responsible for the amphibious training of all forces as assigned for joint amphibious operations in accordance with the policies and doctrines of the Joint Chiefs of Staff.

4. To develop, in coordination with the other services, the doctrines, procedures, and equipment of naval forces for amphibious operations, and the doctrines and procedures for joint amphibious operations.

5. To furnish adequate, timely and reliable intelligence for the Navy and Marine Corps.

6. To be responsible for naval reconnaissance, anti-submarine warfare, the protection of shipping, and for mine laying, including the air aspects thereof, and controlled mine field operations.

7. To provide air support essential for naval operations.

8. To provide sea-based air defense and the sea-based means for coordinating control for defense against air attack, coordinating with the other services in matters of joint concern.

9. To provide naval (including naval air) forces as required for the defense of the United States against air attack, in accordance with joint doctrines and procedures approved by the Joint Chiefs of Staff.

10. To furnish aerial photography as necessary for naval and Marine Corps operations.

11. To maintain the United States Marine Corps, which shall include land combat and service forces and such aviation as may be organic therein. Its specific functions are:

(a) To provide Fleet Marine Forces of combined arms, together with supporting air components, for service with the Fleet in the seizure or defense of advanced naval bases and for the conduct of such land operations as may be essential to the prosecution of a naval campaign. These functions do not contemplate the creation of a second land Army.

(b) To provide detachments and organizations for service on armed vessels of the Navy, and security detachments for the protection of naval property at naval stations and bases.

(c) To develop, in coordination with the Army, the Navy, and the Air Force, the tactics, technique, and equipment employed by landing forces in amphibious operations. The Marine Corps shall have primary interest in the development of those landing force tactics, technique, and equipment which are of common interest to the Army and the Marine Corps.

(d) Tn train and equip, as required, Marine Forces for airborne operations, in coordination with the Army, the Navy, and the Air Force in accordance with policies and doctrines of the Joint Chiefs of Staff.

(e) To develop, in coordination with the Army, the Navy, and the Air Force, doctrines, procedures, and equipment of interest to the Marine Corps for airborne operations and not provided for in Section IV, paragraph A8.

12. To provide forces, as directed by proper authority, for the establishment of military government, pending transfer of this responsibility to other authority.

B. Collateral Functions. - The forces developed and trained to perform the primary functions set forth above shall be employed to support and supplement the other services in carrying out their primary functions, where and whenever such participation will result in increased effectiveness and will contribute to the accomplishment of the over-all military objectives. The Joint Chiefs of Staff member of the service having primary responsibility for a function shall be the agent of the Joint Chiefs of Staff to present to that body the requirements and plans for the employment of all forces to carry out the function. He shall also be responsible for presenting to the Joint Chiefs of Staff for final decision any disagreement within the field of his primary responsibility which has not been resolved. This shall not be construed to prevent any member of the Joint Chiefs of Staff from presenting unilaterally any issue of disagreement with another service. Certain specific collateral functions of the Navy and Marine Corps are listed below:

1. To interdict enemy land and air power and communications through operation at sea.

2. To conduct close air support for land operations.

3. To furnish aerial photography for cartographic purposes.

4. To be prepared to participate in the over-all air effort as directed by the Joint Chiefs of Staff.

SECTION VI - FUNCTIONS OF THE UNITED STATES AIR FORCE

The United States Air Force includes air combat and service forces. It is organized, trained, and equipped primarily for prompt and sustained combat operations in the air. Of the three major services, the Air Force has primary interest in all operations in the air, except in those operations otherwise assigned herein.

A. Primary Functions

1. To organize, train and equip Air Force forces for the conduct of prompt and sustained combat operations in the air. Specifically:

(a) To be responsible for defense of the United States against air attack in accordance with the policies and procedures of the Joint Chiefs of Staff.

(b) To gain and maintain general air supremacy.

(c) To defeat enemy air forces.

(d) To control vital air areas.

(e) To establish local air superiority except as otherwise assigned herein.

2. To formulate joint doctrines and procedures, in coordination with the other services, for the defense of the United States against air attack, and to provide the Air Force units, facilities, and equipment required therefor.

3. To be responsible for strategic air warfare.

4. To organize and equip Air Force forces for joint amphibious and airborne operations, in coordination with the other services, and to provide for their training in accordance with policies and doctrines of the Joint Chiefs of Staff.

5. To furnish close combat and logistical air support to the Army, to include air lift, support, and resupply of air-borne operations, aerial photography, tactical reconnaissance, and interdiction of enemy land power and communications.

6. To provide air transport for the armed forces except as otherwise assigned.

7. To provide Air Force forces for land-based air defense, coordinating with the other services in matters of joint concern.

8. To develop, in coordination with the other services, doctrines, procedures, and equipment for air defense from land areas, including the continental United States.

9. To provide an organization capable of furnishing adequate, timely, and reliable intelligence for the Air Force.

10. To furnish aerial photography for cartographic purposes.

11. To develop, in coordination with the other services, tactics, technique, and equipment of interest to the Air Force for amphibious operations and not provided for in Section V, paragraph A4 and paragraph A11(c).

12. To develop, in coordination with the other services, doctrines, procedures and equipment employed by Air Force forces in air-borne operations.

B. Collateral Functions. - The forces developed and trained to perform the primary functions set forth above shall be employed to support and supplement the other services in carrying out their primary functions, where and whenever such participation will result in increased effectiveness and will contribute to the accomplishment of the over-all military objectives. The Joint Chiefs of Staff member of the service having primary responsibility for a function shall be the agent of the Joint Chiefs of Staff to present to that body the requirements and plans for the employment of all forces to carry out the function. He shall also be responsible for presenting to the Joint Chiefs of Staff for final decision any disagreement within the field of his primary responsibility which has not been resolved. This shall not be construed to prevent any member of the Joint Chiefs of Staff from presenting unilaterally any issue of disagreement with another service. Certain specific collateral functions of the Air Force are listed below:

1. To interdict enemy sea power through air operations.

2. To conduct antisubmarine warfare and to protect shipping.

3. To conduct aerial mine-laying operations.

SECTION VII - GLOSSARY OF TERMS AND DEFINITIONS

The usual and accepted definitions and interpretations of the English language, as contained in Webster's New International Dictionary (Unabridged), are applicable to this document, except that for purposes of clarity and to ensure a common understanding of its intent, certain words and phrases are defined specifically as follows:

Air Defense. - All measures designed to nullify or reduce the effectiveness of the attack of hostile aircraft or guided missiles after they are airborne.

Air Superiority. - That degree of capability (preponderance in morale and material) of one air force over another which permits the conduct of air operations by the former at a given time and place without prohibitive interference by the opposing air force.

Air Supremacy. - That degree of air superiority wherein the opposing air force is incapable of effective interference.

Amphibious Operation. - An attack launched from the sea by naval and landing forces embarked in ships or craft involving a landing on a hostile shore. An amphibious operation includes final preparation of the objective area for the landing and operations of naval, air, and ground elements in over-water movements, assault, and mutual support. An amphibious operation may precede a large-scale land operation, in which case it becomes the amphibious phase of a joint amphibious operation. After the troops are landed and firmly established ashore the operation becomes a land operation.

Antisubmarine Operations. - Operations contributing to the conduct of antisubmarine warfare.

Antisubmarine Warfare. - Operations conducted against submarines, their supporting forces and operating bases.

Base. - A locality from which operations are projected or supported. May be preceded by a descriptive word such as "air" or "submarine", which indicates primary purpose.

Close Air Support. - The attack by aircraft of hostile ground or naval targets which are so close to friendly forces as to require detailed integration of each air mission with the fire and movement of those forces.

Functions. - Responsibilities, missions, and tasks.

In coordination with. - In consultation with. This expression means that agencies "coordinated with" shall participate actively; that their concurrence shall be sought; and that if concurrence is not obtained, the disputed matter shall be referred to the next higher authority in which all participants have a voice.

Joint. - As used in this paper, and generally among the Armed Forces, connotes activities, operations, organizations, etc., in which elements of more than one service of the Department of Defense participate.

Military. - A term used in its broadest sense meaning of or pertaining to war or the affairs of war, whether Army, Navy, or Air Force.

Naval Campaign. - An operation or a connected series of operations conducted essentially by naval forces including all surface, subsurface, air, amphibious, and Marines, for the purpose of gaining, extending, or maintaining control of the sea.

Operation. - A military action, or the carrying out of a military mission, strategic, tactical, service, training, or administrative; the process of carrying on combat on land, on sea, or in the air, including movement, supply, attack, defense, and maneuvers needed to gain the objectives of any battle or campaign.

Strategic Air Operations. - Air operations contributing to the conduct of strategic air warfare.

Strategic Air Warfare. - Air combat and supporting operations designed to effect, through the systematic application of force to a selected series of vital targets, the progressive destruction and disintegration of the enemy's war-making capacity to a point where he no longer retains the ability or the will to wage war. Vital targets may include key manufacturing systems, sources of raw material, critical material, stock piles, power systems, transportation systems, communications facilities, concentration of uncommitted elements of enemy armed forces, key agricultural areas, and other such target systems.

/s/ C. E. WILSON

Changes Made in Key West Agreement by October 1, 1953, Revision

[Underlined items added, struck-through items deleted.]

<u>INTRODUCTION</u>

Congress, in the National Security Act of 1947, has described the basic policy embodied in the Act in the following terms:

"In enacting this legislation, it is the intent of Congress to provide a comprehensive program for the future security of the United States; to provide for the establishment of integrated policies and procedures for the departments, agencies, and functions of the Government relating to the national security; to provide three military departments for the operation and administration of the Army, the Navy (including naval aviation and the United States Marine Corps), and the Air Force, with their assigned combat and service components; to provide for their authoritative coordination and unified direction under civilian control but not to merge them; to provide for the effective strategic direction of the armed forces and for their operation under unified control and for their integration into an efficient team of land, naval, and air forces."

In accordance with the policy declared by Congress, and in accordance with the provisions of the National Security Act of 1947, <u>as amended (including Reorganization Plan No. 6 of 1953),</u> and to provide guidance for the departments and the joint agencies of ~~the National Military Establishment~~ <u>Department of Defense,</u> the Secretary of Defense, by direction of the President, hereby promulgates the following statement of the functions of the armed forces and the Joint Chiefs of Staff.

SECTION I.--PRINCIPLES

<u>1. No function in any part of the Department of Defense, or in any of its component agencies, shall be performed independent of the direction, authority, and control of the Secretary of Defense.</u>

~~1.~~<u>2.</u> There shall be the maximum practicable integration of the policies and procedures of the departments and agencies of the

~~National Military Establishment~~ Department of Defense. This does
not imply a merging of armed forces, but does demand a consonance
and correlation of policies and procedures throughout the ~~National~~
~~Military Establishment~~ Department of Defense, in order to produce
an effective, economical, harmonious, and business-like organization which will insure the military security of the United States.

~~2~~.3. (Same)

~~3~~.4. (Same)

~~4~~.5. (Same)

~~5~~.6. (Same)

SECTION II--COMMON FUNCTIONS OF THE ARMED FORCES

a. General--As prescribed by higher authority and under the
~~general~~ direction of the Secretary of Defense with the advice of
the Joint Chiefs of Staff, the armed forces shall conduct operations wherever and whenever necessary for the following purposes:

1. (Same)

2. (Same)

3. (Same)

4. (Same)

b. (Same)

1. In accordance with continuous guidance from the Joint
Chiefs of Staff, to prepare forces and to establish reserves of
equipment and supplies, for the effective prosecution of war and
to plan for the expansion of peacetime components to meet the
needs of war.

2. (Same)

3. To provide adequate, timely and reliable intelligence for
use within the ~~National Military Establishment~~ Department of
Defense.

4. (Same)

5. (Same)

6. (Same)

7. (Same)

8. (Same)

9. (Same)

10. (Same)

11. (Same)

12. (Same)

13. (Same)

14. <u>Unified Commands</u> - (a) <u>The Secretary of Defense after consultation with the Joint Chiefs of Staff shall designate in each case one of the military departments to serve as the executive agency for unified commands and other matters requiring such designation.</u>

(b) <u>Under the arrangements herein established, the channel of responsibility will be from the Secretary of Defense to the designated civilian Secretary of a military department.</u>

(c) <u>For the strategic direction and for the conduct of combat operations in emergency and wartime situations, the Secretary of the military department designated as executive agent shall forthwith authorize the military chief of each department in such situations to receive and transmit reports and orders and to act for such department in its executive agent capacity. The military chief will keep his Secretary, the Secretary of Defense and the Joint Chiefs of Staff fully informed of decisions made and actions taken under such authority. The military chief will in such circumstances be acting in the name and under the direction of the Secretary of Defense. Promulgated orders will directly state that fact.</u>

SECTION III.--FUNCTIONS OF THE JOINT CHIEFS OF STAFF

A. General.--The Joint Chiefs of Staff, consisting of <u>the Chairman</u>; the Chief of Staff, U. S. Army; the Chief of Naval Operations; <u>and</u> the Chief of Staff, U. S. Air

Force, and the Chief of Staff to the Commander in Chief, if there be one, are the principal military advisers to the President, the National Security Council and to the Secretary of Defense. The Commandant of the Marine Corps has co-equal status with the members of the Joint Chiefs of Staff on matters which directly concern the Marine Corps.

B. Specific.--Subject to the authority and direction of the President and the Secretary of Defense, it shall be the duty of the Joint Chiefs of Staff:

1. To prepare strategic plans and to provide for the strategic direction of the Armed Forces, to include the general direction of all combat operations including guidance for the operational control of forces and for the conduct of combat operations.

(2) (Same)

3. (Same)

4. To promulgate to the individual departments of the National Military Establishment Department of Defense general policies and doctrines in order to provide guidance in the preparation of their respective detailed plans.

5. (Same)

6. To establish unified commands in strategic areas when such unified commands are in the interest of national security and to authorise[sic] commanders thereof to establish such subordinate unified commands as may be necessary.

7. To designate, as necessary, one of their members as their executive agent for:

(a) A unified command;

(b) Certain operations, and specified commands;

(c) The development of special tactics, technique, and equipment, except as otherwise provided herein; and

~~(d) The conduct of joint training, except as otherwise provided herein.~~

8.<u>7</u>. To determine what means are required for the exercise of unified command, and to ~~assign~~ <u>recommend to the Secretary of Defense the assignment</u> to individual ~~members~~ <u>military departments</u> the responsibility of providing such means.

~~9~~.<u>8</u>. (Same)

~~10~~.<u>9</u>. (Same)

~~11~~.<u>10</u>. (Same)

~~12~~.<u>11</u>. (Same)

SECTION IV.--FUNCTIONS OF THE UNITED STATES ARMY - no change

SECTION V.--FUNCTIONS OF THE UNITED STATES NAVY AND MARINE CORPS - no change

SECTION VI.--FUNCTIONS OF THE UNITED STATES AIR FORCE - no change

SECTION VII.--GLOSSARY OF TERMS AND DEFINITIONS - no change except

Joint.--As used in this paper, and generally among the Armed Forces connotes activities, operations, organizations, etc., in which elements of more than one service of the ~~National Military Establishment~~ <u>Department of Defense</u> participate.

(20) Establishment of Continental Air Defense Command, 1 September 1954

Air defense of the United States remained on the back burner after the formation of the Air Force and remained well down on the priority list prior to the Soviet explosion of an atomic weapon. Following the outbreak of the Korean War, the lack of preparedness for air defense, and the magnitude of preparations required to defend the United States prompted apprehension as the population watched warily for the conflict to spread to the American continent. The necessity for dedicated air defense forces had already brought about the split of Air Defense Command (ADC) from Continental Air Command on 1 January 1951. An Army Antiaircraft Command, formed on 1 July 1950, had forces located in close proximity to their air defense counterparts and under the operational control of the air defense commander.

The Air Force was the key element in the air defense scheme, though the Army and Navy also possessed a role in an effective air defense system. In mid-1953 the Joint Chiefs of Staff (JCS) agreed to form a joint (although actually a unified) air defense command after several earlier attempts had failed. Effective 1 September 1954, the Continental Air Defense Command (CONAD) was established under the JCS with the Chief of Staff of the Air Force as executive agent. CONAD's Commander exercised operational control over ADC, the Army's Antiaircraft Command, and such naval forces as were allocated, which in wartime would consist of Navy and Marine Corps fighter aircraft, augmenting the peacetime contingent of radar ships.

****

Alfred Goldberg, ed., A History of the United States Air Force 1907-1957, (Princeton, N.J.: D. Van Nostrand Company, Inc., 1957), pp 129-33, 137.

THE JOINT CHIEFS OF STAFF
Washington 25, D.C.

SM-688-54
2 August 1954

MEMORANDUM FOR: Chief of Staff, U.S. Army
Chief of Naval Operations
Chief of Staff, U.S. Air Force
Commandant of the Marine Corps

Subject: Continental Air Defense Command

1. Under the authority of the Secretary of Defense, the Continental Air Defense Command (CONAD) is established, effective 1 September 1954, as a Joint Command for the air defense of the continental United States, with headquarters at Ent Air Force Base, Colorado Springs, Colorado. The Secretary of Defense has designated the Department of the Air Force as the executive agency for this command.

2. The Joint Chiefs of Staff designate General Benjamin W. Chidlaw as Commander in Chief, Continental Air Defense Command (CINCONAD).

3. The mission of CONAD and the terms of reference for the commander are contained in the annex hereto. CINCONAD will submit to the Joint Chiefs of Staff for approval, revisions to the attachments as experience dictates.

Info copies to:
  Commander in Chief, U.S. European Command
  Commander in Chief, Far East
  Commander in Chief, Pacific
  Commander in Chief, Atlantic
  Commander in Chief, Caribbean
  Commander in Chief, Alaska
  Commander in Chief, U.S. Northeast Command
  Commander, Strategic Air Command
  Commander in Chief, U.S. Naval Forces,
    Eastern Atlantic and Mediterranean
  Commander in Chief, U.S. Air Forces in Europe

277

4. The following forces are initially allocated to CONAD:
   <u>a</u>. The U.S.A.F. Air Defense Command.
   <u>b</u>. The U.S.A. Antiaircraft Command.
   <u>c</u>. Naval forces of the continuous radar coverage system.

5. Initial press releases regarding the establishment of this command will be made by the Secretary of Defense.

6. Addressees are directed to take action as necessary.

signed
EDWIN H. J. CARNS,
Brigadier General, USA,
Secretary

ANNEX

TERMS OF REFERENCE AND MISSION

1. The Continental Air Defense Command (CONAD) is established as a joint command for the defense of the continental United States against air attack. The Department of the Air Force has been designated as the executive agency therefor. Headquarters USAF Air Defense Command is additionally designated as Headquarters, CONAD, the staff of which will be augmented by appropriate representation from all services.

2. The Commander in Chief (CINC) CONAD will exercise operational control# over all forces assigned or otherwise made available by the Joint Chiefs of Staff or other proper authority, for defense of the continental United States against air attack. The command will be established in accordance with the appropriate provisions of Joint Action Armed Forces (JAAF), and the directives contained herein. The command shall consist initially of the U.S. Air Force Air Defense Command, the U.S. Army Antiaircraft Command, and a Naval Command composed of the naval forces of the continuous radar coverage system. During the periods that augmentation forces of the Army, Navy/Marine Corps, and Air Force are employed in air defense of the continental United States, operational control of such forces shall be temporarily vested in CINCONAD.

3. The CINCONAD will be a U.S. Air Force general officer who will be designated Commander, U.S. Air Force Air Defense Command. The Commanding General, Antiaircraft Command, will be the principal advisor to CINCONAD on Army matters pertaining to the CONAD. An appropriate Naval Command, under a flag officer, will be established with headquarters at Ent Air Force Base and the Commander will also be the principal advisor to CINCONAD on Navy matters pertaining to the CONAD. An appropriate Marine Corps representative will be assigned to the Staff of CINCONAD as principal advisor on Marine Corps matters pertaining to the CONAD. In the absence of the Joint Commander, the Senior Component Commander will assume temporary command.

4. Forces and operations of the seaward extensions of the early warning system will continue under the Commander in Chief, Atlantic

---

\# "Operational control" wherever used in this paper is as defined in Tab "D" hereto.

(CINCLANT), and the Commander in Chief, Pacific (CINCPAC), and early warning installations in Alaska and the Northeast Command under the Commander in Chief, Alaska (CINCAL) and the Commander in Chief, Northeast Command (CINCNE). However, the above commanders will support CINCONAD in accordance with plans approved by the Joint Chiefs of Staff and mutual agreements by the Commanders concerned, to insure that plans for, and the operations of, these elements of the early warning system will be responsive to the needs of CINCONAD.

5. The mission of the CINCONAD will be to:
   a. Defend the continental United States against air attack.
   b. Support CINCPAC, CINCLANT, CINCARIB, COMSAC, CINCAL and CINCNE in their missions to the maximum extent consistent with the primary mission outlined in subparagraph a above.

6. In carrying out his mission, CINCONAD will:
   a. Conduct operations to the limit of the capabilities of available forces in the defense of the continental United States against air attack.
   b. Prepare joint plans and requirements for the defense of the continental United States against air attack and submit these plans and requirements to the Joint Chiefs of Staff for approval.
   c. Implement JCS approved plans, through the appropriate component commands; and exercise such emergency powers as may be delegated to him by proper authority.
   d. Coordinate plans, operations and exercises with appropriate United States Commanders and with Canadian and Mexican Commanders in accordance with agreed Canada-United States and Mexico-United States defense policies.
   e. In coordination with# appropriate U.S. and allied commanders, plan for early warning systems and procedures which will provide early warning of air attack for the defense of the continental United States to insure that there [sic] systems are designed and operated in a manner responsive to continental air defense requirements and in consonance with national policy.
   f. In coordination with commanders concerned, establish procedures and methods of operation for all forces allocated, attached or otherwise made available for the air defense of the continental United States.

"In coordination with" whenever used in this paper is as defined in the "Dictionary of U.S. Military Terms for Joint Usage (Second Revision)."

g. In coordination with commanders concerned, prepare and submit to the Joint Chiefs of Staff for approval, plans for the full utilization of all military forces, including reserve forces, which have an air defense capability and which can temporarily augment the air defense forces in event of emergency.

h. When there exists an imminent threat of air attack upon the continental United States, or in case such an attack develops, assume operational control of those forces specifically having been made temporarily available from other commands (augmentation forces). Such operational control over forces having been made temporarily available from other commands, will be relinquished when the imminence of the threat has dissipated or when the attack is ended. In the event that the commander who made the forces available should consider that his primary mission requires their return to their permanent command assignments, he should first take appropriate requests to the Air Defense commander; if such request is not granted his next recourse is to the Joint Chiefs of Staff.

i. Plan for and conduct air defense exercises, including participation by augmentation forces, coordinating plans as appropriate with other U.S. commands and military agencies of Canada and Mexico.

j. Plan for, train, exercise and operate in coordination with appropriate authorities a Ground Observer Corps of necessary military personnel, and civilian volunteers.

k. Coordinate with appropriate military governmental and non-governmental agencies in the development of plans, policies and procedures for the security control of air traffic, the control of electromagnetic radiations, and the control of illumination and, when appropriate, initiate implementing actions therefor in the defense of continental United States against air attack.

l. Coordinate with the Federal Civil Defense Administration, state Civil Defense agencies, and other non-military agencies on matters of participation in air defense.

7. Based on missions or tasks assigned by CINCONAD in consonance with JCS approved plans, detailed planning as to forces and their deployments will be accomplished by component commanders coordinated as necessary with other commanders of their Services.

8. In matters not covered by JCS approved joint plans, doctrines or procedures, interim directives, promulgated by CINCONAD

will govern all Air Defense operations. These will be formulated
in consonance with existing inter-Service and inter-Command
agreements and decisions of the Joint Chiefs of Staff.

   9. Responsibilities of component commanders relating to the
participation of the forces provided by each Service for air
defense of the continental United States are contained in the
appendices to these terms of reference:

> Tab "A" - Air Force Forces
> Tab "B" - Army Forces
> Tab "C" - Naval Forces
> Tab "D" - Command Arrangements
> Tab "E" - Command Chart.

TAB "A"

RESPONSIBILITIES OF THE COMMANDER, AIR FORCE#
AIR DEFENSE COMMAND

1. Serve as the Commander of the Air Force component command of the CONAD.

2. Command all Air Force forces assigned or otherwise made available for air defense of the continental United States.

3. Coordinate with the other Service component commanders on matters of mutual interest.

4. Organize, administer, equip, train, and prepare for combat, units and combat crews of the Air Force as may be designated, assigned or attached to the Air Defense Command.

5. Recommend plans and policies for the employment of the military reserve forces of the Air Force in the air defense of the United States.

6. Develop tactics, techniques, and recommend equipment employed by Air Force forces in defense against air attack.

7. Participate in disaster relief and other domestic emergencies as required.

8. Prepare combat Air Force air defense units for overseas deployment as required, to include organizing, training, and equipping.

Commander, USAF ADC is also CINCONAD

TAB "B"

RESPONSIBILITIES OF THE COMMANDING GENERAL
ARMY ANTIAIRCRAFT COMMAND

1. Serve as the Commander of the Army Component of the CONAD.

2. Command all Army forces assigned or otherwise made available for air defense of the continental United States.

3. Provide above forces for operational control by the CINCONAD, in accordance with Tab "D", on the basis of JCS approved plans, doctrines and procedures pertaining to the air defense of the continental United States.

4. Develop detailed plans for Army forces and their deployments allocated for the air defense of the United States based on missions or tasks assigned by the CINCONAD in consonance with approved JCS plans.

5 Organize and establish a suitable headquarters and subordinate headquarters and commands as deemed necessary to accomplish the assigned missions or tasks.

6. Participate in ground defense, harbor defense, disaster relief, and other domestic emergencies when such participation will not interfere with the air defense mission.

7. Coordinate with the Department of the Army and other Army agencies on matters pertaining to the support, administration, organization, and equipping of Army units assigned or otheriwse[sic] made available for the air defense mission.

8. Prepare combat Army air defense units for overseas deployment as required, to include organizing, training, and equipping.

TAB "C"

RESPONSIBILITIES OF THE COMMANDER, NAVAL FORCES
AIR DEFENSE COMMAND

1. Organize a suitable command under a flag officer with appropriate headquarters necessary to meet the requirements set forth by higher authority.

2. Serve as the Commander of the Naval component command of the CONAD.

3. Coordinate with the other Service component commanders on matters of mutual interest.

4. Command all Naval forces assigned or otherwise allocated for employment in the continuous radar coverage of the continental United States air defense system.

5. Coordinate with appropriate fleet and training command for provision of naval augmentation forces for continental air defense.

6. Provide above forces for operational control by the CINCONAD in accordance with Tab "D", on the basis of JCS approved plans, doctrines and procedures pertaining to the air defense of the United States.

7. Provide appropriate Air Defense Commanders with required information relative to the status and operating characteristics of all Naval forces allocated for the air defense of the continental United States, and Naval augmentation forces and facilities capable of emergency employment in air defense of the United States.

8. Provide for the control of fire of the Antiaircraft batteries of vessels in port by the Air Defense Commander through the local Army, Antiaircraft Control Center, if one is established, otherwise through a Navy AA Control Center.

Tab "D"

COMMAND ARRANGEMENTS

SECTION I

Operational Control

1. The operational control exercised by CINCONAD over all forces assigned or otherwise made available, will consist of the following:

    a. Direct the conduct of the tactical air battle including the engagement and disengagement of air defense weapons.
    b. Control of fighters.
    c. Specify the conditions of alert.
    d. Station the early warning elements of the command and their control elements.
    e. Locate and deploy the combat elements of the command in accordance with plans approved by the Joint Chiefs of Staff.

SECTION II

Implementation of Operational Control

2. Operational control as defined above will be implemented in accordance with the chart, shown in Tab "E", in the following manner.

    a. When reporting on station, naval forces in contiguous radar coverage system come under operational control of the appropriate regional headquarters through the appropriate naval regional component channel.
    b. Naval surface forces made available in case of emergency will report for operational control to the Commander in Chief through the appropriate Naval Regional Component Commander. Limitations on the deployments of these surface forces may be prescribed by the fleet commander making the forces available.
    c. Naval aviation augmentation forces, provided in case of emergency, will report for operational control to the appropriate Air Division Command. The Fleet or Naval Air Training Command Commander making the forces available will prescribe whether such forces may be deployed to other than home bases.

d. Operational control, as defined in paragraph 1 Section I, above will be exercised by the joint air defense commanders in accordance with the chart in Tab "E".

e. Operational control will be exercised over all forces assigned or otherwise made available in a geographical area by the appropriate joint regional or sector air defense commander thereof.

f. Army antiaircraft units will pass to the operational control of the appropriate air defense commander upon deployment to tactical air defense positions.

SECTION III

Organization and Command Arrangements

1. The mission of air defense is a functional mission carried out on a geographical basis. Since time of reaction to the threat is all-important, successful Air Defense must be predicated upon decentralization of control. The United States is now divided into three Air Defense regions which are further subdivided into sectors; each region having an Air Defense Force Commander responsible for the defense of his area against air attack and utilizing all available forces of the military establishment which have an air defense capability.

2. The existing organization of the USAF Air Defense Command, with its air defense system for surveillance, warning and control, and combat is the basic structure which will be utilized for the Joint Command. Each USAF headquarters from command down to air division level will be additionally designated as a joint headquarters commanded by an Air Force officer and with appropriate representation from each Service. The Army Antiaircraft Command and the Naval Command will parallel this organization through the regional level and with a Component Commander or staff representation below regional level as experience dictates. The numbers of personnel who will represent each component commander at the Joint Regional Air Defense Force level will be a matter for agreement between him and the Commander, Joint Regional Air Defense Force.

3. The Chart, Tab "E", shows the lines of operational control and command as set forth in Tab "D".

4. The Service component commanders at regional or lower levels, in addition to their uni-service functions, shall be Army Deputy and Navy Deputy, respectively, to the joint commanders for matters of concern to their Services.

5. The Component Commanders will be responsible for the military command of their components in accordance with directives and procedures of their Services. Logistic and administrative support of the Service components will be provided as directed by the Service concerned.

6. The Joint manning of the staff of the Commander in Chief, due to the proximity of the headquarters of the component commands should be kept to a minimum. Thus, augmentation of the Command will be approximately as follows:

	ARMY	NAVY	MARINE
Operations and Training	1	1	-
Operations Analysis	1	1	-
Communication and Electronics	1	1	-
Plans and Requirements	1	2	-
Assistant to the DCS/O	1	1	1
Intelligence	1	1	-
Material	-	1	-
Comptroller	-	1	-
Information Services	1	1	-
	7	10	1

7. The command of naval forces in the continuous radar coverage system will be exercised at the regional (second echelon) level for the east and west coasts.

288

COMMAND AND OPERATIONAL CONTROL CHART

TAB "E"

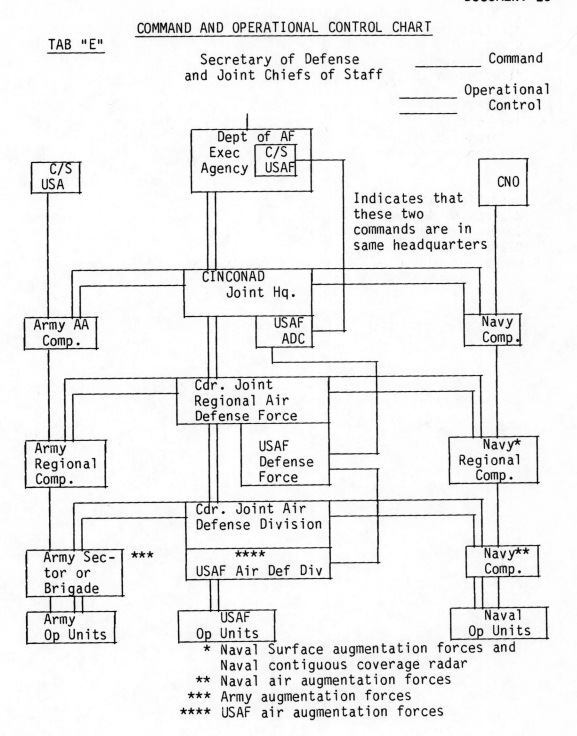

* Naval Surface augmentation forces and
  Naval contiguous coverage radar
** Naval air augmentation forces
*** Army augmentation forces
**** USAF air augmentation forces

(21) Secretary of Defense Wilson's Memorandum, 26 November 1956

Continuing strife within the Defense Department over the limited appropriations prompted the Secretary of Defense, Charles E. Wilson, to clarify several contentious problems existing between the Army and the Air Force. Promulgated in the form of a memorandum for the Armed Forces Policy Council, Secretary Wilson resolved to his own satisfaction several outstanding issues. The paramount one centered on the role of Army aviation, which had not been settled by either of the Pace-Finletter agreements or the 1953 reorganization. Under Eisenhower's "New Look" policy the defense of the United States depended primarily on atomic retaliatory power, with a concomitant lesser emphasis on ground forces and their corresponding air support units within the Air Force. As a result, the Army aircraft forces grew in number, though not necessarily in size, and their presence proved a source of disagreement among the Joint Chiefs of Staff (JCS) and the Defense Department. Secretary Wilson, in this memorandum, set forth the role of aircraft in the Army.

Under its "flexible response" strategy (first mentioned by Army Chief of Staff Gen. Maxwell D. Taylor in 1955), the Army intended to develop its own organic capability for air movement of combat units within the war zone. It was also vitally interested in four air power elements beyond the Army's organic capabilities, such as, air superiority in the battle zone, inter- and intra-theater airlift, and aircraft firepower. Despite emphasis on this new doctrine from the highest Army levels, limited budgets mitigated against its adoption.

Secretary Wilson once again defined the range of the combat zone, which extended normally 100 miles forward of and back from the contact line between opposing forces. He restricted the Army to four basic functions for which it could use aircraft: liaison and communications; observation, fire adjustment and topographic survey; airlift of personnel and materiel; and aeromedical evacuation. Wilson limited Army fixed-wing aircraft to 5,000 pounds and rotary-wing aircraft to 20,000 pounds, although the Secretary reserved the right to provide exemptions. He expressly provided that the allowance for a limited airlift capacity for the Army not be used to alter the size of Air Force forces and prohibited the Army from providing aircraft for such combat functions as close air support,

291

interdiction, and strategic airlift. Wilson deemed adequate the Air Force's airlift capacity for current strategic concepts.

In the realm of air defense, Secretary Wilson divided developmental responsibility for systems among the three services: the Army was assigned point defense surface-to-air missiles; the Air Force area defense missiles; and the Navy and Marine Corps responsibility for weapon systems to carry out their assigned functions (the Marine Corps being permitted to adapt weapons from one of the other three services). Wilson assigned air defense responsibilities in overseas areas to the air component commanders, with appropriate levels of support from other components.

This memorandum allowed the Army to continue development of surface-to-surface missiles for close support of field operations, subject to certain limitations -- specifically, their range was limited to about 200 miles -- and the tactical air support functions, beyond those provided by the missiles, would remain an Air Force responsibility. Although favored by the latter limitation, the Air Force potentially suffered from an Army missile program, since Wilson and the JCS could reduce tactical wings as the Army began to use missiles for close support.

The final provision of this memorandum assigned operational employment of land-based intermediate range ballistic missiles (IRBM) to the Air Force and ship-based IRBMs to the Navy. This limitation was consistent with holding Army missiles to 200 miles. (Operational employment of intercontinental ballistic missiles (ICBM) had already been assigned to the Air Force.) The memorandum represented settlement of an Army-Air Force disagreement over IRBMs, though the Army was allowed to continue limited feasibility studies on IRBMs with ranges exceeding 200 miles.

****

Robert F. Futrell, Ideas, Concepts and Doctrine: A History of Basic Thinking in the United States Air Force 1907-1964, (Maxwell AFB, Ala: Air University, 2nd edition, 1974) pp 228-29, 248, and 407-408.

THE SECRETARY OF DEFENSE
Washington

November 26, 1956

MEMORANDUM FOR: Members of the Armed Forces Policy Council

SUBJECT: Clarification of Roles and Missions to Improve the
          Effectiveness of Operation of the Department of Defense.

        Important changes in organization and in roles and
missions are not easily decided upon or effected. It is not as
though we were starting fresh with a clean sheet of paper, so to
speak, or could set up a theoretically perfect organization and
division of responsibilities between the Military Departments.
Assignment of responsibilities must continue to recognize the pre-
cedents of the past and the availability of men and facilities for
carrying out assigned missions. Problems of this nature would be
easier to solve if there were always complete unanimity of opinion
among all responsible executives of the Defense Department, both
military and civilian. The very nature of the problems, however,
and the varying background and experience of the individuals
serving in responsible positions make some differences of opinion
normal and to be expected.

        In spite of the differences of opinion which may exist,
there are times when conditions require that changes should be
made in administrative responsibilities and at such times decisions are mandatory. That is the situation now.

        The National Security Act of 1947 states:

                    "Declaration of Policy

        "Sec. 2. In enacting this legislation, it is the intent of
        Congress to provide a comprehensive program for the future
        security of the United States; to provide for the establish-
        ment of integrated policies and procedures for the depart-
        ments, agencies, and functions of the Government relating to
        the national security; to provide three military depart-
        ments, separately administered, for the operation and admi-
        nistration of the Army, the Navy (including naval aviation
        and the United States Marine Corps), and the Air Force, with
        their assigned combat and service components; to provide for

their authoritative coordination and unified direction under civilian control of the Secretary of Defense but not to merge them; to provide for the effective strategic direction of the armed forces and for their operation under unified control and for their integration into an efficient team of land, naval and air forces but not to establish a single Chief of Staff over the armed forces nor an armed forces general staff (but this is not to be interpreted as applying to the Joint Chiefs of Staff or Joint Staff)."

Nine years of experience operating under the National Security Act of 1947, as amended, have proved the soundness of this comprehensive program for national security.

The statement of roles and missions recommended by the Joint Chiefs of Staff at Key West and Newport and approved by Secretary of Defense James Forrestal, and as codified in 1953, have also proved to be sound and effectively to implement the intent of Congress as expressed in the National Security Act.

No basic changes in the present roles and missions of the armed services are necessary but the development of new weapons and of new strategic concepts, together with the nine years operating experience by the Department of Defense have pointed up the need for some clarification and clearer interpretation of the roles and missions of the armed services. We have recognized the need for a review of these matters and from time to time certain steps have been taken and we are now taking others to improve the effectiveness of our overall military establishment, to avoid unnecessary duplication of activities and functions, and to utilize most effectively the funds made available by the people through Congress.

I would like to point out that clarification and interpretation of roles and missions does not in itself predetermine the weapons to be used by each of the armed services and their numbers, nor the numbers of men to be trained in various fields. It should be clearly understood that the approval of roles and missions of the armed services for guidance in peacetime does not predetermine the weapons or forces which a commander in the field would be permitted to use in the event of war. Also, the development of a weapon by a particular military department does not in itself predetermine its use. Such determinations rest with the Secretary of Defense after considering the recommendations of the Joint Chiefs of Staff and the Secretaries of the Military Departments.

294

The recent clarification of command responsibilities for commanders should be most helpful in determining weapons and forces to be employed in various missions and should assist the Joint Chiefs of Staff in making recommendations in this regard to the Secretary of Defense in order to determine approved requirements for each of the armed services.

We have recently reviewed five important problem areas which need to be cleared up. The recommendations of the Joint Chiefs of Staff in regard to these matters have been carefully considered and their differences of opinion carefully weighed. In addition, I have given consideration to the opinions in these areas of responsible officials, both military and civilian, in the Office of the Secretary of Defense. These matters are being resolved as follows:

1. Use of Aircraft by U.S. Army.

In matters affecting the use of aircraft by the U.S. Army, the combat zone is defined as extending not more than 100 miles forward of the general line of contact between U. S. and enemy ground forces. Its extension to the rear of the general line of contact will be designated by the appropriate field commander, and normally extends back of the frontlines about 100 miles.

The Army Aviation Program will consist of those types of aircraft required to carry out the following Army functions envisaged within the combat zone:

a. Command, liaison, and communications.

b. Observation, visual and photographic reconnaissance, fire adjustment, and topographical survey.

c. Airlift of Army personnel and materiel.

d. Aeromedical evacuation.

The Army Aircraft Program to carry out these functions will be subject to the following limitations:

a. Fixed wing aircraft, convertiplanes, and vertical/short take-off and landing aircraft will have an empty weight not to exceed 5,000 pounds. Rotary wing aircraft will have an empty weight not to exceed 20,000 pounds. Specific exceptions to weight limitations for specific aircraft for specific purposes may be granted by the Secretary of Defense after consideration of Army requirements and appropriate Air Force functions and capabilities. (For example, the Secretary of Defense has just approved the purchase by the Army of five DeHavilland DHC-4 airplanes, "Twin Otter", for test and evaluation and is giving consideration to another project involving a plane in the development stage.)

b. The provision of a limited airlift capability within the Army Aviation Program shall not serve as a basis for increasing or decreasing Air Force forces necessary to support or protect the Army airlift forces. Provision of this limited airlift capability will apply only to small combat units and limited quantities of materiel to improve local mobility, and not to the provision of an airlift capability sufficient for the large-scale movement of sizeable Army combat units which would infringe on the mission of the Air Force.

c. As limited Army Aviation airlift capability becomes available to active Army forces, provision should be made for compensating reductions in other forms of Army transportation designed to operate within the combat zone.

d. The Army Aviation Program will not provide for aircraft to perform the following functions:

(1) Strategic and tactical airlift.

(a) Airlift of Army supplies, equipment, personnel and units from exterior points to points within Army combat zone.

(b) Airlift for evacuation of personnel and materiel from Army combat zone.

(c) Airlift for air movement of troops, supplies and equipment in the initial and subsequent phases of airborne operations.

(d) Aeromedical evacuation from Air Force operating locations within the combat zone through Air Force casualty staging units to hospital facilities outside combat zone, and aeromedical evacuation from an airhead or an airborne objective area where airborne operation includes air landed logistic support by Air Force.

(2) Tactical reconnaissance.

(3) Interdiction of the battlefield.

(4) Close combat air support.

e. The Army will not maintain unilateral aviation research facilities but will confine itself to development and determination of specific requirements peculiar to Army needs, to evaluation of proposals, and to user testing of equipment. The Army will make maximum use of Air Force and Navy aircraft research and development facilities. The Air Force and the Navy will be responsive to Army needs in such research activities on a reimbursable basis.

f. The Army will use existing types of Navy, Air Force or civilian aircraft when they are suitable, or may be suitably modified, to meet Army requirements, rather than attempt to develop and procure new types.

With regard to the 4 November 1952 Pace-Finletter Memorandum of Understanding, I am directing my staff to prepare an appropriate technical and detailed directive for coordination and issuance. Until this directive is approved, the Memorandum of Understanding will remain applicable except as specifically amended herein or by subsequent Secretary of Defense direction.

2. Adequacy of Airlift.

There has been a great deal of discussion and consideration given to the requirements for the airlift of tactical units and supplies examined, and it appears that it presently provides adequate airborne lift in the light of currently approved strategic concepts.

3. Air Defense

Consideration has been given to distinguishing between Air Force and Army responsibility for surface-to-air guided missile systems for defense of the Continental United States on the basis of area defense and point defense, as well as the criterion of an arbitrary range limitation.

Area and point defense systems cannot be defined with precision. Area defense involves the concept of locating defense units to intercept enemy attacks remote from and without reference to individual vital installations, industrial complexes or population centers. For such a defense system to be effective, extensive information gathering networks such as the Semi-Automatic Ground Environment (SAGE) system are required to trace continuously the enemy attack and transmit and present the data in usable form for guiding the defense weapons to counter the attack. As applied to surface-to-air missiles, this means that area defense missiles, because of their more widespread sitings, will normally receive their guidance information from the network system rather than from acquisition and tracking radars located in the vicinity of the missile launching site.

Point defense has as its purpose the defense of specified geographical areas, cities and vital installations. One distinguishing feature of point defense missiles is that their guidance information is received from radar located near the launching sites.

The present state of the art justifies development of point defense surface-to-air missile systems for use against air targets at expected altitudes out to a horizontal range of the order of 100 nautical miles.

It must be clearly understood that the Commander-in-Chief, Continental Air Defense Command, who has been given the responsibility for the Air Defense of the Continental United States, Alaska, and the United States area of responsibility in the North East, also has the authority and duty for stating his operational need for new or improved weapon systems and for recommending to the Joint Chiefs of Staff all new installations of any type. Therefore, no Service shall unilaterally plan for additional missile installations of either category (point or area defense) in support of CINCONAD's responsibilities until and unless they have been recommended by CINCONAD to the Joint Chiefs of Staff, and approved by that body.

In conformance with the above:

a. The Army is assigned responsibility for the development, procurement and manning of land-based surface-to-air missile systems for point defense. Currently, missile systems in the point defense category are the NIKE I, NIKE B, and land-based TALOS.

b. The Air Force is assigned responsibility for the development, procurement and manning of land-based surface-to-air missile systems for area defense. Currently, the missile system in the area defense category is the BOMARC.

c. The Navy, in close coordination with the Army and Air Force, is assigned responsibility for the development, procurement and employment of ship-based air defense weapon systems for the accomplishment of its assigned functions.

d. The Marine Corps is authorized to adapt to its organic use, such surface-to-air weapons systems developed by the other Services as may be required for the accomplishment of its assigned functions.

e. In overseas areas, the U.S. theater commander should normally assign responsibility for air defense to an air component commander, with appropriate participation by other components. Under this arrangement, Army units in the combat zone should continue to be responsible for their own local defense, employing organic means. Other Army air defense units should carry out point defense missions under the air component commander. Air Force units should carry out the area defense missions. Special emphasis should be given to simplicity, flexibility and mobility of weapon systems employed in air defense in overseas areas. Navy forces should continue to be responsible for their own air defense at sea, employing organic means. As approved by the theater commander, the air component commander should establish such procedures for coordinating Army, Navy, and Air Force air defense forces as may be required to carry out his responsibilities, and, in addition, should establish such detailed procedures as are necessary for proper coordination with national air defense commanders of allied countries.

4. Air Force Tactical Support of the Army.

The Army will continue its development of surface-to-surface missiles for close support of Army field operations with the following limitations:

a. That such missiles be designed and programmed for use against tactical targets within the zone of operations, defined as extending not more than 100 miles beyond the front lines. As such missiles would presumably be deployed behind the combat zone normally extending back of the front lines about 100 miles, this places a range limitation of about 200 miles on the design criteria for such weapons.

b. That the tactical air support functions beyond those that can be provided by Army surface-to-surface missiles as above defined remain the responsibility of the Air Force.

It is evident that the tactical air forces programmed for Army support should be reconsidered and the Joint Chiefs of Staff have been requested to furnish me with their recommendations for specific adjustments as to the number and types of planned Army guided missile and unguided rocket units and with the number of Air Force tactical wings which may be eliminated as a result of these decisions.

In preparing these recommendations, the development of balanced and interrelated Army and Air Force tactical support forces for the accomplishment of overall U.S. national security objectives must be considered, rather than the development of completely independent Army and Air Force forces to accomplish tactical support tasks. In developing force recommendations in this area, as well as for other U.S. military forces, it should be recognized that all operations in which our forces will be employed will be conducted under the command of the designated commanders who will have the necessary forces assigned to them for the conduct of their missions by higher authority.

5. Intermediate Range Ballistic Missile (IRBM)

In regard to the Intermediate Range Ballistic Missiles:

a. Operational employment of the land-based Intermediate Range Ballistic Missile system will be the sole responsibility of the U. S. Air Force.

b. Operational employment of the ship-based Intermediate Range Ballistic Missile system will be the sole responsibility of the U. S. Navy.

c. The U. S. Army will not plan at this time for the operational employment of the Intermediate Range Ballistic Missile or for any other missiles with ranges beyond 200 miles. This does not, however, prohibit the Army from making limited feasibility studies in this area.

(The Intercontinental Ballistic Missile has previously been assigned for operational employment to the U.S. Air Force.)

There are a number of other matters relating to research and development of particular weapons that will affect the choice of weapons to be used for various missions in the armed services. These choices can only be made after a careful technical review of the capabilities of the various weapons under development. I refer particularly to weapons systems such as the NIKE and TALOS and the multiple approach (JUPITER-THOR) to developments such as the Intermediate Range Ballistic Missile. This memorandum does not attempt to answer those questions which can only be decided after studies now in progress are completed, and should not be so interpreted.

In the meantime, these competing weapons systems will be continued with support from Fiscal Year '57 funds until the completion of the technical evaluation referred to above. Budget support in Fiscal Year '58 for the land-based TALOS, as required, will be provided by the U.S. Army. Budget support in Fiscal Year '58 for the land-based Intermediate Range Ballistic Missile Program, as required, will be provided by the U. S. Air Force.

In view of the great interest in these matters in the Congress, copies of this memorandum are being sent to the appropriate Congressional Committees. In addition, in order that there can be full understanding of these decisions within the Military Departments and by the public, copies of this memorandum are being made available to the press.

(signed)
C. E. Wilson

Distribution:
  Members of the Armed Forces Policy Council:
    Secretary of Defense
    Deputy Secretary of Defense
    Secretary of the Army
    Secretary of the Navy
    Secretary of the Air Force
    Chairman, Joint Chiefs of Staff
    Chief of Staff, U.S. Army
    Chief of Naval Operations
    Chief of Staff, U.S. Air Force
    Commandant, Marine Corps
  Assistant Secretaries of Defense
  General Counsel

(22) **Secretary of Defense Wilson's Directive (5160.2)**
    on Single Manager Assignment for Airlift Service,
    7 December 1956.

In 1956, following implementation of Department of
Defense (DOD) policies regarding missions assigned to
various services, Secretary Wilson designated the
Secretary of the Air Force as the single manager for
airlift within the DOD. Since it superseded the
directive of 25 June 1952, the new directive was issued
in the same series. The assignment was meant to ensure
wartime airlift needs were met by providing a peacetime
organization capable of carrying out the wartime
mission, and to provide forces in being possessing
adequate training to meet those wartime needs. It
would also integrate into a single agency all transport
aircraft involved in point-to-point scheduled service
in the most economical manner. A major objective was
"to develop and guide the peacetime employment of
airlift services in a manner that will enhance the
wartime airlift capability...."
No mention was made in the revised directive of
tactical troop transport, combat resupply, or travel
over naval administrative routes. Secretary Wilson was
determined to have a single airlift agency, with a
minimum of non-Military Air Transport Service (MATS)
transport aircraft in the air, thereby promoting
economy and efficiency. However, the military
departments were allowed their own aircraft for
administrative airlift and combat readiness training.
One factor which prompted this assignment was the
proliferation of special-purpose airlift aircraft,
which flourished despite the presence of MATS. In 1955
the Hoover Commission on Government Organization
recommended that all DOD airlift services, except for a
drastically reduced fleet of administrative aircraft,
be assigned to MATS, and that peacetime operation of
MATS be restricted and limited to those persons and
cargoes deemed necessary for military air transport,
and only after maximum utilization of commercial
carriers. As a result, the Air Force transferred
Tactical Air Command's (TAC) C-124 transports to MATS,
and the Navy transferred 15 four-engine aircraft from
its fleet logistics wings. Despite this assignment,
some 920 Air Force and Navy transport aircraft remained
outside the control of MATS.
One significant change brought about by this
directive was the switch in funding methodology which
put MATS in the industrial fund category. That meant

that each agency using MATS services would be forced to purchase these services and pay for them. This method of reimbursement was expected to cause the military users to prioritize their cargoes, relieving MATS of a percentage of the financial burden and promoting economy by making customers scrutinize their need for air transport. MATS industrial funding began on 1 July 1958, when it received a one-time appropriation of $75 million to be used as a revolving fund that would be replenished as airlift was sold to service customers.

The biggest change of all was psychological, the change that said MATS was to use its flying as a way to prepare for war. Rather than simply providing a military airline, MATS was providing airlift while at the same time performing its primary task of being prepared for war.

****

Robert F. Futrell, <u>Ideas, Concepts and Doctrine: A History of Basic Thinking in the United States Air Force 1907-1964</u>, (Maxwell AFB, Ala: Air University, 2nd edition, 1974) pp 322-29.

William H. Tunner, <u>Over the Hump</u>, Reprint Edition, (Washington, D.C.: Office of Air Force History, 1985), pp 281-306.

DEPARTMENT OF DEFENSE DIRECTIVE

SUBJECT   Single Manager Assignment for Airlift Service

References: (a) DOD Directive 4000.8, November 17, 1952, Basic
                    Regulations for Military Supply System.

               (b) DOD Directive 5160.12, January 31, 1956,
                    Policies for Implementation of Single Manager
                    Assignments.

               (c) DOD Directive 5160.2, June 25, 1952, The
                    Military Air Transport Service (MATS)(cancelled
                    herein)

               (d) DOD Directive 4100.15, April 27, 1955,
                    Commercial and Industrial Type Facilities.

               (e) Section 405(a), National Security Act, as
                    amended.

               (f) Memo from the Deputy Secretary of Defense to the
                    Secretary of the Air Force, December 23, 1955,
                    directing the application of the industrial fund
                    principle to transport functions of MATS.

               (g) Regulations Covering the Operation of Working
                    Capital Funds for Industrial and Commercial Type
                    Establishments(Industrial Funds), July 13, 1950.

               (h) Memo from the Deputy Secretary of Defense to the
                    Secretaries of the Military Departments and the
                    Assistant Secretaries of Defense, April 5, 1956,
                    establishing inventory of management positions
                    within the Department of Defense.

I.   AUTHORITY AND PURPOSE

        A. Pursuant to the authority vested in the Secretary of
            Defense by the National Security Act of 1947, as
            amended, a Single Manager Service Assignment is
            hereby directed within the Department of Defense
            with authority, functions responsibilities, and
            relationships as set forth herein.

305

B. The purposes and objectives of this assignment with respect to the military airlift mission are:

1. To ensure that the approved D-Day and wartime airlift requirements of the Department of Defense are met.

2. To provide that level of military airlift capability and organizational structure required for 1. above having due regard for the commercial airlift available.

3. To integrate into a single military agency of the Department of Defense all transport type aircraft engaged in scheduled point-to-point service or aircraft whose operations are susceptible of such scheduling, and such organizational and other transport aircraft as may be specifically designated by the Secretary of Defense.

4. To provide the most effective and economical airlift service to support the Armed Forces under all conditions consistent with references (a) and (b), military requirements, and the airlift service available to the Department of Defense from United States commercial air carriers.

5. To develop and guide the peacetime employment of airlift services in a manner that will enhance the wartime airlift capability, achieve greater flexibility and mobility of forces, and increase logistics effectiveness and economy.

II. CANCELLATION

This Directive cancels and supersedes reference (c)

III. DEFINITIONS

For the purpose of this Directive, the following definitions, in addition to those set forth in reference (b) which are relevant to this assignment, will apply:

A. Military Air Transport Service (MATS) - The Single Manager Operating Agency for Airlift Service (hereinafter referred to as the Agency).

306

B. <u>Airlift Service</u> - The performance or procurement of air transportation and services incident thereto required for the movement of persons, cargo, mail or other goods.

C. <u>Administrative Airlift Service</u> - The airlift service provided by specifically identifiable aircraft assigned to organizations or commands for internal administration.

D. <u>Common User Airlift Service</u> - The airlift service provided on a common basis for all Department of Defense agencies and, as authorized, for other agencies of the United States Government.

E. <u>Attached Airlift Service</u> - The airlift service provided to a military organization or command by an air transport unit of the Agency attached to that organization or command for operational control.

F. <u>Organizational Airlift Service</u> - The airlift service provided by those military aircraft not assigned to the Agency as specified in Section IV B herein.

G. <u>Controlled Transport Aircraft</u> - Transport aircraft designated by the Secretary of Defense for transfer or assignment to the Agency.

H. <u>Air Transport Unit</u> - An organizational unit which provides airlift service or support through the operation of controlled transport aircraft.

I. <u>Military Airlift Capability</u> - The airlift which the Agency is capable of providing for the air movement of passengers and cargo through the use of controlled transport aircraft.

IV.   <u>COMPOSITION</u>

A. The Agency will be composed of Controlled Transport Aircraft together with personnel, facilities, and equipment necessary to support the operation.

B. It is not intended to assign to the Agency transport aircraft in the following categories:

1. Those whose design or configuration limits their employment to specialized tasks.

2. Those required by the Military Departments for Administrative Airlift Service or Combat Readiness Training.

3. Those whose assignment outside of the Agency is required by overriding military considerations.

V. DELEGATION OF AUTHORITIES AND RESPONSIBILITIES

A. The Secretary of the Air Force is hereby designated as the Single Manager for Airlift Service with authorities and responsibilities as assigned herein, subject to overall guidance, policies and programs of the Secretary of Defense.

B. The Secretary of the Air Force will be responsible for utilization of all applicable portions of reference (b) which portions shall be considered to be policy pertinent to this assignment, except where such portions are specifically codified or amplified herein.

C. The Joint Chiefs of Staff will:

1. Review and evaluate requirements of the Military Departments for airlift service, training, and total airlift capacity and the Agency's capability to meet them.

2. Allocate the airlift capacity of the Agency as required to meet approved Joint Chiefs of Staff plans or upon request by the Agency or one of the Military Departments.

3. On their own initiative or on the request of the Secretary of Defense prepare recommendations regarding the designation of additional aircraft to be transferred to the Agency.

4. Review and approve appropriate plans developed by the Agency in support of war plans developed by the Joint Chiefs of Staff and approved by the Secretary of Defense.

VI.   AUTHORITIES AND RESPONSIBILITIES OF THE SINGLE MANAGER

The Secretary of the Air Force as Single Manager will:

A.   Organization and Management

1.   Establish and organize, as a major component of the United States Air Force, the Single Manager Operating Agency for Airlift Service which shall have no functions other than those assigned to it by this Directive.

2.   Designate as Executive Director for Airlift Service a general officer nominated by the Chief of Staff, United States Air Force, subject to the approval of the Secretary of Defense. The Executive Director shall have no other duties but to direct the operations of the Military Air Transport Service, including such technical services as are set forth in Appendix A. The Executive Director shall be responsible to the Secretary of the Air Force through channels prescribed by that Secretary.

3.   Organize the Administrative Committee in accordance with reference (b).

4.   Organize, equip and attach air transport units necessary to meet military requirements as determined by the Joint Chiefs of Staff.

B.   Airlift Requirements

1.   Prescribe, in coordination with the Joint Chiefs of Staff, the procedures to be followed by the Military Departments in reporting their airlift service requirements.

C.   Budgeting and Funding

1.   In accordance with references (e), (f), and (g), take all necessary steps to establish airlift service on an industrial fund basis at an early date and in any case not later than January 1, 1958.

2. Budget and fund for the operation of the Agency in accordance with policies and procedures cooperatively developed with and concurred in by the Assistant Secretary of Defense (Comptroller).

D. Personnel

1. Staff the agency headquarters and its subordinate elements with civilian employees who will be employees of the Department of the Air Force and military personnel from all Services, as appropriate, not necessarily with equal representation. Initially existing personnel, personnel spaces, funds, facilities and equipment will be adjusted among the Military Departments for responsibilities assigned to the Agency in order to meet the support requirements of the Single Manager created by this Directive. Such personnel adjustments will be effected in accordance with DOD Instruction 1404.4, dated April 19, 1955, and other applicable directives.

2. Positions within the Agency will be identified as military or civilian based on criteria established by the Secretary of Defense. Military staff positions subordinate to the Executive Director, at either the Agency Headquarters or its subordinate elements, will be alternated among the Military Services having representation in the Agency on a basis agreed to by the Single Manager and the Secretaries of the other Department or Departments concerned, with due consideration being given to the qualifications of the individuals concerned and career program needs of each Military Department.

E. General Functions

1. Maintain and operate a military airlift service system within limits approved by the Secretary of Defense to

(a) maintain an adequate emergency readiness position,

(b) carry out realistic training programs,

(c) provide attached airlift service as required to all agencies of the Department of Defense, and

(d) provide common user airlift service as required by all agencies of the Department of Defense and, as authorized, for other agencies of the United States Government

 (1) between points in the United States and oversea areas,

 (2) between and within overseas areas, and

 (3) within the United States when necessary for reasons of security or to supplement commercial air carrier service based on determinations of the Military Traffic Management Agency.

2. Augment the airlift capacity of the Agency as required to meet requirements by the use of commercial airlift service in peacetime on a basis which will contribute to the sound economic development of an increased modern civil airlift capacity and enhance the ability of civil carriers to operate with maximum effectiveness in support of the military forces in time of war.

3. Procure by contract or otherwise all commercial airlift service between the United States and overseas areas and within and between overseas areas except individual travel and package air freight or express, and such other airlift service as may be directed by the Secretary of Defense.

4. Control the volume and rate of flow of traffic into the military airlift service system. Loading plans and loading and unloading of cargo and passengers shall be the responsibility of the Agency, utilizing the advice and participation of the shippers, as appropriate.

5. Develop an expanded mobilization base through the maximum feasible use of commercial airlift,

311

maintenance, repair and overhaul, and terminal services, consistent with military requirements and the efficient employment of Department of Defense resources.

F. Planning and Programming

1. Prepare plans in support of approved Joint War Plans consistent with Joint Chiefs of Staff allocations approved by the Secretary of Defense for the employment and expansion of the Agency in time of war or national emergency.

2. Coordinate appropriate plans of the Agency with the Military Services and transmit such plans to the Joint Chiefs of Staff for approval.

3. Prepare and submit to the Secretary of Defense the annual operating plans and programs of the Agency in support of Department of Defense requirements, consistent with approved Joint Chiefs of Staff requirements for the employment of the Agency in time of peace.

IMPLEMENTATION

A. It is the express intent of this Directive that implementation of the Single Manager Assignment for Airlift Service will obviate the requirement for any other activity within the Department of Defense to perform airlift service functions which duplicate the functions of the Agency. Accordingly, the Secretary of each Military Department will abolish any organizational unit or part thereof performing functions which duplicate those assigned to the Agency as soon as the Agency has assumed its responsibilities for such functions.

B. Terms of Reference, regulations and procedures, including plans showing the proposed organization, staffing and personnel requirements of the Agency, together with statements of any adjustments in personnel, personnel spaces, facilities, and equipment required to implement this Directive, will be developed and coordinated with the Military Departments by the Single Manager and transmitted to

the Secretary of Defense for approval. The Assistant
Secretary of Defense (Supply and Logistics) will
coordinate the approval of such matters with other
cognizant elements of the Office of the Secretary of
Defense. Adjustments of funds will continue to be
handled in the statutory manner through the Office
of the Assistant Secretary of Defense (Comptroller).

1. Within 60 days after issuance of this Directive,
    the Single manager will submit to the Secretary
    of Defense for approval recommended Terms of
    Reference governing

    (a) the relationship between the Military
         Departments and the Agency, and between
         the Agency and the Military Traffic
         Management Agency,

    (b) the maintenance of military airlift service
         capability required for war,

    (c) the operation of the Agency, together with
         the detailed plans showing the organiza-
         tion, functions, personnel requirements and
         staffing patterns for the Agency, including
         the schedule of military and civilian posi-
         tions developed in accordance with
         Paragraph VI D 1 above, and

    (d) the delineation of the responsibilities of
         each Military Department for providing
         support to the Agency.

2. Upon approval of the Terms of Reference by the
    Secretary of Defense, the Single Manager will
    activate the Agency.

3. The Secretaries of the Navy and the Air Force
    will take action to transfer transport aircraft
    to the Agency as indicated in Appendix B and
    assign necessary support and operating person-
    nel.

4. The Secretary of Defense will review at least
    annually the assignment of Department of Defense
    transport aircraft to determine the desirability

of designating additional aircraft for transfer to the Agency.

VIII.   <u>EFFECTIVE DATE</u>

This Directive is effective upon issuance.

(signed)
C. E. Wilson
Secretary of Defense

Inclosures - 2
  1. Appendix A
  2. Appendix B

APPENDIX A

TECHNICAL SERVICES (NON-AIRLIFT) OF THE DEPARTMENT OF THE AIR FORCE WHICH MAY BE ASSIGNED UNDER THE CONTROL OF THE EXECUTIVE DIRECTOR, SINGLE MANAGER OPERATING AGENCY FOR AIRLIFT SERVICE

The operations of the following Technical Services (non-airlift) of the Department of the Air Force may be assigned to the Agency at the discretion of the Single Manager for administrative convenience; being non-airlift functions, they are not subject to industrial funding.

1. Air Photographic and Charting Service

2. Air Rescue Service

3. Airways and Air Communications Service

4. Air Weather Service

5. Flight Service

APPENDIX B

TRANSPORT AIRCRAFT TO BE TRANSFERRED BY THE SECRETARIES OF THE
NAVY AND THE AIR FORCE TO THE DEPARTMENT OF DEFENSE
SINGLE MANAGER AGENCY FOR AIRLIFT SERVICE 1/ & 2/

1. The following aircraft will be transferred to the
Department of Defense Single Manager Agency for Airlift Service
upon its activation:

a. All transport aircraft assigned to the existing
Military Air Transport Service including those
assigned to the 1254th Air Transport Group
(Special Missions) and the 1706th Air Transport
Group (Aeromedical Evacuation).

b. All transport aircraft of the Naval components of
the Military Air Transport Service and all four
engine transport aircraft of the Fleet Logistic
Air Wings with the exception of twenty (20) which
may be retained for assignment to the Atlantic
and Pacific Fleets, ten (10) which may be
retained for administrative airlift service, and
all water based transport aircraft.

c. All heavy transport aircraft of the Troop Carrier
elements of the Tactical Air Command.

1/ The actual number of transport aircraft transferred will be
based on the inventory as of July 1, 1956, adjusted to reflect
increases resulting from procurement or transfers and decreases
resulting from attrition as of the date of transfer.

2/ Reimbursement to the Military Air Transport Service for
Special Air Missions, Air Evacuation, and troop carrier operations
will be from the Service having the airlift mission responsibility.

(23) Secretary of Defense Wilson's Directive (5160.22), 18 March 1957

In March 1957, Secretary Wilson issued Department of Defense Directive 5160.22, designed to clarify roles and missions overlaps between the Army and the Air Force. Coming as it did only a few months after his earlier memorandum on roles and missions, it would appear that his 26 November memorandum had met some resistance in the services. The new directive rescinded and cancelled the second Pace-Finletter Agreement, confirmed the principles embodied in the 26 November 1956 memorandum, and clarified roles and missions imparted to the Army aviation program. The directive's stated purpose was to ensure that the Army could employ aircraft for its internal administration without duplicating Air Force capabilities, establish the scope of the Army's aviation program, and explain Air Force responsibilities to provide aviation support for the Army.

The support the Air Force was expected to provide the Army included airlift of supplies from exterior points to the combat zone, evacuation of materiel and personnel from the Army combat zone, airborne operations, and aeromedical evacuation from the combat zone. The Army was authorized aircraft for: command, liaison, and communications; observation, reconnaissance, fire adjustment, and topographical survey; airlift of Army personnel and material (within the combat zone); and aeromedical evacuation within the combat zone, excluding areas under Air Force logistic support. This directive retained the weight limits prescribed for Army aviation by the Pace-Finletter Agreement, that is, 5,000 pounds for fixed-wing aircraft, and 20,000 pounds for rotary-wing aircraft.

However, the limited Army aviation capacity was not to serve as the basis for increasing or decreasing Air Force forces. Moreover, to avoid duplicating Air Force capabilities, it limited the Army's airlift capacity so that the Army could not move sizeable combat units. The Army also had to provide corresponding reductions in surface transportation to balance the inclusion of Army aircraft. The directive urged the Army to use Air Force and Navy services and aircraft.

The Air Force was willing to have the Army assume a greater combat air support capability as the Air Force attempted to upgrade its atomic capability while reducing its conventional commitment.

317

BASIC DOCUMENTS

****

Robert F. Futrell, <u>Ideas, Concepts and Doctrine: A History of Basic Thinking in the United States Air Force 1907-1964</u>, (Maxwell AFB, Ala: Air University, 2nd edition, 1974) pp 264-67.

Alfred Goldberg, ed., <u>A History of the United States Air Force 1907-1957</u>, (Princeton, N.J.: D. Van Nostrand Company, Inc., 1957), pp 143-45.

DEPARTMENT OF DEFENSE DIRECTIVE

SUBJECT   Clarification of Roles and Missions of the
Departments of the Army and the Air Force
Regarding Use of Aircraft

References: (a) Memorandum of Understanding Between the
Secretary of the Army and the Secretary of
the Air Force Relating to Army Organic
Aviation, 4 November 1952(cancelled herein)

              (b) DoD Directive 5100.1, "Functions of the
Armed Forces and the Joint Chiefs of Staff"

              (c) Secretary of Defense Memorandum for the
Members of the Armed Forces Policy Council,
"Clarification of Roles and Missions to Improve
the Effectiveness of Operation of the Department
of Defense," 26 November 1956

I. AUTHORITY AND PURPOSE

Pursuant to the authority contained in the National Security
Act of 1947, as amended, and in consonance with reference
(b), this directive is issued for the purpose of:

1. Defining the scope of the U.S. Army aviation program
and establishment.

2. Insuring that the U.S. Army may employ aircraft necessary for its internal requirements in the conduct of
operations on land, without duplicating the functions
assigned to the U.S. Air Force.

3. Stressing and clarifying the responsibilities of the U.S.
Air Force with regard to providing aviation support for
the U.S. Army.

II. DEFINITION

For purposes of this directive, the combat zone is defined
as extending not more than 100 miles forward of the general
line of contact between U.S. and enemy ground forces. Its
extension to the rear of the general line of contact will be

designated by the appropriate field commander, and normally
extends back of the frontlines about 100 miles.

III. POLICY AND RESPONSIBILITIES

   A. General

   As stated in reference (b), the U.S. Air Force includes
   among its primary responsibilities those of furnishing
   close combat and logistical air support for the U.S.
   Army. These responsibilities are continuing in nature,
   from the immediate outset and throughout the course of
   all combat operations, and for peacetime training.
   While the extent of such support, by nature, is not
   readily susceptible of specific delimitation, it must at
   all times meet the reasonable requirements specified by
   the U.S. Army, either for combat operations or for
   training, and the U.S. Air Force shall be prepared to
   devote an appreciable portion of its resources to such
   support and to the establishment and organization which
   may be required therefor.

      1. U.S. Air Force

      Consistent with its assigned function of furnishing
      logistical air support to the U.S. Army, the U.S.
      Air Force will, as required, provide the following:

      a. Airlift of Army supplies, equipment, personnel
         and units from exterior points to points within
         the Army combat zone.

      b. Airlift for the evacuation of personnel and
         materiel from the Army combat zone.

      c. Airlift for the air movement of troops, supplies,
         and equipment in the initial and subsequent
         phases of airborne operations.

      d. Aeromedical evacuation from Air Force operat-
         ing locations within the combat zone through
         Air Force casualty staging units to hospital
         facilities outside the combat zone; and the aero-
         medical evacuation from an airhead or an airborne
         objective area where airborne operation includes
         air landed logistical support by the Air Force.

320

2. <u>U.S. Army</u>

The U.S. Army Aviation Program will consist of
those types of aircraft required to carry out the
following Army functions envisaged within the combat zone and shall be used by the Army exclusively
as a basis for developing Army requirements for
aircraft and for the normal employment of Army
Aviation. The capability of operation from unim-
proved fields should be adopted as a basic objective
for the development of Army Aviation. This
capability is essential to the quality of responsiveness, and responsiveness is a quality essential to
that aviation whose day-to-day operations must be
intimately coordinated with the actions of surface
forces. Army organic aircraft will be used by the
responsible Army commander as he considers
necessary for the discharge of his military mission.

a. <u>Command, liaison, courier and communications</u> -
This includes aerial wire-laying and aviation to
assist in the direction, coordination and control
of Army forces in the field.

b. <u>Observation, visual and photographic reconnaissance, fire adjustment and topographical survey</u> -
This includes aerial observation to amplify and
supplement other Army methods of observation
for the purpose of locating, verifying and
evaluating targets, adjusting fire, terrain
study, or obtaining information on enemy forces,
complementing that obtained by air reconnaissance
agencies of the other Services; this includes
limited aerial photography incident to these
purposes.

c. <u>Airlift of Army personnel and material</u> -
Transportation of Army supplies, equipment,
personnel, and small units within the Army
combat zone in the course of combat and logistical operation. Includes the movement of small
units to execute small-scale air-landed operations, the movement of reserves, and the shifting
or relocation of small units and individuals
within the combat zone as the situation may dictate. Includes expeditious movement of criti-

cally needed supplies or equipment, or both, within the combat zone, supplementing the ground transportation system operating within the field Army. Does not include the execution of joint airborne operations.

d. <u>Aeromedical evacuation</u> - Aeromedical evacuation within the Army combat zone to include battlefield pickup of casualties (except those from an airhead or airborne objective area which is supported by Air Force air-landed logistical support), air transport to initial point of treatment and any subsequent moves to hospital facilities within the Army combat zone.

B. <u>Limitations</u>

The U.S. Army Aircraft Program, carrying out the functions set forth in A above, will be subject to the following limitations:

1. Fixed wing aircraft, convertiplanes, and vertical/ short take-off and landing aircraft will have an empty weight not to exceed 5,000 pounds. Rotary wing aircraft will have an empty weight not to exceed 20,000 pounds. Specific exceptions to weight limitations for specific aircraft for specific purposes may be granted by the Secretary of Defense after consideration of U.S. Army requirements and appropriate U.S. Air Force functions and capabilities.

2. The provision of a limited airlift capability within the U.S. Army Aviation Program shall not serve as a basis for increasing or decreasing U.S. Air Force forces necessary to support or protect the U.S. Army airlift forces. Provision of this limited airlift capability will apply only to small combat units and limited quantities of materiel to improve local mobility, and not the provision of an airlift capability sufficient for the large-scale movement of sizeable U.S. Army combat units which would duplicate the mission of the U.S. Air Force.

3. As limited Army aviation airlift capability becomes available to active Army forces, provision should be made for compensating reductions in other forms of

Army transportation designed to operate within the combat zone.

4. The U.S. Army Aviation Program will not provide for aircraft to perform the following functions:

   a. Strategic and tactical airlift, as outlined in Section III, Subparagraphs A.1.a. through d., above.

   b. Tactical reconnaissance.

   c. Interdiction of the battlefield.

   d. Close combat air support.

5. The U.S. Army will not maintain unilateral aviation research facilities, but will confine itself to development and determination of specific requirements peculiar to Army needs, to evaluation of proposals, and to user testing of equipment. The U.S. Army will make maximum use of U.S. Air Force and U.S. Navy aircraft research and development facilities. The U.S. Air Force and the U.S. Navy will be responsive to U.S. Army needs in such research activities on a reimbursable basis.

6. The U.S. Army will use existing types of U.S. Navy, U.S. Air Force or civilian aircraft when they are suitable, or may be suitably modified, to meet Army requirements, rather than attempt to develop and procure new types.

C. Army aircraft may, as required by the U.S. Army, be employed in peacetime operations and in training for the functions outlined above.

IV. <u>INTERPRETATION</u>

Nothing contained in this directive is intended to, nor shall be construed as modifying, altering, or rescinding any of the assigned functions of the Armed Forces; it provides a clarification and interpretation of the roles and missions of the armed services, necessitated by the development of new weapons and of new strategic concepts.

V. RESCISSION AND EFFECTIVE DATE

This directive is effective immediately. Reference (a) is hereby superseded.

VI. ACTION REQUIRED

The Secretary of the Army and the Secretary of the Air Force will take appropriate action to insure that the provisions of this directive are fully implemented within their respective Departments.

(signed)
C. E. Wilson
Secretary of Defense

(24) **Department Of Defense Reorganization Act of 1958, 6 August 1958**

The essentials of the Defense Reorganization Act of 1958 have continued basically unchanged through 1985. Desiring greater efficiency and in hopes of eliminating some of the encumbering interservice rivalries, the Eisenhower administration aimed to reorganize the Department of Defense (DOD) in early 1958. During 1957 and 1958 congressional and public policy study groups noted the Defense Department's many problems. The Symington Committee reported in January 1957 that DOD suffered from duplication and triplification, promoting waste and retarding modernization. Several congressional committees, examining the U.S. space and missiles program in the aftermath of Sputnik, blamed interservice rivalries for development delays. A study group sponsored by the Rockefeller Fund disclosed three major defects in DOD structure: service roles and missions had become competitive, rather than complementary as technology and threats evolved; Joint Chiefs of Staff (JCS) organization and responsibilities precluded coherent strategic direction; and the Secretary of Defense, burdened with arbitrating interservice disputes, was unable to initiate and direct military policy development.

Each of the services held different views on reorganization. Air Force Chief of Staff Gen. Nathan F. Twining, in a 1956 address, favored a single service, though he felt that the creation of additional unified commands was more likely. The Air Force endorsed the concept of a single defense chief of staff, supported by a general staff, but the Navy was vigorously opposed. The reorganization which ultimately occurred became the responsibility of the newly-installed Secretary of Defense, Neil H. McElroy.

President Dwight D. Eisenhower's State of the Union message on 9 January 1958 prodded Secretary McElroy into action. He appointed a special assistant for reorganization and an expert consultative group including the incumbent JCS Chairman and two former Chairmen. Over a six-week period, this group interviewed many people and provided draft legislation which McElroy included in his report to the President. On 3 April Eisenhower, in a message to Congress, outlined the essential congressional actions and his own administrative orders to reorganize the Defense Department.

Congress passed the Defense Reorganization Act of

1958 with few changes and President Eisenhower signed it into law on 6 August. The act greatly strengthened the powers of the Secretary of Defense at the expense of the service secretaries. The operational chain of command no longer passed through the service secretaries; rather it ran from the President to the Secretary of Defense, and through the corporate JCS to the unified and specified commanders. The act repealed the previous legislative authority for the Army and Air Force Chiefs of Staff to command their respective services, as it was also for the Navy's Chief of Naval Operations. The 1947 National Security Act provided for "three military departments separately adminis-tered," while the 1958 Reorganization called for a "Department of Defense, including three military departments," to be "separately organized" (a provision insisted upon by Congress). The 1958 act vested control and direction of military research and development in the Secretary of Defense and created a Director of Defense Research and Engineering to oversee it. The Defense Secretary was authorized to establish single agencies to conduct any service or supply activity common to two or more services, and subsequently several were established. Another key measure of the act provided for unified and specified commands to carry out specific military missions, with the forces assigned under the full operational control of the commander, although supported by their respective military departments. This allowed a reexamination of forces and commands, which took place during the last few months of 1958. Administrative and logistic support of unified and specified command headquarters was parceled out in September 1958. The Air Force was assigned to support the Alaskan Command (unified), the Continental Air Defense Command (unified), and the Strategic Air Command (specified). Two lines of command were established: operational command flowed from the President and Secretary of Defense through the corporate JCS, while non-operational command flowed from the President and Secretary of Defense to the secretaries of the military departments.

Ultimately, this reorganization centralized control of the Defense Department in the Secretary's office, but left the military departments intact. Few limitations remained on the Secretary's power. He could not merge the military departments, substantially alter statutory functions without congressional approval; or establish a single armed forces chief of staff or a general staff. Finally, the service secretaries and individual members of the JCS could present any recommendation they deemed proper to Congress.

****

Robert F. Futrell, <u>Ideas, Concepts and Doctrine: A History of Basic Thinking in the United States Air Force 1907-1964</u>, (Maxwell AFB, Ala: Air University, 2nd edition, 1974) pp 284-89.

Public Law 85-599

AN ACT

To Promote the national defense by providing for reorganization of the Department of Defense, and for other purposes.

Be it enacted by the Senate and House of Representatives of the United States of America in Congress assembled, That this Act may be cited as the "Department of Defense Reorganization Act of 1958".

AMENDING THE DECLARATION OF POLICY

SEC. 2. Section 2 of the National Security Act of 1947, as amended (50 U.S.C. 401), is further amended to read as follows:
"SEC. 2. In enacting this legislation, it is the intent of Congress to provide a comprehensive program for the future security of the United States; to provide for the establishment of integrated policies and procedures for the departments, agencies, and functions of the Government relating to the national security; to provide a Department of Defense, including the three military Departments of the Army, the Navy (including naval aviation and the United States Marine Corps), and the Air Force under the direction, authority, and control of the Secretary of Defense; to provide that each military department shall be separately organized under its own Secretary and shall function under the direction, authority, and control of the Secretary of Defense; to provide for their unified direction under civilian control of the Secretary of Defense but not to merge these departments or services; to provide for the establishment of unified or specified combatant commands, and a clear and direct line of command to such commands; to eliminate unnecessary duplication in the Department of Defense, and particularly in the field of research and engineering by vesting its overall direction and control in the Secretary of Defense; to provide more effective, efficient, and economical administration in the Department of Defense; to provide for the unified strategic direction of the combatant forces, for their operation under unified command, and for their integration into an efficient team of land, naval, and air forces but not to establish a single Chief of Staff over the armed forces nor an overall armed forces general staff."

STRENGTHENING THE DIRECTION, AUTHORITY, AND CONTROL OF THE SECRETARY OF DEFENSE

Sec. 3. (a) Section 202 (c) of the National Security Act of

329

1947, as amended (5 U.S.C. 171a (c), is amended to read as follows:

"(c) (1) Within the policy enunciated in section 2, the Secretary of Defense shall take appropriate steps (including the transfer, reassignment, abolition, and consolidation of functions) to provide in the Department of Defense for more effective, efficient, and economical administration and operation and to eliminate duplication. However, except as otherwise provided in this subsection, no function which has been established by law to be performed by the Department of Defense, or any officer or agency thereof, shall be substantially transferred reassigned, abolished, or consolidated until the expiration of the first period of thirty calendar days of continuous session of the Congress following the date on which the Secretary of Defense reports the pertinent details of the action to be taken to the Armed Services Committees of the Senate and of the House of Representatives. If during such period a resolution is reported by either of the said committees stating that the proposed action with respect to the transfer, reassignment, abolition, or consolidation of any function should be rejected by the resolving House because (1) it contemplates the transfer, reassignment, abolition, or consolidation of a major combatant function now or hereafter assigned to the military services by section 3062 (b), 5012, 5013, or 8062 (c) of title 10 of the United States Code, and (2) if carried out it would in the judgment of the said resolving House tend to impair the defense of the United States, such transfer, reassignment, abolition, or consolidation shall take effect after the expiration of the first period of forty calendar days of continuous session of the Congress following the date on which such resolution is reported; but only if, between the date of such reporting in either House and the expiration of such forty-day period such resolution has not been passed by such House.

"(2) For the purposes of paragraph (1)-

"(A) continuity of session shall be considered as broken only by an adjournment of the Congress sine die: but

"(B) in the computation of the thirty-day period or the forty-day period there shall be excluded the days on which either House is not in session because of an adjournment of more than three days to a day certain.

"(3) (A) The provisions of this paragraph are enacted by the Congress-

"(i) as an exercise of the rulemaking power of the Senate and the House of Representatives; and as such they shall be considered as part of the rules of each House, respectively, and such rules shall supersede other rules only to the extent that they are inconsistent therewith; and

330

"(ii) with full recognition of the constitutional right of either House to change such rules (so far as relating to the procedure in such House) at any time, in the same manner and to the same extent as in the case of any other rule of such House.

"(B) For the purposes of this paragraph, any resolution reported to either House pursuant to the provisions of paragraph (1) hereof, shall for the purpose of the consideration of such resolution by either House be treated in the same manner as a resolution with respect to a reorganization plan reported by a committee within the meaning of the Reorganization Act of 1949 as in effect on July 1, 1958 (5 U.S.C. 133z et seq.) and shall be governed by the provisions applicable to the consideration of any such resolution by either House of the Congress as provided by sections 205 and 206 of such Act.

"(4) Notwithstanding the provisions of paragraph (1) hereof, the Secretary of Defense has the authority to assign, or reassign, to one or more departments or services, the development and operational use of new weapons or weapons systems.

"(5) Notwithstanding other provisions of this subsection, if the President determines that it is necessary because of hostilities or imminent threat of hostilities, any function, including those assigned to the military services by sections 3062 (b), 5012, 5013, and 8062 (c) of title 10 of the United States Code, may be transferred, reassigned, or consolidated and subject to the determination of the President shall remain so transferred, reassigned, or consolidated until the termination of such hostilities or threat of hostilities.

"(6) Whenever the Secretary of Defense determines it will be advantageous to the Government in terms of effectiveness, economy, or efficiency, he shall provide for the carrying out of any supply or service activity common to more than one military department by a single agency or such other organizational entities as he deems appropriate. For the purposes of this paragraph, any supply or service activity common to more than one military department shall not be considered a "major combatant function" within the meaning of paragraph (1) hereof.

"(7) Each military department (the Department of the Navy to include naval aviation and the United States Marine Corps) shall be separately organized under its own Secretary and shall function under the direction, authority, and control of the Secretary of Defense. The Secretary of a military department shall be responsible to the Secretary of Defense for the operation of such department as well as its efficiency. Except as otherwise specifically provided by law, no Assistant Secretary of Defense shall have authority to issue orders to a military department unless (1) the Secretary of Defense has specifically delegated in writing to such an Assistant Secretary the authority to issue such orders with respect to a specific subject area, and (2) such orders are issued through the Secretary of such military department or his designee. In the implementation of this paragraph it shall be the duty of each such Secretary, his civilian assistants, and the military personnel in such department to cooperate fully with personnel of the Office of the Secretary of Defense in a continuous effort to achieve efficient administration of the Department of Defense and effectively to carry out the direction, authority, and control of the Secretary of Defense.

"(8) No provision of this Act shall be so construed as to prevent a Secretary of a military department or a member of the Joint Chiefs of Staff from presenting to the Congress, on his own initiative, after first so informing the Secretary of Defense, any recommendations relating to the Department of Defense that he may deem proper."

(b) Section 202 (d), of the National Security Act of 1947, as amended (5 U.S.C. 171a (d)),is further amended to read as follows:

"(d) The Secretary of Defense shall annually submit a written report to the President and the Congress covering expenditures work, and accomplishments of the Department of Defense, accompanied by (1) such recommendations as he shall deem appropriate, (2) separate reports from the military departments covering their expenditures, work, and accomplishments, and (3) itemized statements showing the savings of public funds and the eliminations of unnecessary duplications and overlappings that have been accomplished pursuant to the provisions of this Act."

(c) Section 2201 of title 10, United States Code, is repealed and the analysis of chapter 131 of title 10 is amended by striking out the following item:
"2201. General functions of Secretary of Defense."

(d) Section 2351 of title 10, United States Code, is repealed and the analysis of chapter 139 of title 10 is amended by striking out the following item:
"2351. Policy, plans, and coordination."

CLARIFYING THE CHAIN OF COMMAND OVER MILITARY OPERATIONS

Sec. 4. (a) Section 3034 (d) (4) of title 10, United States Code, is amended to read as follows:
"(4) exercise supervision over such of the members and organizations of the Army as the Secretary of the Army determines. Such supervision shall be exercised in a manner consistent with the full operational command vested in unified or specified combatant commanders pursuant to section 202 (j) of the National Security Act of 1947, as amended."

(b) Section 5081 (c) of title 10, United States Code, is amended to read as follows:

"(c) Under the direction of the Secretary of the Navy, the Chief of Naval Operations shall exercise supervision over such of the members and organizations of the Navy and the Marine Corps as the Secretary of the Navy determines. Such supervision shall be exercised in a manner consistent with the full operational command vested in unified or specified combatant commanders pursuant to section 202 (j) of the National Security Act of 1947, as amended."

(c) Section 5201 of title 10, United States Code, is amended by adding at the end thereof a new subsection (d) to read as follows:

"(d) Under the direction of the Secretary of the Navy, the Commandant of the Marine Corps shall exercise supervision over such of the members and organizations of the Marine Corps and Navy as the Secretary of the Navy determines. Such supervision shall be exercised in a manner consistent with the full operational command vested in unified or specified combatant commanders pursuant to section 202 (j) of the National Security Act of 1947, as amended."

(d) Clause (5) of section 8034 (d) of title 10, United States Code, is renumbered "(4)" and amended to read as follows:

"(4) exercise supervision over such of the members and organizations of the Air Force as the Secretary of the Air Force determines. Such supervision shall be exercised in a manner consistent with the full operational command vested in unified or specified combatant commanders pursuant to section 202 (j) of the National Security Act of 1947, as amended."

(e) Section 8034 (d) is amended by striking out clause (4) and by renumbering clauses (6) and (7) as clauses "(5)" and "(6)", respectively.

(f) (1) Section 8074 (a) of title 10, United States Code, is amended to read as follows:

"(a) The Air Force shall be divided into such organizations as the Secretary of the Air Force may prescribe."

(2) Subsections (b) and (c) of section 8074 of title 10, United States Code, are repealed, and subsection (d) is redesignated as subsection "(b)".

(g) Section 3032 (b) (1) of title 10, United States Code, is amended to read as follows:

"(1) prepare for such employment of the Army, and for such recruiting, organizing, supplying, equipping, training, serving, mobilizing, and demobilizing of the Army, as will assist in the execution of any power, duty, or function of the Secretary or the Chief of Staff;".

(h) Section 8032 (b) (1) of title 10, United States Code, is amended to read as follows:

"(1) prepare for such employment of the Air Force, and for such recruiting, organizing, supplying, equipping, training, serving, mobilizing, and demobilizing of the Air Force, as will assist in the execution of any power, duty, or function of the Secretary or the Chief of staff;".

CLARIFYING THE ORGANIZATION AND DUTIES OF THE JOINT STAFF

Sec. 5. (a) Section 143 of title 10, United States Code, is amended to read as follows:

"§ 143. Joint Staff

"(a) There is under the Joint Chiefs of Staff a Joint Staff consisting of not more than 400 officers selected by the Joint Chiefs of Staff with the approval of the Chairman. The Joint Staff shall be selected in approximately equal numbers from-

"(1) the Army;
"(2) the Navy and the Marine Corps; and
"(3) the Air Force.

The tenure of the members of the Joint Staff is subject to the approval of the Chairman of the Joint Chiefs of Staff, and except in time of war, no such tenure of duty may be more than three years. Except in time of war, officers completing a tour of duty with the Joint Staff may not be reassigned to the Joint Staff for a period of not less than three years following their previous tour of duty on the Joint Staff, except that selected officers may be recalled to Joint Staff duty in less than three years with the approval of the Secretary of Defense in each case. The number of such officers recalled to Joint Staff duty in less than three years shall not exceed 30 serving on the Joint Staff at any one time.

"(b) The Chairman of the Joint Chiefs of Staff in consultation with the Joint Chiefs of Staff, and with the approval of the Secretary of Defense, shall select the Director of the Joint Staff. Except in time of war, the tour of duty of the Director may not exceed three years. Upon the completion of a tour of duty as Director of the Joint Staff, the Director, except in time of war, may not be reassigned to the Joint Staff. The Director must be an officer junior in grade to each member of the Joint Chiefs of Staff.

"(c) The Joint Staff shall perform such duties as the Joint Chiefs of Staff or the Chairman prescribes. The Chairman of the Joint Chiefs of Staff manages the Joint Staff and its Director, on behalf of the Joint Chiefs of Staff.

"(d) The Joint Staff shall not operate or be organized as an overall Armed Forces General Staff and shall have no executive authority. The Joint Staff may be organized and may operate along conventional staff lines to support the Joint Chiefs of Staff in discharging their assigned responsibilities."

(b) Section 202 of the National Security Act of 1947, as amended, is amended by adding at the end thereof the following new subsection:

"(j) With the advice and assistance of the Joint Chiefs of Staff the President, through the Secretary of Defense, shall establish unified or specified combatant commands for the performance of military missions, and shall determine the force structure of such combatant commands to be composed of forces of the Department of the Army, the Department of the Navy, the Department of the Air Force, which shall then be assigned to such combatant commands by the departments concerned for the performance of such military missions. Such combatant commands are responsible to the President and the Secretary of Defense, with the approval of the President. Forces assigned to such unified combatant commands or specified combatant commands shall be under the full operational command of the commander of the unified combatant command or the commander of the specified combatant command. All forces not so assigned remain for all purposes in their respective departments. Under the direction, authority, and control of the Secretary of Defense each military department shall be responsible for the administration of the forces assigned from its department to such combatant commands. The responsibility for the support of forces assigned to combatant commands shall be vested in one or more of the military departments as may be directed by the Secretary of Defense. Forces assigned to such unified or specified combatant commands shall be transferred therefrom only by authority of and under procedures established by the Secretary of Defense, with the approval of the President."

. . . .
[Ed. Note] (Material deleted can be found in Public Law 85-599 (72 Stat.514))

(d) Section 8035 of title 10, United States Code, is amended by adding at the end thereof a new subsection (d) to read as follows:

"(d) The Vice Chief of Staff has such authority and duties with respect to the Department of the Air Force as the Chief of Staff, with the approval of the Secretary of the Air Force, may delegate to or prescribe for him. Orders issued by the Vice Chief of Staff in performing such duties have the same effect as those issued by the Chief of Staff."

CLARIFYING THE ROLE OF THE CHAIRMAN OF THE JOINT CHIEFS OF STAFF

Sec. 7. Section 141 (a) (1) of title 10, United States Code, is amended by striking out the words ", who has no vote".

REDUCING THE NUMBER OF ASSISTANT SECRETARIES OF MILITARY DEPARTMENTS

. . . .

[Ed. Note] (Material deleted can be found in Public Law 85-599 (72 Stat.514))

(c) Section 8013 (a) of title 10, United States Code, is amended to read as follows:
"(a) There are an Under Secretary of the Air Force and three Assistant Secretaries of the Air Force in the Department of the Air Force. They shall be appointed from civilian life by the President, by and with the advice and consent of the Senate."

ESTABLISHING THE DIRECTOR OF DEFENSE RESEARCH AND ENGINEERING

Sec. 9. (a) Section 203 of the National Security Act of 1947, as amended, is amended by redesignating subsections "(b)" and "(c)" as subsections "(c)" and "(d)", respectively, and by inserting a new subsection "(b)" as follows:
(b) (1) There shall be a Director of Defense Research and Engineering who shall be appointed from civilian life by the President, by and with the advice and consent of the Senate, who shall take precedence in the Department of Defense after the Secretary of Defense, the Deputy Secretary of Defense, the Secretary of the Army, the Secretary of the Navy, and the Secretary of the Air Force. The Director performs such duties with respect to research and engineering as the Secretary of Defense may prescribe, including, but not limited to, the following: (i) to be the principal adviser to the Secretary of Defense on scientific and technical matters: (ii) to supervise all research and engineering activities in the Department of Defense; and (iii) to direct and control (including their assignment or reassignment) research and engineering activities that the Secretary of Defense deems to require centralized management. The compensation of the Director is that prescribed by law for the Secretaries of the military departments.
"(2) The Secretary of Defense or his designee, subject to the approval of the President, is authorized to engage in basic and applied research projects essential to the responsibilities of the Department of Defense in the field of basic and applied research and development which pertain to weapons systems and other military requirements. The Secretary or his designee, subject to the

approval of the President, is authorized to perform assigned research and development projects: by contract with private business entities, educational or research institutions, or other agencies of the Government, through one or more of the military departments, or by utilizing employees and consultants of the Department of Defense.

"(3) There is authorized to be appropriated such sums as may be necessary for the purposes of paragraph (2) of this subsection."

(b) Section 7 of Public Law 85-325, dated February 12, 1958, is amended to read as follows:

"Sec. 7. The Secretary of Defense or his designee is authorized to engage in such advanced projects essential to the Defense Department's responsibilities in the field of basic and applied research and development which pertain to weapons systems and military requirements as the Secretary of Defense may determine after consultation with the Joint Chiefs of Staff: and for a period of one year from the effective date of this Act, the Secretary of Defense or his designee is further authorized to engage in such advanced space projects as may be designated by he President.

"Nothing in this provision of law shall preclude the Secretary of Defense from assigning to the military departments the duty of engaging in research and development of weapons systems necessary to fulfill the combatant functions assigned by law to such military departments.

"The Secretary of Defense shall assign any weapons systems developed to such military department or departments for production and operational control as he may determine."

(c) Section 171 (a) of title 10, United States Code, is amended by renumbering clauses "(6)", "(7)", "(8)", and "(9)" as clauses "(7)", "(8)", "(9)", and "(10)", respectively, and inserting the following new clause (6) after clause (5):

"(6) The Director of Defense Research and Engineering;".

REDUCING THE NUMBER OF ASSISTANT SECRETARIES OF DEFENSE

Sec. 10. (a) Subsection (c) of section 203 of the National Security Act of 1947, as amended (5 U.S.C. 171c), as redesignated by section 9 (a) of this act, is amended as follows:

(1) By striking out the word "three" and inserting the word "seven" in place thereof.

(2) By striking out the word "and" after the word "Navy,".

(3) By inserting the words ", and the Director of Defense Research and Engineering" after the words "Air Force".

(b) Section 3 of Reorganization Plan No. 6 of 1953 (67 Stat. 638) is repealed.

AUTHORIZING THE TRANSFER OF OFFICERS BETWEEN THE ARMED FORCES

Sec. 11. Chapter 41 of title 10, United States Code, is amended as follows:

(1) By adding the following new section at the end:

"§ 716. Commissioned officers: transfers between Army, Navy, Air Force, and Marine Corps."

"Notwithstanding any other provision of law, the President may, within authorized strengths, transfer any commissioned officer with his consent from the Army, Navy, Air Force, or Marine Corps to, and appoint him in, any other of those armed forces. The Secretary of Defense shall establish, by regulations approved by the President, policies and procedures for such transfers and appointments. No officer transferred pursuant to this authority shall be assigned precedence or relative rank higher than that which he held on the day prior to such transfer."

NATIONAL GUARD BUREAU

Sec. 12. Section 3015 of title 10, United States Code, is amended by redesignating subsections "(a)", "(b)", and "(c)" as subsections "(b)", "(c)", and "(d)", respectively, and by inserting a new subsection (a) to read as follows:

"(a) There is a National Guard Bureau, which is a Joint Bureau of the Department of the Army and the Department of the Air Force, headed by a chief who is the adviser to the Army Chief of Staff and the Air Force Chief of Staff on National Guard matters. The National Guard Bureau is the channel of communication between the departments concerned and the several States, Territories, Puerto Rico, the Canal Zone, and the District of Columbia on all matters pertaining to the National Guard, the Army National Guard of the United States, and the Air National Guard of the United States."

EFFECTIVE DATE

Sec. 13. Sections 8 and 10 of this Act shall become effective six months after the date of enactment of this Act.

Approved August 6, 1958.

(25) **Department Of Defense Directive 5100.1,**
31 December 1958

Department of Defense (DOD) Directive 5100.1 of 31
December 1958, codified the provisions of the 1958
reorganization and cancelled the 16 March 1954 version.
One provision stipulated that "all functions in the
Department of Defense and its component agencies are
performed under the direction, authority, and control
of the Secretary of Defense." This directive specified
the chains of command required by the Reorganization
Act of 1958. The general responsibilities changed very
little under the terms of this directive, leaving
intact the primary functions of the Air Force,
including the function to "organize, train, and equip
Air Force forces" to conduct air combat operations.
The Air Force also received a new responsibility "to
formulate doctrines and procedures for the organizing,
equipping, training, and employment of Air Force
forces."

There have been four changes and two reissuances of
this basic directive since initial promulgation. This
directive provides the basic guidance undergirding the
division of responsibility in the Defense Department.
Change 1 of 17 June 1966 added functions of certain
defense agencies (like the Defense Intelligence Agency
(DIA), and the Defense Communications Agency), added
the Defense Supply Agency (DSA) to the planning
function for logistical plans, and added the Defense
agencies to the list of groups given military guidance
by the Joint Chiefs of Staff (JCS). Change 2 of 17
June 1969 was merely a technical change to reflect
incorporation of the National Security Act into Title
10, U.S. Code. Also, this change noted different
logistical planning relationships between the JCS and
the Defense agencies. On 31 January 1977, the list of
Defense agencies whose functions were explained in
other functions directives was expanded in change 3.
Later that year, on 24 March, the acronym for the
Defense Intelligence Agency was altered from DSA to DIA
in change 4. This document was reissued on 26 January
1980, and again 1 May 1985, but with only minor changes
in the dates of associated DOD directives for accuracy.
In essence, the operating directive for the Air Force
has changed very little since 1958.

****
This material has been drawn from the documents
themselves.

339

DEPARTMENT OF DEFENSE DIRECTIVE

SUBJECT   Functions of the Department of Defense and
             its Major Components

Refs: (a) DoD Directive 5100.1, "Functions of the Armed Forces
           and the Joint Chiefs of Staff", March 16, 1954
           (cancelled herein)
      (b) DoD Directive 5158.1, "Organization of the Joint Chiefs
           of Staff and Relationships with the Office of the
           Secretary of Defense"

I.   INTRODUCTION

     Congress, in the National Security Act of 1947, as amended,
has described the basic policy embodied in the Act in the
following terms:

     "In enacting this legislation, it is the intent of
Congress to provide a comprehensive program for the future
security of the United States; to provide for the establishment of integrated policies and procedures for the departments, agencies, and functions of the Government relating to
the national security; to provide a Department of Defense,
including the three military departments of the Army, the Navy
(including naval aviation and the United States Marine Corps),
and the Air Force under the direction, authority, and control
of the Secretary of Defense; to provide that each military
department shall be separately organized under its own
Secretary and shall function under the direction, authority,
and control of the Secretary of Defense; to provide for their
unified direction under civilian control of the Secretary of
Defense but not to merge these departments or services; to
provide for the establishment of unified or specified combatant commands, and a clear and direct line of command to
such commands; to eliminate unnecessary duplication in the
Department of Defense, and particularly in the field of
research and engineering by vesting its overall direction and
control in the Secretary of Defense; to provide more effective, efficient, and economical administration in the
Department of Defense; to provide for the unified strategic
direction of the combatant forces, for their operation under
unified command, and for their integration into an efficient
team of land, naval, and air forces but not to establish a

single Chief of Staff over the armed forces nor an overall armed forces general staff."

To provide guidance in accordance with the policy declared by Congress, the Secretary of Defense, with the approval of the President, hereby promulgates the following statement of the functions of the Department of Defense and its major components.

II. ORGANIZATIONAL RELATIONSHIPS IN THE DEPARTMENT OF DEFENSE

1. All functions in the Department of Defense and its component agencies are performed under the direction, authority, and control of the Secretary of Defense.

2. The Department of Defense includes the Office of the Secretary of Defense and the Joint Chiefs of Staff, the military departments and the military Services within those departments, the unified and specified commands, and such other agencies as the Secretary of Defense establishes to meet specific requirements.

    a. In providing immediate staff assistance and advice to the Secretary of Defense, the Office of the Secretary of Defense and the Joint Chiefs of Staff, though separately identified and organized, function in full coordination and cooperation in accordance with Reference (b).

    (1) The Office of the Secretary of Defense includes the offices of the Director of Defense Research and Engineering, the Assistant Secretaries of Defense, and the General Counsel and such other staff offices as the Secretary of Defense establishes to assist him in carrying out his duties and responsibilities. The functions of the heads of these offices shall be as assigned by the Secretary of Defense in accordance with existing laws.

    (2) The Joint Chiefs of Staff, as a group, are directly responsible to the Secretary of Defense for the functions assigned to them. Each member of the Joint Chiefs of Staff, other than the Chairman, is responsible for keeping the Secretary of his military department fully informed on matters considered or acted upon by the Joint Chiefs of Staff.

    b. Each military department (the Department of the Navy to include naval aviation and the United States Marine Corps) shall be separately organized under its own Secretary and shall function under the direction, authority, and control of the

Secretary of Defense. The Secretary of a military department shall be responsible to the Secretary of Defense for the operation of such department as well as its efficiency. Orders to the military departments will be issued through the Secretaries of these departments, or their designees, by the Secretary of Defense or under authority specifically delegated in writing by the Secretary of Defense or provided by law.

      c. Commanders of unified and specified commands are responsible to the President and the Secretary of Defense for the accomplishment of the military missions assigned to them. The chain of command runs from the President to the Secretary of Defense and through the Joint Chiefs of Staff to the commanders of unified and specified commands. Orders to such commanders will be issued by the President or the Secretary of Defense, or by the Joint Chiefs of Staff by authority and direction of the Secretary of Defense. These commanders shall have full operational command over the forces assigned to them and shall perform such functions as are prescribed by the Unified Command Plan and other directives issued by competent authority.

      3. The functions assigned hereinafter may be transferred, reassigned, abolished or consolidated by the Secretary of Defense in accordance with the procedures established and the authorities provided in the National Security Act of 1947, as amended.

III. FUNCTIONS OF THE DEPARTMENT OF DEFENSE

      As prescribed by higher authority, the Department of Defense shall maintain and employ armed forces:

      1. To support and defend the Constitution of the United States against all enemies, foreign and domestic.

      2. To insure, by timely and effective military action, the security of the United States, its possessions, and areas vital to its interest.

      3. To uphold and advance the national policies and interests of the United States.

      4. To safeguard the internal security of the United States.

IV. FUNCTIONS OF THE JOINT CHIEFS OF STAFF

      The Joint Chiefs of Staff, consisting of the Chairman; the

Chief of Staff, U.S. Army; the Chief of Naval Operations; and the Chief of Staff, U.S. Air Force, and supported by the Organization of the Joint Chiefs of Staff, constitute the immediate military staff of the Secretary of Defense. The Joint Chiefs of Staff are the principal military advisers to the President, the National Security Council, and the Secretary of Defense. The Commandant of the U.S. Marine Corps has coequal status with the members of the Joint Chiefs of Staff on matters which directly concern the Marine Corps. In performance of their functions of advising and assisting the Secretary of Defense, and subject to the authority and direction of the President and the Secretary of Defense, it shall be the duty of the Joint Chiefs of Staff:

1. To serve as advisers and as military staff in the chain of operational command with respect to unified and specified commands, to provide a channel of communications from the President and Secretary of Defense to unified and specified commands, and to coordinate all communications on matters of joint interest addressed to the commanders of the unified or specified commands by other authority.

2. To prepare strategic plans and provide for the strategic direction of the armed forces, including the direction of operations conducted by commanders of unified and specified commands and the discharge of any other function of command for such commands directed by the Secretary of Defense.

3. To prepare integrated logistic plans, which may include assignments to the armed forces of logistic responsibilities in accordance with such plans.

4. To prepare integrated plans for military mobilization.

5. To provide adequate, timely, and reliable joint intelligence for use within the Department of Defense.

6. To review major personnel, materiel, and logistic requirements of the armed forces in relation to strategic and logistic plans.

7. To review the plans and programs of commanders of unified and specified commands to determine their adequacy, feasibility, and suitability for the performance of assigned missions.

8. To provide military guidance for use by the military departments and the armed forces as needed in the preparation of their respective detailed plans.

9. To participate, as directed, in the preparation of combined plans for military action in conjunction with the armed forces of other nations.

10. To recommend to the Secretary of Defense the establishment and force structure of unified and specified commands in strategic areas.

11. To determine the headquarters support, such as facilities, personnel, and communications, required by commanders of unified and specified commands and to recommend the assignment to the military departments of the responsibilities for providing such support.

12. To establish doctrines for (a) unified operations and training and (b) coordination of the military education of members of the armed forces.

13. To recommend to the Secretary of Defense the assignment of primary responsibility for any function of the armed forces requiring such determination and the transfer, reassignment, abolition, or consolidation of such functions.

14. To prepare and submit to the Secretary of Defense, for information and consideration in connection with the preparation of budgets, statements of military requirements based upon United States strategic considerations, current national security policy, and strategic war plans. These statements of requirements shall include tasks, priority of tasks, force requirements, and general strategic guidance for the development of military installations and bases and for equipping and maintaining military forces.

15. To advise and assist the Secretary of Defense in research and engineering matters by preparing: (a) statements of broad strategic guidance to be used in the preparation of an integrated Department of Defense program; (b) statements of overall military requirements; (c) statements of the relative military importance of development activities to meet the needs of the unified and specified commanders; and (d) recommendations for the assignment of specific new weapons to the armed forces.

16. To prepare and submit to the Secretary of Defense for information and consideration general strategic guidance for the development of industrial mobilization programs.

17. To prepare and submit to the Secretary of Defense military guidance for use in the development of military aid programs

and other actions relating to foreign military forces, including recommendations for allied military force, materiel, and facilities requirements related to United States strategic objectives, current national security policy, strategic war plans, and the implementation of approved programs; and to make recommendations to the Secretary of Defense, as necessary, for keeping the Military Assistance Program in consonance with agreed strategic concepts.

18.   To provide United States representation on the Military Staff Committee of the United Nations, in accordance with the provisions of the Charter of the United Nations, and representation on other properly authorized military staffs, boards, councils, and missions.

19.   To perform such other duties as the President or the Secretary of Defense may prescribe.

V.   FUNCTIONS OF THE MILITARY DEPARTMENTS AND THE MILITARY SERVICES

The chain of command for purposes other than the operational direction of unified and specified commands runs from the President to the Secretary of Defense to the Secretaries of the military departments.

The military departments, under their respective Secretaries and in accordance with Sections II and IV, shall:

1.   Prepare forces and establish reserves of equipment and supplies for the effective prosecution of war, and plan for the expansion of peacetime components to meet the needs of war.

2.   Maintain in readiness mobile reserve forces, properly organized, trained, and equipped for employment in emergency.

3.   Provide adequate, timely, and reliable departmental intelligence for use within the Department of Defense.

4.   Organize, train, and equip forces for assignment to unified or specified commands.

5.   Prepare and submit to the Secretary of Defense budgets for their respective departments, justify before the Congress budget requests as approved by the Secretary of Defense; and administer the funds made available for maintaining, equipping,

and training the forces of their respective departments, including those assigned to unified and specified commands. The budget submissions to the Secretary of Defense by the military departments shall be prepared on the basis, among other things, of the advice of commanders of forces assigned to unified and specified commands; such advice, in the case of component commanders of unified commands, will be in agreement with the plans and programs of the respective unified commanders.

6. Conduct research, develop tactics, techniques, and organization, and develop and procure weapons, equipment, and supplies essential to the fulfillment of the functions hereinafter assigned.

7. Develop, garrison, supply, equip, and maintain bases and other installations, including lines of communication, and provide administrative and logistical support for all forces and bases.

8. Provide, as directed, such forces, military missions, and detachments for service in foreign countries as may be required to support the national interests of the United States.

9. Assist in training and equipping the military forces of foreign nations.

10. Assist each other in the accomplishment of their respective functions, including the provision of personnel, intelligence, training, facilities, equipment, supplies, and services.

The forces developed and trained to perform the primary functions set forth hereinafter shall be employed to support and supplement the other Services in carrying out their primary functions, where and whenever such participation will result in increased effectiveness and will contribute to the accomplishment of the overall military objectives. As for collateral functions, while the assignment of such functions may establish further justification for stated force requirements, such assignment shall not be used as the basis for establishing additional force requirements.

A. Functions of the Department of the Army

The Department of the Army is responsible for the preparation of land forces necessary for the effective prosecution of war except as otherwise assigned and, in accordance with integrated mobilization plans, for the expansion of the peacetime components of the Army to meet the needs of war.

BASIC DOCUMENTS

The Army, within the Department of the Army, includes land combat and service forces and such aviation and water transport as may be organic therein.

1. Primary Functions of the Army

a. To organize, train, and equip Army forces for the conduct of prompt and sustained combat operations on land -- specifically, forces to defeat enemy land forces and to seize, occupy, and defend land area.

b. To organize, train and equip Army air defense units, including the provision of Army forces as required for the defense of the United States against air attack, in accordance with doctrines established by the Joint Chiefs of Staff.

c. To organize and equip, in coordination with the other Services, and to provide Army forces for joint amphibious and airborne operations, and to provide for the training of such forces, in accordance with doctrines established by the Joint Chiefs of Staff.

(1) To develop, in coordination with the other Services, doctrines, tactics, techniques, and equipment of interest to the Army for amphibious operations and not provided for in Section V, paragraph B 1 b (3) and paragraph B 1 d.

(2) To develop, in coordination with the other Services, the doctrines, procedures, and equipment employed by Army and Marine Forces in airborne operations. The Army shall have primary interest in the development of those airborne doctrines, procedures, and equipment which are of common interest to the Army and the Marine Corps.

d. To provide an organization capable of furnishing adequate, timely, and reliable intelligence for the Army.

e. To provide forces for the occupations of territories abroad, to include initial establishment of military government pending transfer of this responsibility to other authority.

f. To formulate doctrines and procedures for the organizing, equipping, training, and employment of forces operating on land, except that the formulation of doctrines and procedures for the organization, equipping, training, and employment of Marine Corps units for amphibious operations shall be a function of the Department of the Navy, coordinating as required by Section V, paragraph B 1 b (3).

       g.   To conduct the following activities:

       (1)   The administration and operation of the Panama Canal.

       (2)   The authorized civil works program, including projects for improvement of navigation, flood control, beach erosion control, and other water resource developments in the United States, its territories, and its possessions.

       (3)   Certain other civil activities prescribed by law.

    2. <u>Collateral Functions of the Army</u> -- To train forces:

       a.   To interdict enemy sea and air power and communications through operations on or from land.

   B. <u>Functions of the Department of the Navy</u>

     The Department of the Navy is responsible for the preparation of Navy and Marine Corps forces necessary for the effective prosecution of war except as otherwise assigned and, in accordance with integrated mobilization plans, for the expansion of the peacetime components of the Navy and Marine Corps to meet the needs of war.

     Within the Department of the Navy, the Navy includes naval combat and service forces and such aviation as may be organic therein, and the Marine Corps includes not less than three combat divisions and three air wings and such other land combat, aviation, and other services as may be organic therein.

    1. <u>Primary Functions of the Navy and the Marine Corps</u>

       a.   To organize, train, and equip Navy and Marine Corps forces for the conduct of prompt and sustained combat operations at sea, including operations of sea-based aircraft and land-based naval air components -- specifically, forces to seek out and destroy enemy naval forces and to suppress enemy sea commerce, to gain and maintain general naval supremacy, to control vital sea areas and to protect vital sea lines of communication, to establish and maintain local superiority (including air) in an area of naval operations, to seize and defend advanced naval bases, and to conduct such land and air operations as may be essential to the prosecution of a naval campaign.

      b.   To maintain the Marine Corps, having the following specific functions:

      (1) To provide Fleet Marine Forces of combined arms, together with supporting air components, for service with the Fleet in the seizure or defense of advanced naval bases and for the conduct of such land operations as may be essential to the prosecution of a naval campaign. These functions do not contemplate the creation of a second land Army.

      (2) To provide detachments and organizations for service on armed vessels of the Navy, and security detachments for the protection of naval property at naval stations and bases.

      (3) To develop, in coordination with the other Services, the doctrines, tactics, techniques, and equipment employed by landing forces in amphibious operations. The Marine Corps shall have primary interest in the development of those landing force doctrines, tactics, techniques, and equipment which are of common interest to the Army and the Marine Corps.

      (4) To train and equip, as required, Marine Forces for airborne operations, in coordination with the other Services and in accordance with doctrines established by the Joint Chiefs of Staff.

      (5) To develop, in coordination with the other services, doctrines, procedures, and equipment of interest to the Marine Corps for airborne operations and not provided for in Section V, paragraph A 1 c (2).

      c.   To organize and equip, in coordination with the other Services, and to provide naval forces, including naval close air-support forces, for the conduct of joint amphibious operations, and to be responsible for the amphibious training of all forces assigned to joint amphibious operations in accordance with doctrines established by the Joint Chiefs of Staff.

      d.   To develop, in coordination with the other Services, the doctrines, procedures, and equipment of naval forces for amphibious operations, and the doctrines and procedures for joint amphibious operations.

e. To furnish adequate, timely, and reliable intelligence for the Navy and Marine Corps.

f. To organize, train, and equip naval forces for naval reconnaissance, antisubmarine warfare, and protection of shipping, and mine laying, including the air aspects thereof, and controlled mine field operations.

g. To provide air support essential for naval operations.

h. To provide sea-based air defense and the sea-based means for coordinating control for defense against air attack, coordinating with the other Services in matters of joint concern.

i. To provide naval (including naval air) forces as required for the defense of the United States against air attack, in accordance with doctrines established by the Joint Chiefs of Staff.

j. To furnish aerial photography as necessary for Navy and Marine Corps operations.

2. Collateral Functions of the Navy and the Marine Corps -- To train forces:

a. To interdict enemy land and air power and communications through operations at sea.

b. To conduct close air and naval support for land operations.

c. To furnish aerial photography for cartographic purposes.

d. To be prepared to participate in the overall air effort as directed.

e. To establish military government, as directed, pending transfer of this responsibility to other authority.

C. Functions of the Department of the Air Force

The Department of the Air Force is responsible for the preparation of the air forces necessary for the effective prosecution of war except as otherwise assigned and, in accordance with integrated mobilization plans, for the expansion of the peacetime components of the Air Force to meet the needs of war.

The Air Force, within the Department of the Air Force, includes aviation forces, both combat and service, not otherwise assigned.

1. Primary Functions of the Air Force

a. To organize, train, and equip Air Force forces for the conduct of prompt and sustained combat operations in the air --specifically, forces to defend the United States against air attack in accordance with doctrines established by the Joint Chiefs of Staff, to gain and maintain general air supremacy, to defeat enemy air forces, to control vital air areas, and to establish local air superiority except as otherwise assigned herein.

b. To develop doctrines and procedures, in coordination with the other Services, for the unified defense of the United States against air attack.

c. To organize, train, and equip Air Force forces for strategic air warfare.

d. To organize and equip Air Force forces for joint amphibious and airborne operations, in coordination with the other Services, and to provide for their training in accordance with doctrines established by the Joint Chiefs of Staff.

e. To furnish close combat and logistical air support to the Army, to include air lift, support, and resupply of airborne operations, aerial photography, tactical reconnaissance, and interdiction of enemy land power and communications.

f. To provide air transport for the armed forces, except as otherwise assigned.

g. To develop, in coordination with the other Services, doctrines, procedures, and equipment for air defense from land areas, including the continental United States.

h. To formulate doctrines and procedures for the organizing, equipping, training, and employment of Air Force forces.

        i. To provide an organization capable of furnishing adequate, timely, and reliable intelligence for the Air Force.

        j. To furnish aerial photography for cartographic purposes.

        k. To develop, in coordination with the other Services, tactics, techniques, and equipment of interest to the Air Force for amphibious operations and not provided for in Section V, paragraph B 1 b (3) and paragraph b 1 d.

        l. To develop, in coordination with the other Services, doctrines, procedures, and equipment employed by Air Force forces in airborne operations.

    2. Collateral Functions of the Air Force -- To train forces:

        a. To interdict enemy sea power through air operations.

        b. To conduct antisubmarine warfare and to protect shipping.

        c. To conduct aerial mine-laying operations.

VI. CANCELLATION

Reference (a) is cancelled.

VII. EFFECTIVE DATE

This Directive is effective immediately.

                                (signed)
                              Neil McElroy
                          Secretary of Defense

(26) **Assignment of Operational Control of Space Detection and Tracking System to North American Air Defense Command, 7 November 1960**

On 7 November 1960, the Joint Chiefs of Staff (JCS) assigned operational control of the Space Detection and Tracking System (SPADATS) to the Commander in Chief, North American Air Defense Command (CINCNORAD). Simultaneously, it assigned operational command of the system to the Commander in Chief, Continental Air Defense Command (CINCONAD). The purpose of the SPADATS was to detect, identify, and determine the characteristics of all orbiting objects. The distinction between the terms "command and control" implied that the CINCONAD retained legal jurisdiction over the systems, while the CINCNORAD (commander of a binational command) determined operational employment of the system. This marked the first assignment of any space system to an armed forces unit. Intercontinental ballistic missiles and intermediate-range ballistic missiles were parceled out to the Air Force, and the Army had short-range tactical missiles. However, space systems were just coming into being; the Space Detection and Tracking System in many ways represented just a further extension of a North American air defense radar system.

****

Robert F. Futrell, Ideas, Concepts and Doctrine: A History of Basic Thinking in the United States Air Force 1907-1964, (Maxwell AFB, Ala: Air University, 2nd edition, 1974) pp 294-95.

THE JOINT CHIEFS OF STAFF
Washington 25, D. C.

SM-1145-60
7 November 1960

MEMORANDUM FOR THE COMMANDER IN CHIEF, CONTINENTAL
AIR DEFENSE COMMAND

Subject: Assignment of Operational Control of
the Space Detection and Tracking System (U)

1. The Commander in Chief, Continental Air Defense Command is hereby directed to assume operational command of the Space (Satellite) Detection and Tracking System, now consisting of SPASUR and SPACETRACK.

2. An information copy of this memorandum is being provided CINCNORAD.

3. By separate memorandum, CINCNORAD is being informed of his responsibility to exercise operational control of the Space (SATELLITE) Detection and Tracking System.

For the Joint Chiefs of Staff:

Copy to:
  CINCNORAD
  CINCAL
  CINCLANT
  CINCARIB
  USCINCEUR
  CINCPAC
  CINCNELM
  CINCSAC

(signed)

F. J. Blouin
RADM, USN,
Secretary.

Distribution:
  Chairman, JCS (2)
  DCSOPS
  Secy to CNO (JCS)
  Dir/Plans, AF
  MarCorps L/O
  Dir J/S (2)
(JCS 2283/111 - Approved 4 Nov 60)

THE JOINT CHIEFS OF STAFF
Washington 25, D.C.

SM-1146-60
7 November 1960

MEMORANDUM FOR THE COMMANDER IN CHIEF, NORTH AMERICAN AIR
DEFENSE COMMAND

Subject: Assignment of Operational Control of the
Space Detection and Tracking System (U)

1. Reference is made to the Memorandum by the Commander
in Chief, North American Air Defense Command, dated 20 April
1960, subject: "Assignment of Operational Responsibility for
Satellite Detection and Tracking System".

2. After appropriate examination of this proposal it has
been decided that the Commander in Chief, North American Air
Defense Command should exercise operational control of the
Space Detection and Tracking System in accordance with his
Terms of Reference. Operational command of this system has
been assigned to CINCONAD.

3. In the memorandum referenced in paragraph 1, above, an
earlier NORAD desire for operational control of the SPACETRACK
System was reaffirmed. This system as well as SPASUR now comprises the Space Detection and Tracking System, and hence is
assigned to CINCNORAD for operational control.

For the U.S. Joint Chiefs of Staff:

(signed)
F. J. Blouin
RADM, USN,
Secretary.

Copy to:
    CINCAL   USCINCEUR
    CINCLANT   CINCPAC
    CINCARIB   CINCNELM
    CINCONAD   CINCSAC
Distr:
    Chairman, JCS (2)   Dir/Plans, AF
    DCSOPS   MarCorps, L/O
    Secy to CNO (JCS)   Dir J/S (2)
  (JCS 2283/111 - Approved 4 Nov 60)

JCSM-500-60
7 Nov 1960

MEMORANDUM FOR THE CHAIRMAN, CANADIAN CHIEFS OF STAFF

Subject: Assignment of Operational Control of the
Space Detection and Tracking System (U)

1. The United States Joint Chiefs of Staff have assigned to the United States Continental Air Defense Command the operational command of a Space Detection and Tracking System. The purpose of this system is to detect, identify, and determine the orbital characteristics of all objects in orbit, and to disseminate the evaluated information to all cognizant commands and agencies.

2. By memorandum of this date the Commander in Chief, North American Air Defense Command has been assigned operational control of the Space Detection and Tracking System in accordance with his Terms of Reference. This assignment is considered appropriate in that the North American Air Defense Command will be a principal user of the information generated by the system in the execution of his air defense responsibilities.

For the U.S. Joint Chiefs of Staff:

(signed)
L. L. Lemnitzer
Chairman,
Joint Chiefs of Staff

Distr:
  Chairman, JCS (2)
  DCSOPS
  Secy to CNO (JCS)
  Dir/Plans, AF
  MarCorps L/O
  Dir J/S (2)

(JCS 2283/111 - Approved 4 Nov 60)

(27) Secretary of Defense McNamara's Directive Assigning Space System's Development to the Air Force, 6 March 1961 (DOD Directive 5160.32)

With the issuance of Department of Defense (DOD) Directive 5160.32, on 6 March 1961, Secretary of Defense Robert S. McNamara assigned to the Air Force research, development, test, and evaluation (RDT&E) of space programs and projects. Under this directive, each military department and DOD agency could "conduct preliminary research to develop new ways of using space technology" as limited by spending levels and other conditions defined by the Director of Defense Research and Engineering (DDR&E). Proposals beyond the preliminary research stage were to be submitted to the DDR&E. Upon approval they would become DOD space development programs, subject to concurrence of the Secretary of Defense or his deputy. RDT&E of these DOD space programs was assigned to the Air Force after approval, although the Secretary of Defense could make exceptions to that assignment under unusual circumstances.

This directive effectively made the Air Force the DOD executive agent for all space development programs, regardless of service of ultimate use. It enabled the Air Force to determine the shape of space developments to best suit its own requirements.

This directive had antecedents in the late 1950s, when Secretary of Defense Neil McElroy overruled an Air Force bid to disestablish the DOD Advanced Research Projects Agency (ARPA), with the concomitant assignment of space systems' development to the using service. Secretary McElroy had ruled (in a memorandum for the Joint Chiefs of Staff (JCS) on 18 September 1959) against any new joint organization to control space systems operations. He also assigned development of space boosters and payload systems integration to the Air Force. At the same time, he transferred various systems from ARPA to the military services. The Air Force was assigned responsibility for reconnaissance satellites, including the Satellite and Missile Observation System (SAMOS) and the Missile Detection Alarm System (MIDAS).

****

Robert F. Futrell, Ideas, Concepts and Doctrine: A History of Basic Thinking in the United States Air Force 1907-1964, (Maxwell AFB, Ala: Air University, 2nd edition, 1974) pp 292-95 and 386-87.

BASIC DOCUMENTS

Thomas S. Snyder, <u>et al</u>, "Space and Missile Systems Organization: A Chronology 1954-1976," (Norton AFB, Calif: SAMSO History Office, 1978), pp 70-93.

362

March 6, 1961
NUMBER 5160.32

DEPARTMENT OF DEFENSE DIRECTIVE

SUBJECT   Development of Space Systems

References: (a) Memorandum (Conf) from Secretary of Defense
                   to Chairman, Joint Chiefs of Staff, subject:
                   Satellite and Space Vehicles Operations,
                   September 18, 1959

               (b) Memorandum from Director, Advanced Re-
                   search Projects Agency to Secretary of the
                   Army, Secretary of the Navy, and Secretary
                   of the Air Force, subject: Study Contracts
                   for Projects Assigned to the Advanced Research
                   Projects Agency, September 14, 1959

               (c) Memorandum (Conf) from Director of Defense
                   Research and Engineering to the Secretary of
                   the Army, the Secretary of the Navy, the Sec-
                   retary of the Air Force, and Director, Advanced
                   Research Projects Agency, subject: ARPA
                   Programs, June 11, 1959

I.   PURPOSE

     This directive establishes policies and assigns responsi-
     bilities for research, development, test, and engineering
     of satellites, anti-satellites, space probes and supporting
     systems therefor, for all components of the Department
     of Defense.

II. POLICY AND ASSIGNMENT OF RESPONSIBILITIES

     A. Each military department and Department of Defense
         agency is authorized to conduct preliminary research
         to develop new ways of using space technology to
         perform its assigned function. The scope of such re-
         search shall be defined by the Director of Defense
         Research and Engineering in terms of expenditure limi-
         tations and other appropriate conditions.

     B. Proposals for research and development of space programs
         and projects beyond the defined preliminary research

stage shall be submitted to the Director of Defense Research and Engineering for review and determination as to whether such proposals, when transmitted to the Secretary of Defense, will be recommended for approval. Any such proposal will become a Department of Defense space development program or project only upon specific approval by the Secretary of Defense or the Deputy Secretary of Defense.

C. Research, development, test, and engineering of Department of Defense space development programs or projects, which are approved hereafter, will be the responsibility of the Department of the Air Force.

D. Exceptions to paragraph C will be made by the Secretary of Defense or the Deputy Secretary of Defense only in unusual circumstances.

E. The Director of Defense Research and Engineering will maintain a current summary of approved Department of Defense space development programs and projects.

III. <u>CANCELLATION</u>

Reference (a), except as to the assignments of specific projects made therein, and references (b) and (c) are hereby cancelled.

IV. <u>EFFECTIVE DATE</u>

This directive is effective upon publication. Instructions implementing this directive will be issued within thirty (30) days.

> (signed)
> Robert S. McNamara
> Secretary of Defense

(28) LeMay-Decker Agreement, 12 July 1962

On 12 July 1962, the Air Force Chief of Staff, Gen. Curtis E. LeMay, and the Army Chief of Staff, Gen. George H. Decker, signed an agreement on doctrine for Area Air Defense in overseas theaters. This document embodied two basic principles: that a single commander running an integrated air defense was essential to success, and unnecessary restrictions should not hamper optimum employment of air defense systems.

Since early in the 1950s, the Army and Air Force had operated largely under conditions of the Vandenberg-Collins Agreement, which provided for an Air Force air defense commander to exercise operational control over antiaircraft artillery, "insofar as engagement and disengagement of fire is concerned." Citing Secretary of Defense Charles A. Wilson's November 1956 roles and missions memorandum, the Continental Army Command (CONARC) asserted that a field army commander (rather than an air component commander) would be responsible for air defense and would regulate air operations in the airspace over his combat area. Though they noted the success of unified commanders in both Europe and the Pacific in promulgating command control arrangements for battle area air space, the two services could not agree on this issue. Consequently, both Tactical Air Command (TAC) and CONARC began to follow command arrangements similar to those used overseas in their joint maneuvers. This usage was formalized in the LeMay-Decker Agreement

The agreement called for the unified commander (in areas where substantial forces from each service were deployed) to appoint an area air defense commander, normally the air component commander. A deputy in air defense matters would be appointed when a substantial portion of the air defense forces were contributed by a service other than the Air Force. The area air defense commander was assigned to coordinate and integrate the entire air defense effort in his area, including establishing air defense regions and their individual policies and procedures. The appointed commander of an air defense region was expected to delegate authority to field army commanders for control and operational employment of organic Army air defense assets, including surface-to-air missiles.

Coordinated action sought to provide maximum tactical warning and active air defense from diverse forces. Their effectiveness depended upon integrating disparate units into a single air defense system.

BASIC DOCUMENTS

****

Robert F. Futrell, <u>Ideas, Concepts and Doctrine: A</u> <u>History of Basic Thinking in the United States Air</u> <u>Force 1907-1964</u>, (Maxwell AFB, Ala: Air University, 2nd edition, 1974) pp 407-08.

DOCTRINE FOR AREA (OVERSEAS) AIR DEFENSE

Statement of Agreement

1. The undersigned, Chief of Staff of the U.S. Army and the Chief of Staff of the U.S. Air Force agree to the following statement of doctrine for Area (Overseas) Air Defense.

Basic Principles

2. Due to the complexity and efficiency of modern weapon systems, the speed of flight of modern aircraft, the numbers and types of aircraft operating in a theater, and the potential damage which can be inflicted by a single hostile aircraft in the nuclear age, a basic principle is established that a coordinated and integrated air defense system under a single commander is essential to successful theater operations.

3. Unified commanders are assigned a variety of weapon systems for air defense. This mix of weapon systems is chosen to insure that the weaknesses of one are covered by the capabilities of the other. The air defense commander in the area must insure through his organization and through his application of appropriate doctrine that the effectiveness of each system is optimized and that no unnecessary restrictions are placed upon its employment.

Organization

4. In an area of operations where substantial forces of each Service (including allied forces) are deployed, the Unified Commander should normally appoint the Air Component Commander as the Area Air Defense Commander, with appropriate staff representation from the Service components involved. Where a significant portion of the air defense means are contributed by a Service other than the Air Force, a senior officer should be appointed from that Service to serve as deputy in air defense matters to the Area Air Defense Commander.

    a. The mission of the Area Air Defense Commander will be to coordinate and integrate the entire air defense effort within his area. He will establish broad policies and procedures, in the name of the Unified Commander, for the employment of air defense means and the coordination of such means with the operations of other elements within the area.

    b. In the exercise of his responsibility, the Area Air Defense Commander will establish air defense regions. While the number of such regions will vary, the Tactical Air Force Commander will be designated as the Regional Air Defense Commander for his assigned area of responsibility for tactical air operations and such additional area as may be designated by the Area Air Defense Commander. In such a region where a significant portion of the Regional Air Defense are Army air defense means, a senior Army officer should be appointed to serve as deputy in air defense matters to the Regional Air Defense Commander, and Army staff representation should be assigned to the air defense activities of the Regional Commander.

5. In such a region the Air Defense Commander will be fully responsible for and will have full authority in the air defense of his region. He will, however, normally delegate authority to field army(s) commander(s) for control and operational employment of organic Army air defense means within the field Army area. This delegation of authority is for the purpose of permitting optimum employment of surface-to-air missiles in the defense of the forward battle area. Field Army and U.S. Air Force electronic coordination and control means will be compatible and operationally connected for optimum combat effectiveness.

6. In other regions where the situation indicates that there will be no likelihood in war of extensive tactical air offensive operations for attaining air superiority, interdiction or close support; and the threat is essentially that of enemy air attack, the Area Air Defense Commander may establish a Joint Air Defense Command (JADC).

   a. The commander may come from any component depending on the organization and operational situation within the region and air defense means available.

   b. A deputy commander will be appointed from a Service other than that of the commander.

   c. A Joint Staff will be formed in accordance with the principles set forth in JCS PUB 2 (UNAAF) and with appropriate representation from the Service components involved.

Concept of Employment

7. The optimum offensive-defensive relationship exists when friendly defense can limit enemy offensive destruction to an acceptable level. Unlike offensive actions, defensive actions alone cannot be decisive in war. Thus, defensive activities must accommodate themselves to the offense.

8. The primary objective of coordinated and integrated air defense operations is to provide maximum tactical warning and active defense for all forces in the area. To achieve this objective, early identification of air traffic, rapid dissemination of air defense information, and effective application of air defense weapons are essential.

9. The respective efforts of each Service must be integrated into a single air defense system to achieve maximum effectiveness. Surface-to-air missiles, command and control systems, and manned interceptors, regardless of type or Service, will be integrated into this single system. Each force will augment the others in furtherance of the common air defense objective. Each force must be aware of the needs, capabilities and limitations of the others.

(signed)   (signed)
CURTIS E. LeMAY   GEORGE H. DECKER
General, USAF   General, USA
Chief of Staff   Chief of Staff

(29) Redesignation of Military Air Transport Service to Military Airlift Command, 11 October 1965

With the evolution of Air Force transport from primarily a transport service to a more combat-oriented airlift organization, Military Air Transport Service (MATS) was redesignated Military Airlift Command (MAC) on 11 October 1965, effective on 1 January 1966. As early as 1960, MATS was evolving into the role of combat airlift support rather than scheduled airlift support of overseas forces. The result was more money and effort spent on preparing for and practicing combat deployments, rather than on running a peacetime passenger and freight service. In 1961, the MATS Commander, Lt. Gen. Joe W. Kelly, wanted to redesignate his units to common descriptors since both troop carrier and air transport units performed the same mission. Yet, each operated under different restrictions regarding numbers of crews, unit equipment, and flying hours. Headquarters USAF had approved the redesignations in 1962, but reversed itself prior to implementation due to the expense and inconvenience involved.

In June 1962, Congressman L. Mendel Rivers had proposed redesignating MATS to MAC, making MAC a specified command under the Joint Chiefs of Staff (JCS), and consolidating all strategic airlift resources within the new command. Rivers' bill failed, and the issue lay dormant for three years.

On 5 May 1965, the House of Representatives passed a bill changing MATS to MAC, and President Lyndon B. Johnson signed it into law on 11 June 1965. There was no mention of a change in status to a JCS specified command. As a result of the new law, Headquarters USAF issued an order, under the authority of the Secretary of the Air Force, directing the redesignation. At the same time, MATS was authorized to redesignate its transport air forces to numbered air forces and its air transport/troop carrier units to military airlift units, effective on 8 January 1966. The change marked the reorientation of air transport back to its combat role by providing the organizational structure to support it.

****
History of MAC, 1 July 1965-30 June 1966, pp 22-26.

DEPARTMENT OF THE AIR FORCE
HEADQUARTERS UNITED STATES AIR FORCE
WASHINGTON, D. C. 20330

AFOMO 461n   11 October 1965

SUBJECT: Redesignation of the Headquarters, Military Air
          Transport Service

TO: MATS

1. By order of the Secretary of the Air Force, effective 1
January 1966:

    a. Military Air Transport Service is redesignated <u>Military
Airlift Command</u>. Concurrently, the headquarters is redesignated
from Headquarters, Military Air Transport Service to Headquarters,
Military Airlift Command.

2. Report completed action using the Air Force Organization
Status Change Report (Reports Control Symbol AF-01) in compliance
with current instructions.

3. Forward copies of the orders issued pursuant to this letter in
accordance with paragraph 28, AFM 10-3, 28 June 1961.

FOR THE CHIEF OF STAFF

BERTRAM C. HARRISON
Major General, USAF
Director of Mpr & Orgn, DCS/P&R

                              DISTRIBUTION:
                                 Joint Chiefs of Staff   (15)
                                 Armed Services Medical
                                    Regulating Office   (1)
                                 Hq USAF (1 cy AFTAC M&O)   (115)
                                 AF Logistics Command   (12)
                                 AMAs & AFVCG (Mat Svcs Div)   (3)
                                    except SAAMA   (4)
                                 Air University Library   (24)
                                 USAF Historical Div, ASI   (1)
                                 Military Air Transport
                                    Service   (10)

(30) **Secretary of Defense McNamara's Memorandum for Navy Withdrawal from Military Airlift Command, 5 April 1966**

Late in 1965, the Secretary of the Navy, Paul Nitze, reiterated his earlier request to Air Force Secretary Harold Brown that they recommend withdrawing Navy personnel from Military Air Transport Service (MATS). Nitze reasoned that the Navy contribution to MATS had shrunk from 36 to 14 percent, with a concomitant reduction in advancement opportunities for Navy officers in MATS; MATS tours retarded promotion opportunities for Navy assignees since MATS and Navy transport aircraft were different models; and the cost of training the few Navy enlisted personnel assigned to MATS was high.

Secretary Brown backed Nitze, provided that the proposed phase-out did not retard the current and projected MATS (by then redesignated Military Airlift Command (MAC)) build-up and that the Defense Department would provide the resources, including manpower, that the Navy withdrew. Secretary of Defense Robert S. McNamara approved the proposal on 5 April 1966 and it was publicly announced on 26 April. The Air Force-owned, Navy-operated C-130s were transferred to Air Force units, and the last Navy squadron was inactivated on 2 June 1967.

****
History of MAC, 1 July 1965-30 June 1966, pp. 41-45.

THE SECRETARY OF DEFENSE
WASHINGTON

5 April 1966

MEMORANDUM FOR SECRETARY OF THE NAVY
                SECRETARY OF THE AIR FORCE

SUBJECT: Navy Withdrawal from the Military Airlift Command
          (MAC) (U)

I have reviewed your joint memorandum, dated March 19, 1966, subject as above, which requests approval of the phased withdrawal of Navy airlift squadrons from MAC beginning in the third quarter of FY 1967. I understand that this withdrawal involves (a) necessary adjustments to the manning levels of the Navy and the Air Force, (b) retention of all aircraft and other physical assets by the Air Force unless exceptions are approved by OSD, and (c) appropriate steps to insure that MAC airlift capability is not degraded by the transfer.

I concur in your rationale for this proposed action and approve the requested withdrawal of Navy airlift squadrons from MAC. Please submit a simplified program change proposal covering the force, manpower, and TOA implications of this action.

(signed)
Robert S. McNamara

(31) McConnell-Johnson Agreement, 6 April 1966

The issue of who would control tactical airlift was settled with the signing of an agreement between Army Chief of Staff Gen. Harold K. Johnson and Air Force Chief of Staff Gen. John P. McConnell on 6 April 1966. Announced on 15 April 1966, the agreement set an effective date of 1 January 1967 for an end to years of dispute over tactical airlift responsibility.

The impetus for the agreement was provided by air supply operations in Vietnam. In the years up to 1964, Army special forces camps were supplied by a variety of airlifters, both Army and Air Force. The Army special forces wanted their own dedicated airlift force, but its own commanders would not provide it, although ironically the Air Force did with their C-123s. Bad weather and muddy ground conditions prompted the Army to loan its CV-2 Caribou aircraft to the Air Force airlift allocation system at times. The later adoption of the Army airmobile division, with its dependence on aerial re-supply, brought the airlift allocation issue to the surface. Productive Air Force supply performances blunted Army reluctance to rely on its sister service, and reduced Army contentions that it required organic airlift for main base supply lines. In addition, airmobile divisions needed to use their organic, rotary-wing airlift in tactical deployments rather than supply. The Air Force led by General McConnell wanted to bring the Caribous under its centralized airlift allocation system, hoping to utilize more fully the aircraft's capacity.

The agreement grew out of a series of conferences between the two chiefs and represented a number of tradeoffs. The Army relinquished its claims to the de Havilland CV-2, later designated the C-7 (Caribou), the CV-7 (Buffalo), and all future fixed-wing aircraft designed to fulfill the tactical airlift role. The Army would transfer these aircraft to the Air Force. In return, the Air Force would relinquish all claims for rotary-wing aircraft designed and operated for intra-theater movement, fire support, and supply and resupply of Army forces. This did not preclude the Air Force from operating helicopters for search and rescue and special air warfare.

It permitted the Army to develop and employ armed helicopters without entering into a roles and missions controversy, while also eliminating a source of Army-Air Force friction in armed, fixed-wing aircraft which impinged on the Air Force close air support mission. The Air Force gained clear title to the tactical airlift role, which it was supposed to have in any case, while recognizing an accomplished fact (that the Army owned the helicopter combat role). In addition, the Air Force gained overriding influence in tactical transport development, though required to consult the Army for its needs.

****

"Air Force, Army Agree on Roles and Missions," Aviation Week and Space Technology, 25 April 1966, pp 26, 27.

Frederic A. Bergerson, The Army Gets an Air Force, (Baltimore, Md: Johns Hopkins University Press, 1980), pp 117-20.

Ray L. Bowers, The United States Air Force in Southeast Asia: Tactical Airlift, (Washington, D.C.: Office of Air Force History, 1983), pp 149-65, 208-16, 233-39.

INITIAL AGREEMENT BETWEEN CHIEF OF STAFF, U. S. ARMY, AND CHIEF OF STAFF, U. S. AIR FORCE (U)

The Chief of Staff, U.S. Army, and the Chief of Staff, U.S. Air Force, have reached an initial understanding with respect to employment of ARDF aircraft in SEA and are individually and jointly agreed as follows:

a. There is a requirement for both direct support and general support ARDF aircraft in SEA. Current estimate, pending the outcome of the OSD directed test, is 57 Army U6/U8 ARDF aircraft, and 47 USAF C-47 HAWKEYE ARDF aircraft. These aircraft can be made available in accordance with the following schedule:

	U6/U8	C-47
On Hand SEA	25	1 (test to be withdrawn)
April	29	1
May	31	5
June	34	11
July	47	19
August	56	27
September	57	35
October		43
November		47

b. A proper mix of aircraft and the employment thereof will be considered by the JCS following receipt of the OSD directed test results now being conducted by the Director, NSA. Specific recommendations will be made by the JCS upon conclusion of their review of the test. Pending this receipt, the CofSA and CofSAF are being directed by the JCS to proceed with deployment of aircraft in accordance with the schedule in paragraph a.

(signed)
J. P. McConnell
General, USAF
Chief of Staff

(signed)
HAROLD K. JOHNSON
General, USA
Chief of Staff

6 April 1966

AGREEMENT BETWEEN CHIEF OF STAFF, U. S. ARMY,
AND CHIEF OF STAFF, U. S. AIR FORCE (U)

The Chief of Staff, U. S. Army, and the Chief of Staff, U. S. Air Force, have reached an understanding on the control and employment of certain types of fixed and rotary wing aircraft and are individually and jointly agreed as follows:

a. The Chief of Staff, U. S. Army, agrees to relinquish all claims for CV-2 and CV-7 aircraft and for future fixed wing aircraft designed for tactical airlift. These assets now in the Army inventory will be transferred to the Air Force. (CSA and CSAF agree that this does not apply to administrative mission support fixed wing aircraft).

b. The Chief of Staff, U. S. Air Force, agrees:

(1) To relinquish all claims for helicopters and follow-on rotary wing aircraft which are designed and operated for intra-theater movement, fire support, supply and resupply of Army forces and those Air Force control elements assigned to DASC and subordinate thereto. (CSA and CSAF agree that this does not include rotary wing aircraft employed by Air Force SAW and SAR forces and rotary wing administrative mission support aircraft). (CSA and CSAF agree that the Army and Air Force jointly will continue to develop VTOL aircraft. Dependent upon evolution of this type aircraft, methods of employment and control will be matters for continuing joint consideration by the Army and Air Force).

(2) That, in cases of operational need, the CV-2, CV-7 and C-123 type aircraft performing supply, resupply, or troop-lift functions in the field army area, may be attached to the subordinate tactical echelons of the field army (corps, division, or subordinate commander), as determined by the appropriate joint/unified commander. (NOTE: Authority for attachment is established by Subsection 6, Section 2 of JCS Pub 2, Unified Action Armed Forces (UNAAF).)

(3) To retain the CV-2 and CV-7 aircraft in the Air Force structure and to consult with the Chief of Staff, U.S. Army, prior to changing the force levels of, or replacing these aircraft.

(4) To consult with the Chief of Staff, U.S. Army, in order to arrive at take off, landing, and load carrying charac-

teristics of follow-on fixed wing aircraft to meet the needs of the Army for supply, resupply, and troop movement functions.

c. The Chief of Staff, U.S. Army, and the Chief of Staff, U.S. Air Force, jointly agree:

(1) To revise all Service doctrinal statements, manuals, and other material in variance with the substance and spirit of this agreement.

(2) That the necessary actions resulting from this agreement will be completed by 1 January 1967.

(signed)
J. P. McConnell
General, USAF
Chief of Staff

(signed)
HAROLD K. JOHNSON
General, USA
Chief of Staff

ADDENDUM TO THE AGREEMENT OF 6 APRIL 1966
BETWEEN CHIEF OF STAFF, U. S. ARMY, AND
CHIEF OF STAFF, U. S. AIR FORCE

19 May 1967

The Chief of Staff, U. S. Army, and the Chief of Staff, U.S. Air Force, agree to amend their agreement of 6 April 1966 concerning the control and employment of certain types of fixed and rotary wing aircraft by adding the following clarifying sentences to paragraph b (1):

"SAW rotary wing aircraft - armed if required - will be employed to train foreign air forces in the operation and employment of helicopters and to support U. S. Air Force forces, other government agencies, and indigenous forces only when operating without U. S. Army advisors or not under U. S. Army control."

J. P. McConnell
General, USAF
Chief of Staff

HAROLD K. JOHNSON
General, USA
Chief of Staff

(32) **Deputy Secretary of Defense Directive on Space**
System Development, 8 September 1970

On 8 September 1970, Deputy Secretary of Defense
David Packard issued an updated Department of Defense
(DOD) Directive 5160.32 on developing space systems,
which superseded the one of 6 March 1961. In the new
document, Mr. Packard reiterated the assignment of
development, production, and deployment of space
systems (for "warning and surveillance of enemy nuclear
delivery capabilities and all launch vehicles,
including launch and orbital support operations...") to
the Air Force. However, future development of space
systems would fall under the same guidelines as other
major weapon systems. No assignment of responsibility
for existing systems changed under this new directive
and proposals from the military departments to develop
space systems still required Office of the Secretary of
Defense (OSD) approval based on normal DOD acquisition
policies.

The Director of Defense Research and Engineering
(DDR&E) would monitor all space technology activity to
prevent duplication and minimize technical risk and
cost. The DDR&E served as a focal point for space where
more than one service was involved. In February 1971,
Air Force Under Secretary John L. McLucas persuaded
Secretary of Defense Melvin R. Laird to require
coordination with the Air Force as a prior condition
for space system development. This also aimed at
avoiding wasteful duplication of effort. In the four
years following publication of this new directive, only
one space system, the Navy's Fleet Satellite
Communications (FLTSATCOM) program, was managed and
funded by a service other than the Air Force, and today
the Air Force continues to dominate space systems
development.

```
**********************************************************
```

Jacob Neufeld, "The Air Force in Space 1970-1974,"
(Washington, D.C.: Office of Air Force History, 1976),
pp v-vi.

DEPARTMENT OF DEFENSE DIRECTIVE

SUBJECT   Development of Space Systems

Ref: (a) DoD Directive 5160.32, March 6, 1961, subject as
          above (hereby cancelled)

I.   PURPOSE

This Directive establishes policies and assigns responsibilities for research, development, test, and engineering
of satellites, anti-satellites, space probes and supporting
systems therefor, for all components of the Department of
Defense.

II. CANCELLATION

Reference (a) is hereby superseded and cancelled.

III. POLICY AND ASSIGNMENT OF RESPONSIBILITIES

A.   Functional responsibilities within OSD and the
     Military Departments for acquiring major weapon
     systems will be applied to the development and acqui-
     sition of space systems.

B.   Existing assignment of responsibilities for on-going
     space systems are not changed by this Directive.
     The Air Force will have the responsibility for develop-
     ment, production and deployment of space systems for
     warning and surveillance of enemy nuclear delivery
     capabilities and all launch vehicles, including launch
     and orbital support operations. Military Department
     proposals for space development programs will require
     specific OSD approval based on DCP and DSARC
     policies. DCP's for space communications, naviga-
     tion, unique surveillance (i.e., ocean or battlefield),
     meteorology, defense/offense, mapping/charting/
     geodesy, and major technology programs will desig-
     nate the Military Department or DOD agency responsi-
     ble for execution of the program.

C.   Exceptions to B above will be made only by the Secretary
     of Defense or Deputy Secretary of Defense.

387

D. The Director of Defense Research and Engineering will
    monitor all space technology activity to minimize system
    technical risk and cost, to prevent unwarranted duplica-
    tion, and to assure that a space program assigned to
    one department meets the needs of other departments.
    Other departments may appoint program/project monitors
    to report progress to their departments and perform
    liaison between their departments and the responsible
    department. DDR&E continue to serve as a focal point
    for space technology and space systems where the
    interests of more than one department are involved.

IV. <u>EFFECTIVE DATE AND IMPLEMENTATION</u>

This Directive is effective upon publication. Two(2) copies
of implementing instructions shall be forwarded to the
Director of Defense Research and Engineering within sixty
(60) days.

(signed)
David Packard
Deputy Secretary of Defense

(33) Consolidation of Airlift Forces, 1974

On 29 July 1974, a Department of Defense (DOD) Program Decision Memorandum (PDM) (amended on 22 August) directed the Air Force to consolidate all DOD airlift under Military Airlift Command (MAC) as single manager, primarily as part of an effort to achieve greater service interdependence. MAC would assume responsibility for all airlift except Navy on-board delivery and Marine KC-130 tanker operations. On 21 November 1974, Headquarters USAF announced its program to consolidate all strategic and tactical airlift under MAC's control, including transports flown by Tactical Air Command (TAC), Pacific Air Forces (PACAF), United States Air Forces Europe (USAFE), and United States Air Force Southern Air Division (USAFSO) (the Caribbean air units) and Alaskan Air Command (AAC). One facet of this consolidation was to remove the MAC C-5s and C-141s from industrial funding in order to provide greater flexibility to the MAC Commander for efficient allocation of airlift. In addition, MAC would become a Joint Chiefs of Staff (JCS) specified command.

Under the Air Force plan, the first step was to transfer administratively (in place and as is) the TAC airlift aircraft to MAC, effective 1 December 1974. Next, on 31 March 1975, the airlift aircraft of PACAF, USAFE, and AAC were transferred to MAC in the same manner. MAC then reorganized, without any new headquarters structure, to effectively utilize all of its airlift resources. MAC finally became a JCS specified Command on 1 February 1977.

****
History of MAC, July 1974-December 1975, pp. 42-44.

Extract from OSD Program Decision Memorandum, dated 29 July 1974.

IV. GENERAL PURPOSE FORCES

A. Consolidation of Airlift Forces: The consolidation of all DoD airlift forces under a single manager will be accomplished by the end of FY 77. Airlift for all services, including the Navy and Marine Corps will be provided by the Air Force. All Navy and Marine Corps funding for procurement of airlift (Fleet Tactical Support) aircraft in FY 76 and beyond is cancelled with the exception of aircraft for Carrier Onboard Delivery (COD) Operations. All Navy and Marine Corps airlift (Fleet Tactical Support) operations will be phased out in FY 77 with the exception of COD operations. The Marines will continue to operate their KC-130 tankers. The Navy CY 75 POM will address specific disposition of their current airlift assets. The Air Force will consolidate in FY 76 all Strategic and Tactical airlift under MAC as a single manager which will be designated as a Specified Command for Airlift. This will be accomplished without the addition of a new headquarters structure by relying on the use of the current MAC headquarters structure. The C-5 and C-141 aircraft will be removed from industrially funded operations to provide the new Specified Commander with greater flexibility in the efficient allocation of his airlift assets. The single manager together with the JCS and OSD will establish an allocation system for inter-theater airlift (C-5, C-141 and that fixed commercial cargo procurement needed to insure a viable CRAF) to be implemented by the JCS. In recognition of the new "allocation" system for the C-5 and C-141, the Air Force Program IV O&M account will be increased to fully fund the C-5 and C-141 peacetime operations. The funds are being transferred from each of the DoD users, taking into account the amount of "industrially funded" cargo airlift purchased during the past three years. The new Specified Commander with the JCS and appropriate CINCS will establish, prior to FY 77, a plan to be implemented in FY 77 by the CINCS which assures that the entire airlift force will be responsive to the various theater component commanders. By end-FY 77, the Air Force will assume all inter-theater (Strategic) and intra-theater (Tactical) airlift missions for all Services.

(34) Memorandum of Agreement on the Concept of Operations for USAF Collateral Functions Training, 2 September 1975

In response to declining resources in the early 1970s, the Chief of Naval Operations, Adm. Elmo Zumwalt, solicited the aid of the other services in helping the Navy meet the Soviet threat. This solicitation fell largely upon the Air Force, since it had three collateral missions in support of the Navy: interdiction of enemy sea power through air operations; conducting antisubmarine warfare and protecting shipping; and conducting aerial minelaying operations. The Strategic Air Command had been involved in aerial minelaying operations incident to training for these collateral missions and as a further justification for retaining additional squadrons of aircraft beyond their scheduled retirement date.

Between 1971 and 1982, the two services signed five agreements, the last on 9 September 1982, to promote joint efforts to utilize Air Force resources to enhance the effectiveness of maritime operations. The agreement signed by the two services on 2 September 1975, covered three areas of employment. The first was ocean surface surveillance and reconnaissance, including locating, identifying, and reporting of enemy or potential enemy surface vessels. The second area involved attrition operations, whereby the unified commander identified targets for Air Force action. The third involved aerial minelaying operations, in which the Air Force had already indulged in some practice. This helped set the stage for more training for collateral missions, and provided more explicit guidance to allow the forces to maximize their training results. Subsequent agreements in 1979 and 1982 increased the scope and frequency of joint training exercises.

The agreement authorized direct coordination between the major air commanders and the fleet commanders-in-chief, and provided that the training would support maritime operational requirements set forth by the unified commanders. Command arrangements would remain unaltered, with Air Force forces under the operational control of Air Force commanders, in support of the naval commander. The costs were to be borne by the Air Force and the intelligence for training supplied by the Navy. The result was more joint Navy-Air Force exercises with the Air Force providing reconnaissance and mine-laying support.

BASIC DOCUMENTS

****

Maurice A. Miller, "The Collateral Maritime Mission of the Strategic Air Command," (Offutt AFB, Nebr: SAC Office of History, 1980), pp 113-14, 119, 125.

Memo, Chief of Naval Operations and Air Force Chief of Staff, "Memorandum of Agreement on Joint USN/USAF Efforts to Enhance USAF Contribution to Maritime Operations," 9 September 1982.

DEPARTMENT OF THE AIR FORCE
Headquarters United States Air Force
Washington, D. C.

10 September 1975

Reply to
Attn of: XO

Subject: Memorandum of Agreement for USAF Forces Collateral
Functions Training

To: AF/IN   AF/LG   AF/RD   AF/SA   AF/PR

1. As a result of the liaison established between the
USAF and the USN initiated by CNO Memorandum to CSAF of 6
February 1975 and CSAF Memorandum to CNO of 19 February
1975, agreement has been reached on USAF forces colla-
teral functions training with the Navy. The enclosed
Memorandum of Agreement is considered a significant
milestone in implementing the policy of Mutual
Reinforcement.

2. Attachment 1 is forwarded for your information and
use as appropriate.

1 Atch
Memorandum of Agreement
on Concept of Operations for
USAF Forces Collateral
Functions Training, 2 Sep 75

OTIS C. MOORE, Maj Gen, USAF
Assistant Deputy Chief of Staff
Plans and Operations

Info copies to: AF/XOO
AF/XOD
AF/XOXX

395

Department of the Air Force
Headquarters, U.S. Air Force
Washington, D.C.

Department of the Navy
Office of the
Chief of Naval Operations
Washington, D.C.

MEMORANDUM OF AGREEMENT

ON

THE CONCEPT OF OPERATIONS FOR USAF
FORCES COLLATERAL FUNCTIONS TRAINING

References:

   a.   CNO Memorandum to CSAF of 6 February 1975, Subj:
Employment of USAF Augmentation Forces in Collateral Functions.

   b.   CSAF Memorandum to CNO of 19 February 1975, Subj:
Employment of U.S. Forces in Collateral Functions.

   c.   DOD Directive 5100.1, Subj: Functions of the
Department of Defense and its Major Components.

   d.   JCS Pub 2, Unified Action Armed Forces (UNAAF).

   e.   JCS Pub 1, Dictionary of Military and Associated
Terms.

   f.   Agreement between the Department of the Navy and the
Department of the Air Force of 22 May 1974 governing B-52
aircraft aerial delivery of Navy sea mines.

PURPOSE

1.   (U) To set forth the joint USAF/USN agreement in accordance
with references (a) and (b) concerning a general concept of
operations for U.S. Air Force resources training to perform
collateral functions.

BACKGROUND

2.   (U) The Department of Defense Reorganization Act of 1958,
supported and implemented by references (c) and (d), states
the collateral functions of the Air Force -- "To train forces:

a. To interdict enemy sea power through air operations.

b. To conduct antisubmarine warfare and to protect shipping.

c. To conduct aerial minelaying operations."

3. (U) One of the primary functions of the Navy listed in references (c) and (d) is to "organize, train, and equip naval forces for naval reconnaissance, antisubmarine warfare, protection of shipping, and minelaying, including the air aspects thereof, and controlled minefield operations."

4. (U) JCS Pub 2 specifies that each Service has the responsibility for "planning for the utilization and exploitation of the intrinsic capabilities of forces of the other Services which may be made available." Training for unified and joint operations is to be conducted in accordance with Chapter III of JCS Pub 2. Specifically, joint exercises may be held on the initiative of one or more of the Service Chiefs and the initiating directive for exercises held by agreement between Service Chiefs or commanders acting directly under them will be issued jointly. This concept of operations, therefore, represents the broad guidance necessary for the development of plans for enhancing, through training, Air Force collateral functions capabilities to support naval operations at sea.

5. (U) The definitions and functions outlined in references (c), (d), (e), and (f) remain unchanged by this agreement.

DISCUSSION

6. (U) It is becoming increasingly more important for the Unified Commander to utilize effectively any resources that are made available to conduct sea control operations in accordance with the spirit and intent of mutual reinforcement.

7. (U) Sea control operations involve a variety of surface, subsurface and aviation functions, most of which are beyond the scope of this agreement. This general concept of operations for training Air Force resources in collateral maritime functions is limited to those aspects of sea control which are within the intrinsic capabilities of those resources. That is, Air Force resources will be trained for tasks (a) which complement and supplement sea control

operations, and (b) for which an inherent Air Force capability already exists. Further, since primary functions may necessarily preempt the availability of Air Force resources, it is recognized that a primary organic Navy capability must be maintained.

8. (U) It is envisioned that Air Force capabilities might be employed to perform the following tasks:

    a. Search and identification.

    b. Electronic warfare.

    c. Tactical deception.

    d. Attack against surface and air units.

    e. Aerial minelaying.

9. (U) Considering the scope of sea control operations and the degree of existing Air Force maritime capability, the following tasks are considered appropriate:

    a. Performance of ocean surface surveillance/reconnaissance to include real-time location, identification, determination of movement and reporting of enemy or potential enemy surface combatants and merchant ships. Such tasking could conceivably be implemented in the following scenarios:

        (1) Establishment of radar and visual barriers at specified choke points and key locations.

        (2) Establishment of search sectors in oceans remote from naval task force operations for purposes of general strategic assessment or for deceptive operations.

        (3) Establishment of search operations in support of naval task force operations.

    b. Performance of attrition operations wherein the Unified Commander, or when authorized, the supported naval component commander could assign specifically designated and identified enemy surface combatant/merchant shipping as targets. This task could be performed by either an airborne or ground alert reaction force.

c. Aerial minelaying operations.

10. (U) Training of Air Force resources in collateral functions
will be based on the following agreed precepts:

a. Direct liaison is authorized between the Major Air
Commanders and the Fleet Commanders-in-Chief to effect training
programs for Air Force units which may be made available to
perform collateral functions.

b. Training will be conducted to support maritime
operational requirements set forth by the Unified Commanders.

c. Reports will be in accordance with joint, Navy, and
Air Force requirements using inbeing communications nets and
will be reported as near real time as possible.

d. Command arrangements for training normally shall
be the same as those established for operational employment;
i.e., Air Force forces remain under the operational control
of the appropriate Air Force commander and operate in support
of the naval commander.

e. Training plans will be prepared by Major Air
Commanders or their designated subordinates in coordination
with the appropriate Fleet Commanders-In-Chief or their
designated subordinates.

f. Training rules of engagement (ROE) will be established
by the Major Air Commanders and the Fleet Commanders-In-Chief
or their designated subordinates.

11. (U) Areas of Responsibility:

a. Air Force is responsible for the training of its
personnel in collateral functions as specified in JCS Pub 2.

b. Air Force is responsible for its portion of all costs
associated with training, operations, material, logistic
support, personnel support and any other funding aspects of
these collateral functions.

c. Navy is responsible for providing the essential
intelligence information to Air Force forces that are
designated to train in collateral functions during the
periods in which such training is underway.

399

    d. Navy will make available training periods to Air Force taking into consideration such factors as Navy training and operational requirements, sensitivity of operations, and capabilities and limitations of available forces.

    e. In the event that formal schooling of Air Force personnel is deemed necessary, such schooling will be provided by the Navy on a space-available basis. Funding of travel expenses for Air Force personnel associated with such schooling will be borne by the Air Force.

12. (U) <u>Effective Date</u>. This agreement is effective immediately and shall remain in effect until amended by actual written agreement between Navy and Air Force.

<u>J. L. Holloway (signed)</u>   <u>David C. Jones (signed)</u>
Chief of Naval Operations   Chief of Staff, U.S. Air Force

(35) <u>US Army/US Air Force Understanding of Relationship</u>
<u>of Helicopters and Fixed-Wing Aircraft in Close</u>
<u>Air Support, 16 September 1975</u>

As a result of their experience in Vietnam, the
Army and Air Force agreed on a concept of relationships
regarding close air support assets. When given the
opportunity, the Army had been unwilling to specify its
requirements for a fixed-wing, close air support
aircraft. The Air Force had adopted the Vought A-7D as
an interim aircraft in the late 1960s and early 1970s,
while it developed its A-X (which became the Fairchild
Republic A-10) close air support aircraft. When viewed
from outside the services, the A-10 appeared to
duplicate the mission filled by the Army's armed attack
helicopters, whose numbers had vastly increased as a
result of the McConnell-Johnson Agreement of 6 April
1966 and the successful employment of rotary-wing
aircraft in Vietnam.

Due to the appearance of duplication, the House
Committee on Armed Services sanctioned hearings on the
matter. It resulted in a letter (included below, see
p. 404) from the two chiefs of staff to the Chairman of
the House Armed Services Committee which explained the
complementary nature of Army-Air Force close air
support assets. The Army viewed the attack helicopter
as an extension of its ground units' organic firepower,
while Air Force fixed-wing assets were centrally
controlled and were more flexible in responding to
theaterwide exigencies.

****

Frederic A. Bergerson, <u>The Army Gets an Air Force</u>,
(Baltimore, Md: Johns Hopkins University Press, 1980),
pp 121-42.

NEW AIR FORCE AND ARMY UNDERSTANDING ON AIRPOWER USE. The role of the Army attack helicopter in close air support (CAS) has been the subject of controversy for years. Army and Air Force have recently agreed on the relationship of the attack helicopter and Air Force fixed-wing CAS.

The attack helicopter is integral to the Army ground maneuver unit and is an extension of organic firepower. It is to be employed with, or to the rear of, ground forces along the forward edge of the battle area (FEBA) to provide helicopter escort and suppressive fire, to counter enemy armor at the FEBA, and to counter surprise enemy armor penetrations behind friendly lines.

The Army and Air Force agree that the attack helicopter does not perform CAS but is intended to complement Air Force CAS capabilities. The attack helicopter and Air Force close air support offer the ground commander a complementary capability in terms of a wider spectrum of fire support, enhanced responsiveness, flexibility and capability. Because of the limited range, speed and firepower of attack helicopters as compared to Air Force fixed-wing CAS capabilities, the Air Force does not consider the attack helicopter as duplicating Air Force CAS.

Air Force CAS resources are centrally controlled by the Air Force component commander and respond to the theater-wide CAS requirements of the ground commander -- whereas attack helicopter elements are integral to the the Army's combined arms team and are under control of, and employed directly by, the various ground commanders to which they are assigned. Through centralized control of Air Force resources, the Air Force provides a means to fully exploit the broader operational capabilities of tactical airpower.

DEPARTMENT OF THE ARMY
HEADQUARTERS UNITED STATES ARMY
OFFICE OF THE CHIEF OF STAFF

DEPARTMENT OF THE AIR FORCE
HEADQUARTERS UNITED STATES AIR FORCE
OFFICE OF THE CHIEF OF STAFF

WASHINGTON, D.C.

7 April 1976

Honorable Melvin Price
Chairman, Committee on
  Armed Services
House of Representatives

Dear Mr. Chairman:

We appreciate the opportunity to express our views on Army attack helicopters, such as the Advanced Attack Helicopter (AAH), and Air Force close air support capabilities, including the A-10.

It is our view that the attack helicopter is organic to the Army ground maneuver unit and is integral to organic firepower. It is to be employed with, or to the rear of, ground forces along the Forward Edge of the Battle Area (FEBA) to counter enemy armor at the FEBA, to counter enemy armor penetrations behind friendly lines, and to provide helicopter escort and suppressive fire. The Army attack helicopter does not perform close air support but is intended to complement Air Force close air support capabilities. For example, the attack helicopter is a mobile weapons system capable of providing organic fire support to local Army units. Because of the limited range, speed and firepower of the attack helicopter as compared to Air Force fixed wing close air support capabilities, we do not consider the attack helicopter as duplicating Air Force close air support.

Air Force close air support capabilities, including A-10 assets, are centrally controlled in order to be able to respond to theater-wide close air support requirements. Conversely, the attack helicopter elements are integral to each of the Army's combined arms teams, and therefore, are under the direct command and control of the ground commander. The Army philosophy of decentralized control of attack helicopter resources is appropriate to Army operational functions as is centralized control of the Air Force close air support assets. In this regard, the principle of centralized control of Air Force resources at the highest control system level, with decentralized execution of air tasks to lower echelon Tactical Air Control Systems elements provides the Air Force with the optimum control capability to conduct air operations theater-wide.

The attack helicopter, as an integral part of the Army's organic firepower, and Air Force close air support offer the ground commander a complementary capability in terms of a wider spectrum of fire support, enhanced responsiveness, flexibility and capability. It is our view that both the Army Advanced Attack Helicopter and the Air Force A-10 close air support aircraft are essential.

Sincerely,

(signed)
DAVID C. JONES, General, USAF
Chief of Staff

(signed)
FRED C. WEYAND
General, United States Army
Chief of Staff

(36) Establishment of Air Force Space Command, 1 September 1982

By 1980, the Air Force had split its air defense and space-based missile warning and attack assessment functions, and disestablished Aerospace Defense Command (ADCOM) as a major Air Force command, although the Air Force organization continued as the Aerospace Defense Center (a direct reporting unit) which comprised the principal component of the Joint Chiefs of Staff (JCS)-specified command ADCOM. Tactical Air Command had taken over resource management of Air Force air defense aircraft, while operational control of these aircraft rested with North American Air Defense Command (NORAD) (of which ADCOM composed the American portion). The space systems resource management had been absorbed into the Strategic Air Command, with their operational control resting with ADCOM. Many of these space systems were managed in conjunction with Air Force Systems Command (AFSC), based on their determination that these systems were unique research and development systems. The fragmentation in control of its space system assets prompted the Air Force to look towards the formation of an Air Force space command to control and operate these systems.

Effective 1 September 1982, the Air Force formed Space Command (SPACECOM) to manage its space systems, while ADCOM remained a JCS-specified command, though many positions were dual- and triple-hatted as SPACECOM, ADCOM, and NORAD. The incumbent commander of ADCOM and NORAD headed SPACECOM, while the commander of AFSC's Space Division took on the additional role of vice commander of SPACECOM. According to Air Force Chief of Staff Gen. Lew Allen, the new command's function was to "provide a focus initially for operational planning, coordination and consolidation of activities relating to space mission areas." This organizational change set the stage for formation of a unified space command. Under the reorganization attending the command's formation, some systems would remain temporarily under AFSC direction until construction of new control facilities allowed SPACECOM to take over.

The Air Force was not alone in recognizing the need to centralize space operations in a single command. In a January 1982 report, the General Accounting Office criticized Department of Defense (DOD) space systems management. This action came as the Executive Branch and DOD were conducting a space policy examination of their own. The Air Force viewed SPACECOM as a link between the research and operational segments of the space community, and as a precursor to a unified space command which would give the Air Force significant control over military space endeavors, while allowing for individual service programs. The unified space command would put space systems into the operational chain of command that ran from the National Command Authorities, through the JCS, to the operational forces.

The Air Force acted to consolidate its position as the lead service for space by petitioning the JCS on 7 June 1983 for creation of a unified space command. The JCS approved the request (despite Navy disagreement) and recommended on 7 November 1983 to Secretary of Defense Caspar W. Weinberger that one be established. Secretary Weinberger approved the recommendation on 26 November 1983 and forwarded the request to the President, who approved it on 20 November 1984. The one-year delay came about due to disagreements over command relationships and responsibilities. The unified command (USSPACECOM) activated on 23 September 1985, the intervening year being spent on the details of activation.

The mission of the Air Force Space Command (AFSPACECOM) was to provide resource management and operation of assigned assets for: space control (anti-satellite and satellite defense systems), space force application (defensive), force enhancement (including surveillance of objects in or from space), space support, and strategic aerospace defense. Space support included launching and deploying space vehicles, as well as sustaining and recovering them. USSPACECOM's mission included the above Air Force mission elements, in addition to operational command of JCS-designated systems. Both the AFSPACECOM and USSPACECOM were responsible for integrated tactical warning. These organizational arrangements presaged further changes in space operations and mission assignments.

****
Henry M. Narducci, Jr., "Strategic Air Command and the Space Mission 1977-1984," SAC Historical Monograph Number 209, 10 October 1985.

Memo, CJCS to SECDEF, subject: USCINCSPACE Organization and Relationships, JCSM-287-85, 2 Aug 85.

Memo, Col. Donald W. Williams to Unified and Specified Commanders, subject: USCINCSPACE Mission Responsibilities, SM-94-85, 12 Feb 85.

DEPARTMENT OF THE AIR FORCE
Office of the Chief of Staff
United States Air Force
Washington, D.C. 20330

26 July 1982

Reply to
Attn of : CV

Subject: Space Command

To: Distribution B

1. On 21 Jun 82, the Air Force announced the formation of a new
MAJCOM, USAF Space Command (SPACECOM). This decision followed a
lengthy period of debate concerning the evolution of an Air
Force organization for space. As a result, the Air Force is now
committed to a major restructuring involving a myriad of actions
which need to be finalized before SPACECOM becomes fully functional. Needless to say, the Air Force is under close scrutiny
as we accomplish this task.

2. SPACECOM will officially come into existence on 1 Sep 82,
with full implementation scheduled prior to the end of FY 83.
Much work is required to meet this goal and is well underway.
However, many implementation details have resource impacts, and
we must insure that the necessary actions are taken so that
SPACECOM is fully operational before Oct 83. Accordingly, I
ask that each of you and your organizations take the necessary
steps to achieve this goal.

(signed)
JEROME F. O'MALLEY, General, USAF
Vice Chief of Staff

DEPARTMENT OF THE AIR FORCE
Headquarters United States Air Force
Washington, D.C. 20330

DAF/MPM 443q   17 August 1982

SUBJECT: HQ Space Command, A Major Command

    TO: SPACECOM/CC

1. By order of the Secretary of the Air Force, HQ Space Command
is constituted and activated as a major command of the United
States Air Force, effective 1 September 1982.

    a. A mission directive will be published in accordance with
HOI 5-21 as soon as practicable by AF/XOS.

    b. The organization configuration of this unit will be in
accordance with applicable provisions of AFR 26-2.

2. Report completed action using the Air Force Organization
Status Change Report (RCS: HAF-CHO(M)7401) and Unit Status and
Identity Report (UNITREP), in compliance with current instruc-
tions.

FOR THE CHIEF OF STAFF

(signed)
KEITH D. McCARTNEY, Maj Gen, USAF
Director of Manpower & Organization
DCS/Manpower & Personnel

(37) US Army/US Air Force Memorandum of Agreement (31 Initiatives),22 May 1984

On 22 May 1984, the Army and the Air Force Chiefs of Staff signed a memorandum of agreement which promised an unprecedented degree of interservice cooperation. This agreement became known as the 31 Initiatives, since it came out with that many initiatives for action appended. The agreement was designed to provide for "the fielding of the most affordable and effective airland combat forces." The two services sought to provide complementary, but not duplicative, forces capable of executing the airland battle. One result of this would be an annual exchange of priority lists of programs to ensure that each joint area was properly, and not redundantly, provided for.

The 31 Initiatives fell into several broad categories, including air defense, defense of rear echelon areas, electronic combat, and command and control systems and operations. Each initiative represented merely "the tip of the iceberg," with a long implementation process tailing each one.

Initiative #1 allowed Air Force participation in surface-to-air missile development efforts, heretofore an exclusive Army preserve. Initiative #17 promised to rationalize rotary-wing aircraft forces, by transferring to the Army all Air Force Special Operations Forces helicopters, leaving the Air Force with just a few helicopters for search and rescue forces and intercontinental ballistic missile (ICBM) operations. This initiative ran afoul of congressional advocates, and its implementation lagged at the end of 1985. Initiative #24 reiterated the Air Force commitment to provide close air support to Army forces. The necessity of its inclusion spoke loudly to the disagreements which had arisen in the past over the support issue. Initiative #26 provided for coordinated joint positions on manned aircraft to support ground combat operations. The thrust of this initiative pointed towards allowing the Army a voice in close air support aircraft development.

A series of agreements grew out of the process which produced the 31 Initiatives. In April 1985, the two chiefs and the service secretaries signed a memorandum of understanding on follow-on, close air support aircraft. This helped implement initiative #26, and initiative #33 (which had followed the original 31). The two services were able to agree on the need for, and the capabilities of, a new aircraft for the airland battle. In May 1986, the two chiefs signed a memorandum of agreement on manned aircraft systems, which further implemented initiative #26, and also replaced the McConnell-Johnson Agreement of April 1966 (see Doc. #30). This new agreement committed the services to an established joint position on manned aircraft, but also reinforced the division of responsibility for combat support, with the Army in charge of rotary-wing aircraft, and the Air Force responsible for fixed-wing aircraft.

While the long-term impact of these agreements remained unclear, the simple fact of their existence marked a watershed in Army-Air Force relations. The hitherto unrelenting contentiousness which marked discussion of Air Force support of Army combat operations had been muted by the start of a process which provided a forum for discussion and agreement on issues outside the traditional congressional budget process.

****

Richard G. Davis, "The 31 Initiatives: A Study in Air Force-Army Cooperation," (Washington, D.C.: Office of Air Force History, 1987), pp 75-129.

Department of the Army
Headquarters, U.S. Army
Washington, D.C.

Department of the Air Force
Headquarters, U.S. Air Force
Washington, D.C.

22 May 1984

MEMORANDUM OF AGREEMENT

ON

U.S. ARMY - U.S. AIR FORCE
JOINT FORCE DEVELOPMENT PROCESS

1. The Army and the Air Force affirm that to fulfill their
roles in meeting the national security objectives of deterrence
and defense, they must organize, train, and equip a compatible,
complementary and affordable Total Force that will maximize our
joint combat capability to execute airland combat operations.
To that end, broad, across-the-board, warfighting issues have
been addressed. We believe the resulting agreements listed in
the attachment will significantly enhance the country's military
posture and have a major positive impact on the way future
combat operations are conducted.

2. The Army and the Air Force view this MOA as the initial
step in the establishment of a long-term, dynamic process whose
objective will continue to be the fielding of the most affordable and effective airland combat forces. Consequently, the
joint agreements embodied in the attached initiatives will be
updated and reviewed by the services annually to confirm their
continued advisability, feasibility, and adequacy. We will
expand this MOA (and attachments) to include future joint
initiatives, as appropriate.

3. As an integral part of the joint effort to ensure the development of the optimum airland combat capability, the services
will annually exchange a formal priority list of those sister
service programs essential to the support of their conduct of
successful airland combat operations, the purpose of which is
to ensure the development of complementary systems without
duplication. The services will resolve joint or complementary
system differences prior to program development. The services
will ensure that those programs supporting joint airland combat
operations will receive high priority in their respective development and acquisition processes. This MOA confirms our mutual
dedication to ensuring that the provision of the best combat

capability to the Unified and Specified Commanders remains the top priority of the Army and the Air Force.

(signed)
_____
JOHN A. WICKHAM, JR.
General, United States Army
Chief of Staff

(signed)
_____
CHARLES A. GABRIEL
General, United States Air Force
Chief of Staff

1 Atch
Initiatives for Action

CSA/CSAF INITIATIVES FOR ACTION

1. Initiatives on Area Surface-to-Air Missiles/Air Defense Fighters:

    a. The Air Force will participate in the requirement and development process for follow-on area surface-to-air missile (SAM) systems.

    b. The Air Force will lead a joint net sensitivity analysis to determine the optimum program mix of current area SAMs and air defense fighters.

    c. The Army will lead a joint effort to study the advisability and feasibility of transferring proponency for area SAMs from the Army to the Air Force.

2. Initiatives of Point Air Defense:

    a. The Army and Air Force will jointly develop a plan to resolve air base point air defense (PAD) requirements.

        (1) The Air Force will provide to the Army an updated list of outstanding worldwide PAD requirements.

        (2) This joint plan will be reviewed annually.

    b. The Army and Air Force will develop a joint statement of need for future rear-area PAD systems.

    c. The Air Force will participate in the on-going Army effort to review air defense requirements and capacity at Corps and Echelons above Corps.

3. Initiatives to Counter Heliborne Assault Threat:

    a. The Army will lead a joint assessment of the technical characteristics and operational implications of the future heliborne assault threat.

    b. Based on the joint assessment the Army and Air Force will jointly develop and field the capabilities to detect and counter the threat.

4. Initiatives on the Tactical Missile Threat:

a.   The Army and Air Force will complete the tactical missile threat assessment, to include evaluation of the operational impact of anticipated threat technical capabilities.

b.   Using this threat assessment as the baseline, the Army and Air Force will establish a joint Anti-Tactical Missile Program.

5.   Initiatives on Identification Friend or Foe (IFF) Systems:

a.   The Army and Air Force will continue joint research in cooperative friendly identification systems to identify cost-effective refinements for the Mark XV Question and Answer (Q&A) identification program.

b.   The Army and Air Force will develop an IFF system (to include non-cooperative, positive hostile identification) that will enable the effective employment of beyond visual range weapons against hostile aircraft.

6.   Initiatives on Rear Area Operations Centers (RAOCs):

a.   The Army will increase full-time manning of RAOCs as part of the on-going Army Reserve/Army National Guard program to expand manning by full-time support personnel.

b.   The Army will establish the appropriate number of ARNG long tour (OCONUS) positions in each RAOC unit.

7.   Initiative on Host Nation Support Security Equipment.
The Army and Air Force support equipage of FRG reserve security units with German equipment and weapons; with US to FRG equipment ratios to be determined in conjunction with overseas commanders.

8.   Initiatives on Air Base Ground Defense:

a.   The Army and Air Force will develop a Joint Service Agreement for:

(1)   Army units to provide air base ground defense (ABGD) outside the base perimeter.

(2)   Operational control of Army units performing the ABGD mission by the appropriate air component commanders.

b.   The Air Force will transfer Air Force Reserve Component manpower spaces to the Army, if the Air Force ABGD requirements exceed Army capabilities.

c. The Army and Air Force will develop joint procedures for rear area security reflecting these initiatives.

9. Initiative for ABGD Flight Training. The Army and Air Force will execute a Joint Service Agreement for the Army to provide initial and follow-on training for Air Force on-site security flights.

10. Initiative for Rear Area Close Air Support. The Army and Air Force will develop joint doctrine and procedures for the employment of Close Air Support (CAS) in the rear area.

11. Initiative on the Mobile Weapon System. The Air Force will terminate development of the Mobile Weapon System.

12. Initiatives on Ground-based Electronic Combat against Enemy Air Attacks:

a. The Army and Air Force will reconcile their joint requirements and restructure the Air Defense Electronic Warfare System (ADEWS) program accordingly.

b. The Air Force will terminate the Comfy Challenge program.

c. The Army will develop ADEWS to incorporate the required capabilities for both services.

13. Initiative on the Airborne Radar Jamming System (ARJS). The Army will terminate the ARJS program. The Air Force will provide airborne jamming support.

14. Initiative on the Precision Location Strike System (PLSS). The Army and Air Force will develop a joint concept and attendant hardware to broadcast PLSS target information to designated Army units in near-real-time.

15. Initiatives on Joint Suppression of Enemy Air Defenses (J-SEAD):

a. The Army's analytical agencies will model J-SEAD to determine the overall contribution of an effective SEAD campaign and the impact of SEAD on ammunition expenditure rates. The Air Force will provide full time participation.

b. Army Field Manuals will be updated to address transmittal of PLSS targeting information direct to designated Army units.

16. Initiatives on Combat Search and Rescue:

    a. The Air Force will remain proponent for Air Force Search and Rescue (SAR) with Special Operations Forces (SOF) providing a back-up capability in special situations.

    b. The Air Force will:

        (1) Determine Air Force combat SAR objectives in relation to depths on the battlefield defined by capability.

        (2) Develop tactics, techniques, and procedures for conduct of SAR in Air Force zones.

    c. The Army and Air Force will develop tactics, techniques, and procedures for SOF to conduct SAR beyond Air Force zones.

17. Rotary Wing Lift Support for Special Operations Forces (SOF). The Air Force will transfer the responsibility for providing rotary wing lift support for SOF to the Army. A detailed implementation plan will be jointly developed.

18. Initiatives on the Joint Tactical Missile System (JTACMS):

    a. The Army and Air Force will develop a joint statement of need for the JTACMS. The restructured program will include the joint development of procedures to ensure that respective service components of JTACMS are fully complementary.

    b. The Army will refocus its current development efforts on a shorter range ground-launched system.

    c. The Air Force will develop an air-launched system.

19. Initiative on Army and Air Force Munitions RDT&E. The Army and Air Force will develop procedures for a joint and recurring review of munitions technical base programs keyed to the budget/POM cycle. This review will use the Joint Logistics Commanders structure and include Army and Air Staff participation.

20. Initiatives on Night Combat:

    a. The Army and Air Force will jointly determine the requirements for night operations.

    b. The Air Force will pursue a spectrum of night capabilities based on the joint requirements and resolve associated training issues.

c. The Air Force will designate a single Air Staff point of contact for night systems and establish an Air Force liaison to the Army Night Vision and Electro-Optics Laboratory.

21. Initiatives on Battlefield Air Interdiction:

a. The Army and Air Force will develop procedures, that can be tailored to theater specific requirements, to synchronize Battlefield Air Interdiction (BAI) with maneuver.

b. The Army and Air Force will field test these procedures.

c. The Army will automate the Battlefield Coordination Element (BCE) and connect BCE/Corps/Land Component Commanders via near-real-time data links.

22. Initiative on a Joint Target Set. The Army and Air Force will conduct a joint target assessment for use in establishing a consensus on attack of enemy surface targets and development of coordinated munitions acquisition plans.

23. Initiatives on Theater Interdiction Systems:

a. In theater, the Air Component Commander is responsible for the execution of the interdiction campaign.

b. The Air Force will lead a joint study to:

(1) Establish procedures to jointly develop requirements for interdiction systems.

(2) Define future conventional interdiction requirements.

(3) Determine optimum service proponencies for Intermediate Nuclear Force (INF) systems.

24. Initiative on Close Air Support (CAS). The Army and Air Force reaffirm the Air Force mission of providing fixed-wing CAS to the Army.

25. Initiatives on Air Liaison Officers and Forward Air Controllers:

a. The Army and the Air Force will provide enhanced training in maneuver unit operations for Air Liaison Officers (ALOs) and selected Forward Air Controllers (FACs).

b. The Army and Air Force will conduct an in-depth review and evaluation of FAC operations and Tactical Air Control Party (TACP) structure to include:

(1) Enhancing maneuver unit ground FAC capability with organic Army helicopter support.

(2) Executing ground FAC functions while operating from organic maneuver unit vehicles.

(3) Performance of battalion FAC duties by non-rated officers in order to expand the full time Air Force representation at the maneuver battalion.

c. The review and evaluation will be conducted in the following phases:

(1) Phase I: An internal review conducted by Tactical Air Command (TAC).

(2) Phase II: A joint TAC and Training and Doctrine Command (TRADOC) review, to include development of a joint field test plan of the proposed FAC/TACP concepts.

(3) Phase III: Joint field test.

26. Initiatives on Manned Aircraft Systems:

a. The Army and Air Force will establish specific service responsibilities for manned aircraft systems.

b. The Army and Air Force will establish procedures for developing coordinated joint positions on new aircraft starts prior to program initiation.

27. Initiatives on Joint Surveillance and Target Attack Radar System (JSTARS):

a. The Army and Air Force will support the C-18 as the single JSTARS platform.

b. The Army and Air Force will develop a joint Memorandum of Agreement to:

(1) Outline procedures to ensure dedicated support of ground commander requirements.

(2) Ensure adequate platform procurement to provide required support.

28. Initiatives on TR-1 Program. The Air Force and Army will restructure the current TR-1 program to enhance its wartime survivability and effectiveness, within the bounds of affordability.

29. Initiatives for Manned Tactical Reconnaissance Systems:

a. The Army and Air Force will jointly develop requirements for common platforms to meet follow-on manned Special Electronic Mission Aircraft (SEMA) and Tactical Reconnaissance needs.

b. When joint requirements can best be met by a single service platform (Army or Air Force), that service will assume single service mission and development proponency. In parallel with this, procedures will be jointly developed and adequate platforms procured by the responsible service, to ensure dedicated support of the other service's requirements.

30. Initiatives on Intratheater Airlift:

a. The Army and Air Force will establish a joint office to determine intratheater airlift requirements to support movement from Aerial Port of Debarkation/Sea Port of Debarkation to destination; resupply by airland/airdrop; reposition/redeployment of forces, equipment, munitions, and war reserve; and medical/noncombatant evacuation.

b. The Army and the Air Force will develop joint positions, as required, on intratheater airlift programs.

31. Initiative on POM Priority List. The Army and Air Force will formalize cross-service participation in the POM development process. This formalization will include the annual exchange of a formal priority list of those sister service programs essential to the joint conduct of airland combat operations.

Bibliography

"Air Force, Army Agree on Roles and Missions,"
Aviation Week and Space Technology, 25 April 1966, pp.
26, 27.

Bergerson, Frederic A. _The Army Gets an Air Force_.
Baltimore, Md: Johns Hopkins University Press, 1980.

Bowers, Ray L. _The United States Air Force in Southeast
Asia: Tactical Airlift_. Washington, D.C.: Office of Air
Force History, 1983.

Cole, Alice C., Alfred Goldberg, Samuel A Tucker,
Rudolph A. Winnacker, eds. _The Department of Defense,
Documents on Establishment and Organization 1944-1978_.
Washington, D.C.: OSD Historical Office, 1978.

Futrell, Robert F. _Ideas, Concepts and Doctrine: A
History of Basic Thinking in the United States Air
Force 1907-1964_. Maxwell AFB, Ala: Air University,
2nd edition 1974.

Goldberg, Alfred, ed. _A History of the United States
Air Force 1907-1957_. New York: D. Van Nostrand
Company, Inc, 1957.

Goldberg, Alfred, and Lt. Col. Donald Smith. RAND Report
Number R-906-PR, "Army-Air Force Relations: The Close
Air Support Issue." October 1971.

History of Military Airlift Command, 1 July 1965-30
June 1966.

History of Military Airlift Command, July 1974-December
1975.

JCS Publication 1, "Department of Defense Dictionary of
Military and Associated Terms," Washington, D.C.:
Joint Chiefs of Staff, 1986.

JCS Special Historical Study, "History of the Unified
Command Plan," Washington, D.C.: Historical Division,
Joint Secretariat, JCS, 1977.

Narducci, Henry M., Jr. "Strategic Air Command and the
Space Mission 1977-1984." SAC Historical Monograph
Number 209, 10 October 1985.

BASIC DOCUMENTS

Neufeld, Jacob. "The Air Force in Space 1970-1974." Washington, D.C.: Office of Air Force History, 1976.

Miller, Maurice A. "The Collateral Maritime Mission of the Strategic Air Command." Offutt AFB, Nebr: SAC Office of History, 1980.

Rearden, Steven L. History of the Office of the Secretary of Defense, The Formative Years 1947-1950. Washington, D.C.: OSD History Office, 1984.

Snyder, Thomas S. et al. "Space and Missile Systems Organization A Chronology 1954-1976." Norton AFB, Calif: SAMSO History Office, 1978.

Tunner, William H. Over the Hump. Reprint Edition, Washington, D.C.: Office of Air Force History, 1985.

Wolk, Herman S. Planning and Organizing the Postwar Air Force, 1943-1947. Washington, D.C.: Office of Air Force History, 1984.

426

INDEX

Information and Education

✩U.S. G.P.O. 1988-201-372:80632